RADIO MOMENTS

'Reminded me fondly of my early days in radio – a fantastic read.'
SCOTT MILLS, BBC RADIO 1

'David Lloyd has forgotten more about radio than most of us will ever know. Luckily, he has remembered enough about his uniquely varied career to fill these pages with insights, anecdotes and experiences which will prove invaluable, and often hugely entertaining, to people in every corner and at every level of the industry. It is the story of a love affair with a medium that continues to touch people in ways that no other media can and few professionals have expressed that love better than Lloyd. His blue patent shoes, however, are a disgrace.'
JAMES O'BRIEN, LBC PRESENTER

'A passionate love letter to commercial radio. David Lloyd's sparkling stories and wry humour evoke several decades of bad haircuts, big shoulder pads and fine pop music. *Radio Moments* is a delight.'
HELEN BOADEN, FORMER DIRECTOR OF BBC RADIO AND FORMER CONTROLLER AT BBC RADIO 4

'Anyone who is interested in radio should read this book. Written by a man who got to work in the industry he grew up loving, on both sides of the microphone, as broadcaster and station boss. Laced with wonderful dry humour, it tells how radio has changed and developed over the years. If you love radio, you'll love this.'
DAVID HAMILTON, BBC RADIO 1 AND 2 AND COMMERCIAL RADIO BROADCASTER

'This is as good as it gets. A love-in with radio that pulls no punches and spares no blushes.'
JOHN MYERS, RADIO EXECUTIVE

'David has written an autobiographical book that details not only his extensive career but also the life of commercial radio, from its difficult birth pangs in the early '70s through to the present day. Full of fascinating insights into who did what to whom, it will inspire you.'
JOHNNY BEERLING, FELLOW OF THE RADIO ACADEMY AND CONTROLLER OF BBC RADIO 1 (1985–1993)

50 YEARS OF RADIO – LIFE ON THE INSIDE

RADIO MOMENTS

DAVID LLOYD

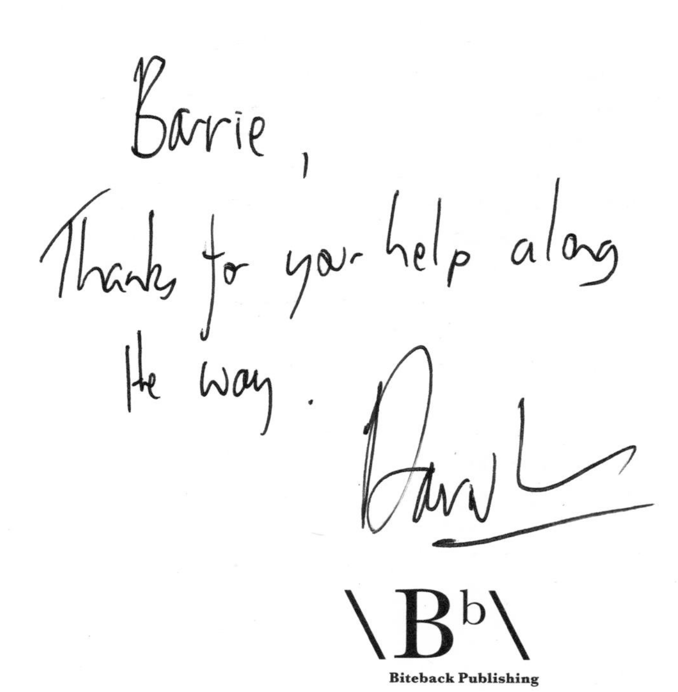

Biteback Publishing

First published in Great Britain in 2017 by
Biteback Publishing Ltd
Westminster Tower
3 Albert Embankment
London SE1 7SP

ISBN 978-1-78590-272-7

10 9 8 7 6 5 4 3 2 1

A CIP catalogue record for this book is available from the British Library.

Set in Adobe Caslon Pro

Printed and bound in Great Britain by
CPI Group (UK) Ltd, Croydon CR0 4YY

CONTENTS

PREFACE

NEW BEGINNINGS

I looked back over my shoulder at the Free Radio premises in Birmingham, the station's bright green logos glimmering. As I strode across the pointlessly well-hoed gravel for the last time, I realised that never again would my key work in the door. The station, which had grown up as BRMB, was now under energetic new ownership and I was about to become an eccentric memory.

It's a reality in any business now that, if you're fortunate enough to have been running something from the top table and someone else buys it, they'll want to do it their way and the likelihood is that they may not need you. There's a thoroughly grown-up response to that. They've bought the train set; they can play with it how they like. But given this is radio, a medium for which those involved feel such genuine passion, there's the private temptation to want to lie on your back in the office, legs flailing, and scream like a spoilt three-year-old because the runny-nosed lad next door has stolen your toy.

A little like splitting from a lover, for a while it hurts to turn on the radio and spend time with your old station. But after a decent amount of time elapses you can become friends again.

Free Radio in Birmingham was one of four Free-branded stations in the West Midlands. Those FM radio stations, plus the successful Gem 106 station serving the East Midlands, formed our Midlands company Orion Media. The roots of our organisation had sprung from collateral damage in 2009 as the UK commercial radio sector consolidated further, edging ever closer to the state in which it will fight the battle for the ear through the twenty-first century.

The UK commercial radio network launched in the 1970s and comprised a few valiant independent companies that were headed by colourful characters. Now, it has become a more grown-up affair. Efficiency is critical if the medium is to survive in a fast-changing world. If the first age of radio was the halcyon spell before the Queen's Coronation and mass-market television, the second age now looks set for its finale, ready for a digital future.

Forty years ago, if you were lucky, your city had a single, lonely commercial radio station. Vinyl songs blared from medium-wave radios; everyone in a city tuned to the same station; and I witnessed the antics of some truly fascinating characters on and off air. As a presenter and then as a boss, I've seen happiness and heartache, success and frustration, canniness and stupidity. And, most recently, after forty years in radio, I've had a taste of owning an appreciable part of a radio company and playing a key role in forging the destiny of its stations.

I wasn't better than many others, I was simply luckier. For the little lad who grew up with dreams of just wanting to play a few songs on the radio, it has been a fascinating journey through a radio era which will never be repeated.

1

DREAMS

The neighbours assembled dutifully in the large scruffy kitchen at our suburban semi. Ours was the only house on the street with an FM radio and my mother was determined that the whole of Lady Bay should hear the whiny ramblings of her youngest son.

Budgets in our noisy home were stretched. Our family of five kids, me being the accidental and late fifth, couldn't afford washing up liquid, mended our own shoes and lived off Fray Bentos steak and kidney pie. Twenty minutes at gas mark five.

Our family possessed an FM radio, which was then known as VHF, only because my tall oldest brother, Martyn, had built it. Like DAB radio sets in the late '90s, few people owned FM sets in the '60s, and listening choices were limited. Such was the rarity of this new gadget that it could not yet be purchased in exchange for Green Shield stamps, which were the source of most things in our house. The smell of solder flux drifted down from the attic and my clever brother emerged with two new radio sets: one white and one faux teak, painstakingly veneered with the sort of sticky back plastic favoured by *Blue Peter*'s Valerie Singleton.

These miracle radio sets picked up radio stations in a hitherto unheard-of quality. No more AM hiss and crackle, which would only get worse if you switched on the twin-tub. Few stations could be received by the new sets at this stage, but one notable spot on the dial in our neighbourhood was the fledgling BBC Radio Nottingham.

BBC local radio was a reluctant addition to the broadcasting landscape. The Corporation's ex-war correspondent Frank Gillard had pursued its launch with single-mindedness. Sufficient BBC funding was not available, so the cities whose local authorities chipped in got their station. Accordingly, Leicester came first, not Manchester, as had originally been planned, with BBC Radio Nottingham following a couple of months later in January 1968.

Back then, every radio programme had a title. My debut appearance came in a programme called *The Magic Microphone Club*. The BBC reporter turned up, clutching a microphone topped with a branded red pop shield, ready to tease out some cute ramblings from the innocents at our Victorian infant school.

My wonderful headmistress had prepared us all with our party pieces. I was offered prime time, reciting a poem about the Great Fire of London. I still recall the opening words to this day, as I stood there in my short trousers and braided blazer: 'It was the year 1666, just after the year of the plague…'

Radio was woven into the infant school curriculum. We'd sit cross-legged on the parquet flooring, gazing at the large speaker grille as Julia Lang, with her vibraphone chimes, delivered the words, which I still associate with the smell of Izal disinfectant and warm milk to this day: 'Are you sitting comfortably? Then we'll begin.'

It would be poetic to suggest my soprano performance on BBC Radio Nottingham was the start of my love affair with radio, but I will never know. It was certainly a vivid memory – and about the only thing I remember from infant school days, apart from an unfortunate lad wetting himself in the first year and my being lent a box of Cuisenaire rods after the head teacher concluded that I was clever at arithmetic. Or maybe she was seeking to make amends, having rightly judged I could not be trusted with the class hamster during the holidays.

At the bottom of our huge rambling garden, hidden behind unkempt blackberry bushes, was a rotting shed. As I progressed through junior school and into secondary school, this became my den. Having clambered on the roof to lay roofing felt and painted the front with leftover turquoise and orange paint, I put my mark on my space. In the corner, all manner of plugs, sockets, loudspeakers and batteries were installed. I also made the early discovery that a small, old loudspeaker could serve as a microphone, and programmes were duly recorded on what remained of a portable reel-to-reel tape machine which I had dismantled and repurposed.

Powered by some PP9 batteries, a radio station was thus created, which I called Radio Anchor, named after the motif on the front of a sailor's hat I'd brought back from a dull weekend in a leaky caravan in Ingoldmells. It wasn't until adolescence that I realised that a sloppily pronounced 'Radio Anchor' was a brand riddled with difficulties. It wasn't to be my last challenge with radio station brand names.

Programmes for Radio Anchor were recorded on tape and relayed to our house, which lay some way up the garden, and to my long-suffering friend Harry's house, whose long garden backed onto ours, by means of lengthy cables Sellotaped together and draped over the weeds.

I was becoming what the industry calls an 'anorak', supposedly named after the dedicated listeners who would journey out to the ship that housed their favourite 1960s pirate radio station. Their intrepid journey across the North Sea, made with the hope of seeing their disc jockey idols, was aboard a small tender, necessitating warm, waterproof clothing.

My listening to proper radio became ever more frequent. Programmes on the young BBC Radio Nottingham were generally short and purposeful, with a theme tune, a name, and a pithy *Radio Times* description usually ending with the words '... and the very best in music'. The schedule ranged from the arts programme *Spectrum*, and the rock programme *Extravaganza*, to a puzzling request programme called *Bran Tub* which featured a homely presenter, helped out by a couple of squeaking characters.

A journey across the country would have heard similar offerings. Launch day of BBC Radio Leeds included an Alan Bennett monologue and a talking budgerigar; and BBC Radio Stoke featured 'The Esperanto Family Robinson', where a local headmaster recorded conversations in Esperanto with his family in their front room. Two stations, which now no longer exist in their original form, excelled themselves with *Heavy Pressure* on BBC Radio Birmingham and *Dad's Music* on Radio Cleveland.

The early BBC local radio stations were staffed by hugely gifted communicators and intelligent producers, led by managers with steely determination. The BBC had only reluctantly agreed to the swathe of early stations and deemed the initial eight 'an experiment'. The local managers, however, eschewed the word and referred to themselves as pioneers.

Like many, my local BBC station was to become an accidental training ground for Radio 1. It created an early home for a young Trevor Dann and Matthew Bannister, who were later to spearhead controversial moves to revive the national station in the '90s;

and for Simon Mayo, who was to become the sixth person to present the hallowed Radio 1 breakfast show.

I also witnessed Dennis McCarthy on BBC Radio Nottingham, a rare character and one of the best examples of the sort of local personality who ruled that generation of stations by simply being himself. Like Billy Butler at Radio Merseyside or Tony Capstick at Radio Sheffield, Dennis chatted effortlessly with understated humour to the people of the city he'd come to call his own. Authenticity is now regarded as a key word in contemporary radio, but back then, given the paucity of radio, these characters likely achieved that through simply having no one else to influence them.

Dennis mastered the pause as well as the art of identifying and exploiting the real value in any programme item. His phone-in segments were legendary. Dennis had the gift of being able to turn the dullest of callers, and the most mundane of features, into pure entertainment. Anyone who can breathe life into 'swap shop' and 'wanted column of the air' deserves recognition. It was to be expected that when Dennis died suddenly, aged just sixty-two, listeners would line the route of his funeral procession. Mention Dennis to anyone over fifty in Nottingham even now, and they'll likely draw from a wealth of anecdotes from the days when his voice would purr from their radio sets over the Sunday Brussels sprouts. Few broadcasters achieve such a legacy.

Late nights on Radio Nottingham featured an experiment called *The Moonlight Mile*, a rambling, yet engaging show which sounded as if management did not know it existed, symbolising the independence of the stations. I recall it seemed to end when the presenters felt like calling it a day. When Radio Nottingham presumably decided late-night radio was not such a good idea, I'd tune down the dial to enjoy Radio Derby's very different late offering. There was always something addictive about radio after dark.

Apart from BBC local radio stations, there was little else of interest on the new FM waveband. Like many, I'd derive some naughty joy from tuning in to the police transmissions, which occupied the swathe of FM spectrum on which no one had bothered to launch radio stations. Back then, I gather, prisoners were not allowed FM radios in their cells lest they heard something to their advantage.

BBC Radio 1, however, was altogether fine for reprobates when it launched in 1967, as it only commanded a crackly 247m wavelength on AM. It would be some twenty years before FM frequencies were bestowed, making use of the spectrum eventually relinquished by the police walkie-talkies. Like BBC local radio, Radio 1 was only just tolerated by a cautious BBC. Reception in the Midlands was almost as bad as it had been for the pirate stations. During the course of the short '60s life of the offshore Radio London, which went on to influence Radio 1, my brother used to dangle a red transistor radio near the electricity meter to render the station vaguely audible.

In those days before social media, you never knew whether your unusual penchant was shared by anyone else. You feared not. I could sing all the Radio 1 jingles, and felt I was the only person in the world who could belt them out word for word. Whilst my friends would be annoyed by disc jockeys talking over the songs they were trying to record, I sat listening impatiently for them to end so I could lift the pause button and hope to capture fifteen seconds of a close harmony radio station identification. I was already discovering I wasn't quite like my friends.

In our school, bringing in a radio was an offence for which you could be hanged. It was even more serious than wearing platform shoes or the wrong colour shirt. Nevertheless, just as in totalitarian states where media is forbidden, we ignored the law because radio meant that much to us. The '60s also made the transgression easier to commit, given radios had shrunk from the sturdy valve sets to affordable pocket-sized transistor sets in pastel colours.

Admittedly, we only risked the teachers' wrath so we could hear the charts, rather than the latest news from the Empire. This was a period when Tuesday lunchtime was sacred, as Paul Burnett would effortlessly run down the new chart. As Paul told me recently, he got the feeling the world appeared to stop as he announced the latest chart topper.

Back then, blackberries, apples and oranges were confined to orchards; and radio was the only way to get our music news. Anxious to hear who was up and who was down, we would assemble in frozen huddles, rather hoping that the marauding teachers would pursue the smell of smoke from neighbouring miscreants rather than the sound of jingles from our small crowd.

Having caught the update between geography and double maths on a Tuesday, we could then look forward to Sunday. The chart was the only exciting thing about a day on which all shops were closed, the lukewarm weekly bath was taken, and that back to school feeling would hit the pit of the stomach when the miserable theme tune to Radio 2's *Sing Something Simple* rang out as you searched for your smelly PE kit.

Six o'clock pipped, and mother would busy herself with the evening ironing, before relaxing by watching *Upstairs Downstairs* on the TV. Meanwhile, in our icy bedrooms, we would crank up the radio to enjoy the Top 20. It was broadcast in stereo on FM, as Radio 1 hijacked Radio 2's frequencies on occasions at the weekend, presumably when the Light's delirious management had gone home for a sherry. Not that anyone had a stereo radio, but mono FM was certainly better than crackly AM.

Sunday evening was self-evidently inspired scheduling for the chart rundown. It had not always been thus. When Alan Dell first took a Biro to a copy of the music press in 1957 and ran down the numbers that mattered most, it was scheduled late on a Sunday night. David Jacobs then started to assemble something more akin to our current chart, broadcast on Saturdays, before Alan Freeman barged in, preferring to work Sunday teatimes. From that moment, whatever its name or the programme in which it was housed, the chart has been part of our Sunday evening listening ritual.

2

AFTER THE BREAK

By 1975, in my small, Anaglypta-papered bedroom in Nottingham, I was discovering all sorts of things, as teenagers do. And I discovered commercial radio.

The Bee Gees faded in and out, and a friendly voice told me I was listening to an 'IBA test', long before I knew much about the Independent Broadcasting Authority, or indeed test transmissions. These early announcements sought to establish whether new stations were effectively pumping out their signals to the right homes.

Although I was to be a suited regulator in later life, I was more fascinated by the '70s summer hits beaming out 'in stereo' across what were truly beautiful Fahrenheit months. I'd rush out with a bowl to give to the local ice cream man to fill with vanilla, before dashing back to shout 'do the hustle' at just the right moment in that luscious Van McCoy hit.

Radio Trent became the thirteenth local commercial radio station to come on air. London's LBC had been first, in 1973, with Capital launching a week later, both of which faced their share of early crises. LBC was beset by painful industrial disputes, and the first chairman of Capital Radio, Richard Attenborough, had resorted to offering to sell some paintings to pay the bills of his station.

The term 'independent local radio' was the official moniker for the grand plan, and the regulator even troubled to write to one station asking it to desist from using the dirty term 'commercial radio'.

Having won the Nottingham franchise in a regulatory beauty parade against Radio Robin Hood, Trent was big news in my home city. On making the award, the IBA had observed there were 'major differences between the two applications' and that the successful applicant would need about £300,000 to come on air.[1] The company, like all those launching commercial stations across the UK, enjoyed a variety of local shareholders, as the regulator demanded, including, in this case, three trade unions, the Co-op and the *Nottingham Evening Post*, for which a shareholding had to be reserved to help protect the press from this annoying newcomer.

The original company, again like many, had been formed in the 1960s, when the first sniff of commercial radio became evident. Indeed, it was expected at that stage that commercial local radio would arrive before any BBC local radio. June 1962 had seen the formation of the Newark & Notts Broadcasting Company, with those around the original board table expecting commercial radio to debut a little earlier than it did. After a decade of presumably dull board meetings, the company changed its name to Radio Trent Ltd in November 1973, and Radio Trent made its debut on air in July 1975, with the deep voice of presenter John Peters.

Commercial radio proper was a late arrival to the UK, whereas in most countries around the world, it had predated commercial television. There had been early commercial influences here in the 1920s; the British Broadcasting Company had formed from a trusted group of radio manufacturers, but they were stamped out as the Company became a Corporation. John Reith, the first general manager of the Company and first director general of the Corporation, referred to radio as being 'of almost incalculable importance'. He was certainly in no mood for double glazing ads on his radio stations and advocated the public corporation model, at arm's length from the government, which we still recognise.

Radio Luxembourg was also an early taste of commercial radio to our shores, beamed in from the Grand Duchy. Broadcasting from the Villa Louvigny, an impressive 1920s building built on the foundations of a seventeenth-century fortress, the English service, established in 1933, became home to a generation of talent to become familiar to BBC listeners. Early presenters often came from acting or singing stock, from Pete Murray to Teddy Johnson and Keith Fordyce.

By the '70s, the station was still huge in the UK. Its more recent presenters, like Paul Burnett, Rob Jones and Kid Jensen, were also to play a key role in due course on our domestic stations.

Only broadcasting at night, Luxy was compulsory listening for a teenage Briton, with its signal fading in and out on its famous 208m wavelength, oddly even becoming part of its charm. A copy of *Fab 208* magazine would be devoured by its avid listeners and centre spread pictures of favourite long-haired artistes cut out and stuck on my sister's headboard. We'd listen on the rowdy return journey from Skegness in our spacious Ford Zephyr, the transistor radio perched precariously on the parcel shelf.

This powerful station had moved on from deeply sponsored programmes and shows solely featuring discs from a single record company to a more familiar Top 40 radio.

Ad breaks on Radio Luxembourg were glossy: shampoo, spot cream and cigarettes, featuring big-name fast-moving consumer goods (FMCG) brands which, to this day, have rarely been heard on home-grown commercial radio. Luxy brought lush, sung ads for the likes of Marlboro and Peter Stuyvesant. Cigarette advertising had been heard on the pirates but was never to be heard on commercial radio proper. Sponsorships were commonplace too, in a way which was only to arrive tentatively on UK commercial radio more than a decade later.

Commercial radio arrived formally in Britain in 1973, under the auspices of the Independent Broadcasting Authority, a hastily rebranded Independent Television Authority with a proud new turquoise logo. It might never have happened, had the Conservatives not won the 1970 election. As former Labour PM Harold Wilson said on the opening day of LBC, the nation's first station: 'It is well known that the Labour Party opposed the introduction of commercial radio, but that in no way prevents me from offering my best wishes to the Independent Broadcasting News service.' Given that's a little like saying 'I don't like you, but here's a birthday card anyway', I'm puzzled they even troubled to air it.

From its lofty premises on Brompton Road in London, the new IBA cautiously licensed its first programme contractors around the country. Anticipating the new services would be less formal than the BBC, its new director of radio, John Thompson, dubbed them 'radio in jeans'. The regulator awarded franchises to produce radio programmes, but not to transmit them, and decisions on the winning contractors were made after painful *Opportunity Knocks*-type auditions. Predator companies could not pounce to acquire the franchisees – and 'excess profit' was shaved off and handed back to the regulator for distribution to worthy radio projects. For those who had invested in the early stations from their own pockets, this was a peculiar form of capitalism.

The regulator was very firmly in charge, and even served as a dating agency. Capital Radio's first managing director, and later director general of the IBA, John Whitney, told me that when Capital Radio won its licence, the IBA ensured that its chairman secured the services of appropriate executives from the rival losing bidder. John himself had been such an appointee.

Key staff changes needed to be cleared by the rubber-stamping IBA officials, as did programme schedules. All transmission was arranged by the regulator's engineering division itself, and the codes of conduct for all matters were as rigorous for radio as they had been for the more lucrative business of television. The IBA's Tony Stoller, in charge of radio programming for a time, conceded to me that technical regulation had indeed been a little overenthusiastic.

The regulator's goal was to license stand-alone stations in markets of various sizes: from the mighty London operations to the smaller ones like Radio Orwell in Ipswich. Following a Labour government's return in 1974, however, the number of stations licensed in the first tranche was curtailed suddenly at just nineteen.

The great commercial radio experiment had thus begun, with an overregulated patchwork quilt of random stations of varying quality all doing different things, covering under a third of the population. Radio was hardly going to be top of Procter & Gamble's list as a favoured choice of advertising media.

I was unimpressed too. In the mid-70s, I was moved to write a disgruntled note to the letters page of *Radio Guide*, a short-lived *TV Times* for radio, which boasted regional opt-outs and pictures of David Essex. In my embarrassing missive, I declared the whole network not fit for purpose and suggested it should all be closed down. Nowadays, when my colleagues curse the ill-informed, and often wildly inaccurate, statements from radio anoraks on social media, I wince and recall the angry and younger me.

The early commercial stations appeared to divide between those with a BBC gene, and those with a music radio influence from the pirates or overseas. Trent, like the mischievous Beacon 303 in Wolverhampton, was one of the latter. These stations were unsurprisingly not top of the IBA's Christmas card list, with the regulator despatching angry notes and refusing to extend the contracts at various stages, threatening the stations' futures. Beacon had been launched by two colourful characters: American managing director Jay Oliver and Scottish/Canadian programme controller Allen McKenzie. It contrasted starkly with its conservative and traditional West Midlands neighbour BRMB.

At launch, Trent had pirate radio DNA, spiced with flavourings from Radio Luxembourg and the excellent biscuit factory radio network, UBN, thanks to the provenance of the staff it appointed.

In the top office sat Trent's first managing director, Dennis Maitland. Dennis, like those who launched Manchester's Piccadilly Radio, was one of the generation who left the pirate ships for the earliest land-based licensed commercial stations. His radio career had begun in 1964, on board offshore Radio London; he then joined Radio Luxembourg, before eventually moving to Nottingham. His first programme director, Bob Snyder, was also of pirate pedigree, having been aboard one of the smaller stations, Radio 270.

Whilst some of the new commercial stations recruited pseudo-continuity announcers to host programmes in traditional BBC stentorian fashion punctuated by sing-song jingles, Trent sounded like a decent music station from day one. It even troubled to define its format in a manner that would be commonplace decades later, but back then was absent from many stations: 'Mainstream pop, over and towards contemporary sounds ... forty oldies a day, mainly during the peak housewife listening times.'

Years before many brands were defining target audiences specifically, and certainly long before BBC local radio spoke of targeting your average 'Dave and Sue', Trent sought to serve 'a West Bridgford housewife, aged twenty-eight'.

The station boasted decent jingles at launch. Apart from some forgetting to mention the station name: 'When you're down, pick us up.' The catchy theme, composed by hit maker Johnny Arthey, and performed by, amongst others, '70s vocalist Tony 'Beach Baby' Burrows, was to be the soundtrack to Nottingham's warmest summers. The identification packages were sufficiently impressive to prompt me to phone in to ask the programme director, who doubled as a gifted presenter, about them on his Boxing Day show in 1976.

I had caught the radio bug.

3

A START

Like Kenny Everett, being given a second tape recorder for Christmas was an important moment for me. My messy bedroom, with its 'cracked ice' polystyrene tiles on the ceiling, now accommodated a home-made mixer, and, at last, I could dub from one machine to another. Editing was even possible, albeit cutting and splicing cassette tapes demanded a special set of implements, available from Woolworths, and the precision of a heart surgeon.

Whilst classmates busied themselves with painting rock band logos on their haversacks, I could make 'radio'.

As inspiration, I would listen to programmes from all stations, savouring the delights of a fading World Service AM signal and relishing a vibrant Radio 1. I'd enjoy the charm of an embroidered Radio 2 and I'd worship my local Radio Trent. The attraction of that proud new commercial station became a magnet. As the station and I grew, fresh exciting presenters heralded more excitement and, like most wannabe presenters, I was subconsciously to adopt a slice of each of them as my model.

Lying in the bath one night, hating the thought of returning to school the following morning, I recall hearing a frizzy-haired, flared-trousered Guy Morris on air, having the sort of fun presenters have on the radio. How could he be so happy and me so miserable? I had all the worries of the world on my teenage shoulders and he appeared to have none. Radio was surely a great job to have. Remembering that feeling now, I cringe when I hear presenters refer on air to 'coming into work today', not acknowledging that their listeners don't want you to describe presenting as a job – you should sound like you're doing it for kicks.

I'd participate in Trent competitions and, usually, I would win. On the *Len Groat Get Together*, an LP was the prize for dreaming up a radio contest. The brown cardboard LP sleeve arrived belatedly in the post – bearing a Stranglers album. This twelve inches of punk would have been a great prize for most lads my age – but not me.

Half a dozen eggs were the mystery prize on Steve Merike's afternoon show, in recognition for writing a jingle – and I was invited in to collect them. On arrival, he dragged me down the stone stairs to the legendary underground Studio A, where the Trent magic was made. I watched the last hour of his show, transfixed. Afterwards, we walked together to Marks & Spencer on an egg-shopping trip.

I wanted to work in radio. I wanted to be on Trent – everything else was pointless.

4

ON THE WARDS

Hospital radio used to be a trunk road to a career in the medium, as aspirant disc jockeys across the country honed their skills by delivering requests to the dying in disinfected wards, in the hope that a Lena Martell song would take their mind off their major surgery the following day.

Thankfully, my city enjoyed a well-respected hospital radio station, launched in the early '70s when even commercial radio had yet to begin in Robin Hood's City. I was initially turned away from its dusty, prefab building for being too young, but I battled through and, aged sixteen, I finally won my blue membership badge. I grew up as a desperately shy teenager, and catching two buses twice a week to mix with all these grown-ups took all of the little courage I had.

Pete Murray, former long-standing Radio 2 host and Tony Blackburn influence, confessed to me recently that he, too, was dangerously shy. For many people who tend to be more timid, radio offers an ideal platform where they can behave as they'd like to, away from the pressure of prying eyes.

Nottingham Hospitals' Radio was frighteningly well managed, with a clear focus on its audience. It was run by the impressive and towering Barrie 'James' Pierpoint, who later would become chief executive of Leicester City Football Club. Anyone whose career was born there knew about promotion,

PR, preparation, pre-fading and PPM levels. Here, I found an early inspiration in Steve Voce, a warm, instinctive presenter and fine producer who helped fine-tune my radio ear. It was Steve whom I first witnessed broadcasting live close-up. I watched his technique and discovered for the first time how the radio I listened to was created.

All broadcasters begin on air with a very high voice. Thankfully, no recordings remain of my first ever hospital radio show on 17 December 1977, although I do recall 'Underneath the Arches' from a warped Flanagan and Allen LP being my first song, which tells a little of how genuinely well targeted the station was.

In the studio, our equipment was sufficient. Sonifex tape cartridge machines with a loud click played out our stolen, poorly edited jingles. A few battered Ferrograph reel-to-reel tape machines with an editing block nailed near the heads were reserved for audio production, and a swish new Revox tape machine played out the evening's recorded shows from their huge spools. Phone calls could be taken to air by the flicking of a switch in the adjacent office, which was most quickly accessed by climbing through a window.

'Sig (signature) tunes' for each show, which appeared to be near-compulsory in the '70s, were kept on baby 5-inch tape spools: yellow leader tape at the front, red at the rear. Turntables were slow to start, so each had a felt slipmat that one gripped until the required moment. Like the BBC a generation before, we even often had technical operators who would play in the records for us as we focused on what needed to be said. I was very much a junior partner in the whole affair, and strong characters with names like Beryl, Betty and Hilda ruled the roost.

Early lessons were learned about the importance of

vocabulary. 'Listeners' were referred to as just that on air, never 'patients'. We received a crash course on how radio is a one-to-one medium, not least because, on lucky days, we did indeed amass that single listener.

An early duty for me was to present the programme for those in the long-stay geriatric hospitals – one popular feature within was the birthday list: 'Hello Agnes, happy ninety-third birthday. Here's George Formby – and the one entitled…' I'd be instructed to run down the shiny tiled corridors to conduct a last-minute check that Agnes was still alive just minutes before the show, on the pretext of delivering a branded birthday card.

Promotion to a Saturday morning upbeat music show followed swiftly a few months later. To this day, when I hear Kate Bush wailing 'Wuthering Heights', I see a red and beige EMI record label and think warmly of those hospital radio days. Having my first chance to do what I felt I was born to do makes those memories amongst the happiest in my life. And – like so many people who join hospital radio – I met my life partner there, too.

Although a voluntary organisation, the station was militarily structured and even had a hefty staff organogram. I brought a photocopy home to show my mother. Pointing to my role, as a lowly 'features producer', she asked where I wanted to be in the future. My finger moved to the box at the top of the sheet.

Meanwhile, at school, the top ancient universities were being flagged up to me by my doddery head of year, encouraged by what she considered my impressive list of O-Levels. Caps and gowns, however, seemed to me highly unlikely, given my attention had wandered to wireless. Distracted by afternoons and evenings at the hospital, I anticipated my A-Level results would fail to impress Balliol College.

At that stage, commercial radio stations were being pressured by the regulator to provide more 'meaningful speech'. Lord Gordon, who, as Jimmy Gordon, had won the Glasgow radio licence with Radio Clyde in '73, observed recently that he felt the implied denigration of entertaining presentation was unwarranted. As he suggested to me with his owlish smile, giving a great best man's speech demands far more talent than delivering a serious announcement.

To feed the meaningful speech quota, devices such as 'hospital radio link-up' programmes were hurriedly added to commercial radio schedules, and I was duly asked by Trent if I'd supply some interviews with patients.

Desperate for a professional break, I dragged a heavy Uher round the wards so I could record dedications from patients in pyjamas. A generation will recall the Uher tape recorder, possibly by the affliction of a lop-sided gait, given that this German machine weighed as much as a large Christmas turkey. I was despatched to the maternity wards and, as a shy, innocent youth, learned more there about the female body than I had ever before.

Down the road, BBC Radio Nottingham staged a worthy jingle contest in conjunction with the local police. The Constabulary brief called for an anti-car-theft ad campaign, as these were the days when car radios were not line-fitted by manufacturers but bought from the Freeman's catalogue and installed by dads in driveways. Vehicle doors did not lock automatically, so spotty delinquents would steal unlocked cars, or at the very least pilfer the radio inside. I was disappointed only to win second prize – and I often wonder what the chap who beat me has gone on to do in life. The prize for winning the competition was a radio.

BBC local stations were expected to belong to their communities. BBC Radio Nottingham, accordingly, boasted a programme slot called *Open Air* in which listeners could devise their own quarter-hour programme on a subject of their choice. Whilst most punters presumably arrived at the station with a few vague ideas scribbled on a napkin, I turned up with a black briefcase full of scripts and edited audio. My topic was pirate radio, and the programme was produced and broadcast with considerable ease.

A few weeks later, I took a call from Radio Nottingham's long-haired producer Trevor Dann: 'I heard your programme. Bloody good. What are you doing with your life? Are you into rock music?' To this day, I have regretted my honest answers: 'I'm at school still' and 'no'.

Every person working in radio has had a different entry route and it is a matter of seizing the moment and making the most of it. Had I possessed the seeming confidence of many of today's aspirant presenters, I would have bluffed better and who knows where I might have ended up, as this hippie Dann chap wended his way through the highest offices of national radio. Years later, Trevor confessed that my battered tape sat on a dusty shelf at the BBC for years, and he'd often point to it and say: 'We should get this chap in.' It would be almost thirty years before they ever did.

Sadly, my tatty comprehensive school was typically ill equipped to prepare anyone for anything resembling an interesting career. The one rebellious teacher, who dared to wear jeans with his corduroy jacket, handed me a couple of misspelt, smelly pink Banda worksheets that offered the sort of elementary advice on media jobs I'd already worked out for myself.

As Margaret Thatcher settled into her first term of government in 1979, and I won the sixth form sweepstake for guessing her majority correctly, I walked out of school into the big wide world with just a dream and absolutely no idea quite how to pursue it.

5

BREAKING IN

Terry Wogan worked in a bank once, so that seemed like a decent job to tide me over. Interviews were duly arranged with cheap-suited nice blokes at three high street banks. I was offered jobs by each, not least because the seemingly interesting hobby of hospital radio had dominated all interviews, apparently setting me apart from all the other acned school leavers.

The best job offer was accepted – a position at Lloyds, although I opted for it mainly because I shared the same name. This marked the beginning of what was to be a depressing few months. I would stamp cheques, remove staples and fetch packs of twenty Lambert & Butler cigarettes for the sexist boss. I remain grateful for this period, purely because an insight into real life is critical for a decent broadcaster. Counting the minutes to the end of a day for a pitiful wage is something too few on-air presenters in the radio business have had to do.

Planning my escape, I targeted one of the BBC station assistant posts, the first possible rung on the BBC ladder, marginally above that of coffee maker. I filled in the necessary forms and Auntie quickly wrote back a foolscap rejection letter, headed by the old slanted Corporation lettering, with typing so determined that the Os had been punched out.

Commercial radio was the only other option, and here, it was more about demonstrating what you sounded like rather than your result in A-Level Art. I'd make desperately poor audition recordings in the hospital radio studios and despatch them to every one of the new stations around the country, not even knowing where on the map they served.

Having posted the Dymo-labelled tapes off to the relevant programme controller with a personally addressed typed letter, I'd count the days on my fingers, anticipating the earliest date a reply might conceivably be received in the post. As the dog barked and my letterbox eventually thudded, just seeing the franked envelope and handling a sheet of paper headed with a colourful wobbly-font radio station logo felt exciting. Even if they were all rejections.

A junior position as 'traffic assistant' emerged at my beloved Radio Trent. I applied – and was turned down. Maybe it was because I was under the impression that this glamorous job was on the front line, assembling crucial travel news, whereas the role really involved scheduling the ads into their time slots across the day. Not knowing what a job entails is probably not the most promising start.

My disappointment was common. Hundreds of applicants were seeking jobs at just nineteen stations across the country in this exciting new industry. Many candidates boasted experience from the United Biscuits Network, a factory radio station which operated on a professional basis to help cheer and retain the workforce in London, Manchester, Liverpool and Glasgow. UBN, based in Osterley, was an early home for the likes of Roger Scott, Dale Winton, Adrian Love, Nicky Horne, Graham Dene, Peter Young and John Peters. UBN-grown talent was seemingly preferred to a wiry hospital radio lad who wouldn't say boo to a goose.

Radio 210 in Reading was my first real interview. An

encouraging letter suggested that my audition tape had shown 'good promise' and I was invited to drop in to have a chat the next time I was in Reading.

The Trevor Dann experience had taught me that if I were to succeed, I needed to be bolder. So, despite the fact that I'd never even journeyed to London without holding mother's hand, I ventured south to visit the programme controller. Like many stations in that first generation, 210's premises were full of character. The operation was housed in a former civil defence base for Berkshire, described to me recently by former 210 MD Tony Stoller as 'a slightly rundown out of town hotel'.[2]

The programme controller sat in his swivel chair wearing a jacket with his name on, surveying his kingdom below, where the presentation office and newsroom were accommodated. I sat perched nearby on a less important chair.

Given the chap had appeared moderately enthusiastic when writing to me, I was taken aback when he asked me why I had turned up. Luckily, I'd brought my treasured letter with me and I handed over his crumpled communiqué. He snorted and suggested he couldn't remember the tape. Fortunately, I had a copy with me which I handed over eagerly so that he might play through the opening few minutes. Swivelling round, he grimaced and told me: 'It's pretty shit.'

I gather this man is fondly remembered and was respected by many, so maybe his tactics went over my head, or perhaps he'd mixed up the letters, but it was a disappointing start. I did get the chance to turn him down for a job later in life – he never knew why.

By this stage, the Conservatives were back at No. 10 and in 1980 the commercial radio network began to grow once more, with stations licensed initially for Cardiff (CBC), Coventry

(Mercia), Peterborough (Hereward) and Bournemouth (2CR). Whilst government focused on its new broadcasting strategy and radio stations rushed to launch at breakneck speed, I was journeying to the Post Office to despatch yet more audition tapes.

CBC invited me to an interview in Cardiff some months before the station went on air. In the absence of official premises, I met the programme controller in a community centre hall, where we sat on hard benches to discuss his station and my aspirations. CBC had community radio ideals and I felt it was likely to be a little different from my beloved home-town Trent. The boss volunteered he'd get back to me within a week. Indeed, I recall he went to great pains to explain how well he understood the irritation of not hearing the results of interviews. Over thirty years on, as I hear Dan Damon delivering news reports on the BBC World Service, I think of reminding him that I'm still waiting for his call.

Evidently, it was difficult to get a job without experience. Without a job, it was difficult to get experience. Wrestling with the challenge, I came up with an idea for an audition tape that might stand out from the others. Rather than fifteen laboured minutes of pretend dedications, imaginary weather forecasts and 'that was/this is', I assembled a two-minute ad that began by explaining the circularity of my position – and how 'your radio station can break the cycle'.

The novel approach earned me several interviews. Sadly, the quality of creativity that had seemed evident in the demo was belied by the frightened youngster who turned up for interview. The radio me was ahead of the physical me.

Impressed with the production values of the audition tape, Beacon Radio in Wolverhampton invited me to interview for a commercial producer's job. To this day I still recall arriving for a six o'clock evening appointment and ringing the doorbell, staring at the polished brass plaque outside, bearing the company name. Over thirty years later, I would become a founding member of a company which owned that radio station. When it moved premises in 2013, I took away the plaque, polished it with Brasso and restored it to its original splendour.

Beacon didn't quite find what they wanted from me that evening. I was asked to play in the studio for a while and then sent on my way. Rightly, they suspected I would be ill equipped to handle moaning double glazing company owners who didn't like the commercial I'd made.

In February 1980, one of the letters back from Trent was certainly not a carbon copy of everyone else's. It was much worse. This lengthy yet accurate note from head of presentation Len Groat was mired in colourful criticism and long tetchy paragraphs of all that was wrong with my audition tapes. Apparently, I was a 'breathy' version of Radio 1 presenter Peter Powell. Tempted to write back angrily to Len with a list of what I'd found wrong in his last show, I simply bit my tongue and penned an effusive response in Quink ink thanking him for the feedback and expressing just how much it was valued.

My grovelling reply obviously struck the right note, so when my novel audition tape was subsequently received, I was invited in by Len to discuss a job opportunity.

At that point, Trent was being run by a shadow government, as there had been unrest at senior level and the programme controller and managing director were no longer in office. Such turmoil was commonplace in the challenging early years of commercial radio. Across the network, this highly unionised business was caught between what the unions wanted, what the regulator wanted and a distinct lack of enthusiasm from advertisers. The last thing anyone was too concerned about was what the listener wanted.

LBC and Trent were amongst the worst affected by industrial strife, with notable episodes in Nottingham of sit-ins, lock-outs, food being smuggled in to those who carried on, and presenters protesting outside with placards. Indeed, the Trent chairman had been summoned to the IBA at one stage to sort things out: 'You must please now take all practicable steps to achieve an effective resolution to the recent internal problems.'

By the start of the '80s, Trent was run by an acting MD and an acting programme controller and it was those understudies who signed off my employment to the mongrel post of broadcast assistant, earning the princely sum of £3,047 per annum. Len Groat seemed keen, and the acting MD – suited, smooth sales director Tony Churcher – nodded off on the salary 'so long as he starts to dress a little better'. I'd never given any thought to how I looked. Folklore suggests I wore a duffel coat and vest to the interview. I vehemently deny this.

I'd got a job in radio. It was one of the happiest days of my life. Shoppers looked on bemused as I ran past Mac Fisheries, jumping in the air. Life felt good. Maybe unfairly, I still expect people to respond in the same way that I did when they are given their first opening into the exciting radio world. Sadly, it seems not to be the case – and not just because Mac Fisheries has closed.

6

THE DREAM COMES TRUE

Driving into a new city and catching the first distinctive crackles of its dedicated local station was exciting for those of us who loved radio. Online listening was decades away, so the only way a local station could be heard was by being close enough to its pulsing transmitters. A few stations did experiment with making their output available on a phone line, but it seemed undue effort – and phone calls were expensive. On FM, the excitement of hearing different jingles, formats and presentation styles was welcome collateral benefit from a glorious ragbag network.

Each of the country's early commercial radio stations was deliciously different. A glance at the network's map revealed further anomalies: Bradford had a station, but Leeds didn't. The capital cities of England and Scotland had one, but not Wales. London had two, but only in the West Midlands was there any appreciable competition between the new stations, with the significant overlap of BRMB and Beacon.

Nottingham's Trent 301 was based in the rambling Burlington House on Castle Gate, an eighteenth-century pair of dwelling houses, which had been united for a host of purposes over the years, most notably as a women's hospital. With two storeys having been added to the original two in the late nineteenth century, there was ample room for larger-than-life presenters.

The roomy basement, carved out of the city's caves – and a former morgue – was an ideal home for a studio suite. Impeccable sound quality in this era was deemed imperative, as a tribe of regulatory engineers would traverse the country at launch, and periodically, ensuring that the equipment and soundproofing in every studio was fit for purpose.

Ian Rufus, who was part of Radio Hallam's launch in Sheffield, recalls how officious IBA engineers nearly prevented the station from going on air when they heard a whisper of noise seeping into the studio: 'The MD, who was a mild-mannered man, virtually squared up to the engineer, saying: "I'll have you thrown off the premises. We'll lock the doors and we'll go on air whether you like it or not."'[3]

In Nottingham, Trent programmes pulsed from the roomy Studio A, a darkened underground hovel, smelling of cigarette smoke and decorated with red and brown acoustic tiles. It was illuminated by an Anglepoise lamp and a touch of daylight escaping down the fire escape. The studio was equipped with Technics turntables, after the hefty Gates models were retired, ITC triple-stack cartridge tape machines, AKG D202 microphones and a sturdy and expensive Neve mixer with a puzzling 'solo' function, where songs were 'pre-faded' with the fader up. The mic sound powered through and was the best I've ever heard on any station. Every radio presenter likes to hear their own voice sounding the best that it possibly can.

Through a couple of heavy red doors lay MCR – the 'Master Control Room', so-called as the designers originally felt that all signals from the main studio would need to pass through a second studio to be monitored by someone other than a careless disc jockey before transmission. MCR became a backup and production studio, and boasted a unit to handle incoming telephone calls which was the size of a fridge.

Upstairs at Trent, the reception area was always brimming with Nottingham folk: these included listeners collecting prizes that presenters had forgotten to leave; insistent charity representatives demanding exposure for their bric-a-brac stall; and grubby radio 'anorak' characters in battered baseball caps wearing last season's Trent shirt and clutching a carrier bag of contents unknown. The hard-working smiling receptionists, who also had to answer busy incoming phone calls in those days before direct lines and emails, did their bit to keep the blue and white curtained area tidy and professional.

Radio station reception areas formed impromptu community centres. David Mansfield, one of Capital Radio's managing directors, told me about his reception area at Euston Tower in its early days: 'Full of weird people camping out all day. It was grubby and badly lit, just terrible. Have you seen the look of disappointment on people's faces when they come in? They come into the famous Capital foyer ... and it's a shithole.' With TV cameras in studios some decades away, and negligible competition for audiences, this early generation of stations invested little in how they looked.

Open-plan working was not a feature in any business in this more hierarchical age. Offices lay behind closed doors, reflecting the compartmentalisation of the radio industry at a time when programming and commercialisation were compulsorily separate on air. Commercial content of any kind was allowed only to exist within an ad break; no sponsorships or other brand integration were permitted. The regulator further insisted such breaks be 'clearly defined' from programming by means of a jingle 'or similar device'. In BRMB's proposals for its Birmingham licence, the station had suggested the use of 'an electric gong', but wisely cautioned that it could become irritating.

It was not to be until the late '80s, following significant industry pressure, that the IBA began to permit what it called 'co-funded' programming – such as *The Network Chart Show in Association with Nescafé*. Following further relaxations, a pithier *The Nescafé Chart* was allowed. Such weasel words appeared to satisfy the regulator but the distinction likely meant little to listeners.

The messy presenters' office at Trent became my first home as I joined the industry. There I sat, at a huge desk, with broken drawers, listening to the authentic voices of the presenters I had idolised. How eerie it is when those who made you tingle as a youngster become your colleagues, and often friends.

Compiling travel news remains one route into the industry to this day. With little grasp of the field of travel information, not least because I had yet to pass my driving test, it seemed odd that I was deemed sufficiently expert to compile traffic information for the breakfast show. My responsibility was to hammer out timely updates on a battered old manual typewriter, before rushing downstairs to the studios clutching a gaudy coloured sheet of paper, which appeared to garner little interest from presenter Peter Tait.

I would grasp the receiver of my trimphone and contact the police stations, the bus and train services, local traffic control and the AA. The results of the hourly calls would fuel the updates, as at the time there was no access to traffic cameras or online feeds. Whilst people now look back fondly to this seemingly ultra-local heyday, the reality was a little different.

Travel news and the like were only adequately assembled; many broadcasters on many stations were parachuted in from stations afar; and, in the absence of neighbouring stations, the 'local' services blatantly embraced as large a geographic patch as they could.

'What's-ons' were the *sine qua non* of the reputation of many commercial stations. These titbits about beetle drives and amateur dramatic shows could be integrated reasonably well on air in talented hands, and met a regulatory tick box without undue intrusion. My job was to translate the scrappy charity circulars into pithy material on printed cards for on-air use. With scant consultation, I formed the view that no one was really going to be deterred by a 25 pence admission charge or enticed by free orange cordial, so distilled the information to the essentials. Whether anyone ever went to a coffee morning or found a dog thanks to a mention on local commercial radio in the '80s has yet to be ascertained.

Another of my duties at Trent was general production, which included serving the needs of mid-morning show presenter Dale Winton. The station had recognised, before some others, that warm, tight, female-friendly radio would cut the daytime mustard. Dale led the way in his field.

Dale's programme, like so many of its vintage, included horoscopes, which arrived by post. Apart from when they failed to arrive. On those occasions, Dale would scream from the top of the stairs: 'David, darling, can you find me some horrors?' I would thumb through the relevant pages of a tabloid newspaper for inspiration, before conjuring up my own version which was delivered by Dale with his usual conviction.

As a handbrake turn from Dale's froth, a daily lunchtime chat show followed his programme. *Trent Topic* featured a veritable shoebox of random items. As one of its presenters, Martin Campbell (later appointed to the regulators, the Radio Authority and Ofcom) confessed, he was left to his own devices: 'It was actually whatever I wanted to do. I wasn't quite sure what the ratings were. Given it was just an hour long, you could hide.'[4] The *Trent Topic* programme even boasted its own merchandising, although when the boxes of bargain basement pens arrived, we found the supplier had inscribed 'Trent Tropic' in silver lettering on each one. In those make-do-and-mend days, they were retained, in the hope we could conjure up a fitting promotion on a warm day.

I was an honorary member of the substantial features unit which helped secure appropriate guests and speech items for programmes. The regulator laboured under the impression that the fast-moving evening drivetime show would be enhanced by an occasional four-minute feature on such topics as mice in windmills. Presenter John Peters thought otherwise, judging by his wry remarks around the pieces.

Dave Newman headed the newsroom, which was a noisy affair, buzzing with the sounds of typewriters, teleprinters, incoming national audio reports and tough ex-press journalists arguing the toss. Dave was a posh ex-*Daily Mail* journalist of stature, who would demand that, for the bigger stories, we 'take the wagon'. The 'wagon' was a converted dirty white Vauxhall Chevette OB vehicle with a bent aerial, awash with Spangles wrappers.

Dave had worn a wig for years but chose to part company with it. To prepare them for the shock, he took colleagues aside and told them discreetly of his intention. As a humble presenter, I only discovered the truth when I glanced through the glass from the studio to the news booth whilst preparing to introduce a bulletin, and spied an unknown bald head through the glass. With good humour, Dave buzzed the talkback switch and said: 'It's Dave Newman, by the way.'

A Trent tradition led to every departing journalist affixing the Dymo label from their old pigeon hole to an extensive list on the side of a wobbly bookshelf, with their length of time served scribbled alongside each. One read 'three hours'. Apparently, that new female journalist had gone out on a story, never to return. Dashing blond breakfast newsreader Lee Peck was another infamous character. Immensely popular in the building and living the life, he'd struggle in to read the six o'clock morning update, and then catch up on a little sleep, spread-eagled across the large news desk, before dashing down for the six-thirty headlines.

As the '80s began, commercial radio across the country was seeking to placate its regulator whilst providing decent radio – and was getting better at it. I did my bit by producing numerous earnest public service announcements, delivered in as deep a voice as I could muster, for all manner of worthy causes. These were played out straight after commercial breaks.

At that stage, ad breaks were not overlong, as the IBA imposed a statutory nine-minute limit per hour, which remained in place until the end of the 1980s. Whilst freedom in this regard became an obvious industry objective, there are those now who feel that the absence of a compulsory maximum has served to drive down the value of advertising spots. Had it been retained, revenues equivalent to current levels may have been amassed through much lower 'minutage', to the advantage of listeners who must surely object to the unbearable loads currently being carried by some UK stations.

Ads for local businesses were produced in house at each station, originally in durations of multiples of fifteen seconds, as befits a country which had only just gone decimal. Capital had to be persuaded to adopt the same duration ad spots as the remainder of the network. At Trent, creativity lay in the skilled hands of Al Bailey, who'd learned his craft at Radio Luxembourg where he'd assembled many commercials and spun in the discs on music shows for some of the all-time great presenters such as Alan Freeman.

The Trent ambition, boasted at launch by its sales director, was that the quality of local ads should be indistinguishable from national ads, and its shelves of awards suggested the ambition was realised. National ads, however, were easily outnumbered by local material, given it was still challenging for a national advertising agency to buy airtime on all stations in the fragmented network.

7

THE FIRST SHOWS

My mother greeted me as I arrived home on the Number 14 bus after my first show on Trent. 'It didn't go very well, did it,' she said, in the way only mothers can get away with. It was a brutal but accurate assessment of my performance in March 1980.

These were the days when Nottingham was associated instantly with Clough's cup-winning team at Forest. Like many radio stations in a pre-satellite TV world, sports coverage on Trent was duly comprehensive, featuring lengthy bulletins and live commentary. On my debut day, a key Ajax vs Forest match was due to end at a quarter past nine, with the ensuing programme beginning at ten o'clock. I was told to pick up immediately if the line carrying the commentary 'went down', and, if it didn't, to wait for the full-time whistle before filling in with a few songs and chat until the next programme. My initial appearance was accordingly destined to be brief. Whilst a programme lasting less than an hour was hardly sensible scheduling, I now recognise it was likely simply a bribe for being a diligent technical operator.

A first show is always nail-biting, let alone when you are obliged to wait poised for the two hours prior. The 'cue-burn' crackle of Dexy's Midnight Runners kicked off my sweaty-palm on-air performance. At least the disc did not 'wow in', as had the Beach Boys in the opening moments of Piccadilly Radio's existence, or stuck, as had poor Kiki Dee, as the first song ever on Radio Hallam.

I spoke nonsense. My voice was pale and thin. I simply did not yet possess the skills to deliver the entertaining conversation which lived in my head.

A couple of days prior to the programme, Len Groat, the angel who had recruited me – and by now promoted to deputy programme controller – had summoned me to his spacious office upstairs. To me and all the young 'jocks', this Clarice Cliff pottery collector was an intimidating character, sat at his large desk. His office doubled as a record library, with a smaller desk piled high with vinyl 7-inch singles in the corner, at which sat record librarian Jane, who would chip into any presenter–boss conversations with clever, well-timed acerbic comments.

Sat in his high chair looking down at me – lost in the huge low chair across the room like the Dennis Waterman character in *Little Britain* – he pushed his spectacles up the bridge of his nose and commanded: 'You need to change your name.' It seemed to worry management that listeners might be confused between the talented existing presenter Tony Lyman and me, the awful Tony Lloyd. The name David was selected randomly, and thus began David Lloyd's life. I had just missed the era of presenters adopting double Christian names.

Thankfully, I was spared a complete rebrand. Len 'Groat' had taken his radio name from a historic retail district in Newcastle, 'the Groat Market', and evidently was such a fan of the strategy that he became renowned for taking away all of his new recruits' identities. Presenters were known to arrive for a one-off relief shift, only to disappear bearing the name of a local town.

Aspirant presenters always relish bank holidays, as they're most likely to get offered shifts, when the regular hosts have a day off to eat sandwiches in trunk road lay-bys with their families. 'David' duly returned for a second show, a few weeks later, on Easter Monday. The content was the usual music and chat, peppered with contributions from Nottingham's Old Market Square marking 'mushroom day'. A second presenter, Graham Knight, was delegated to link into my programme from time to time, supported by two chatty engineers in a dirty Land Rover with a tall mast. Four people were accordingly involved in what was billed as a broadcast about 'cooking mushrooms in various dishes'.

Those who now shake their heads fondly at how wonderful radio used to be must have missed that show, and countless ones like it at the time across the country. There were some very pretty flowers, but quite a lot of weeds.

8

COMMERCIAL RADIO GROWS

My treasured Radio Trent was effectively under threat of closure. Despite all efforts on the meaningful speech front, the regulator remained uncomfortable with the station's performance, although we on the shop floor were not made explicitly aware.

A new management team was appointed, with two key candidates bringing the respectability the IBA sought. Ron Coles, an ex-teacher with Eric Morecambe spectacles who'd been seconded to the Corporation's local stations in their early days, was imported from BBC Radio Sheffield. Ron was a man who did not tower above others in height, but commanded the respect that good teachers do as they walk into a classroom. He recruited a new programme controller, Chris Hughes. Chris was also a BBC stalwart and, amongst more respectable programmes, he had worked on Radio 1's *Junior Choice*, where he recalled listeners would send in dedications recorded on the old quarter-inch tape wrapped around a pencil.

With the sort of blond messy hair which would become fashionable in the next century and sporting a long crème gabardine mac, Chris seemed as reserved as I was when he was introduced to his new squad. As this intelligent man turned his back on me and stared out of the presentation office window to the graveyard above, I felt it did not augur well. For any presenter, getting a new boss is a worrying time. Paranoia is the third line of any radio presenter's job description.

Ron and Chris knew that changes were imperative for the station to survive. The community careline duly arrived, with tomes of talk about trestle tables and venereal disease. The project, run in conjunction with the Council for Voluntary Services, inserted short and worthy bulletins into programmes, broadcast every few hours from a random office half a mile away. No topic was taboo, and the Trent programme presenters integrated the interruptions with decent enthusiasm, heralded by pretty acapella jingles.

The careline was typical of the 'action desks' which germinated across the network; and they likely contributed more to socially useful broadcasting than had the endless hours of programmes an era before. Many stations also created their own social action initiatives such as the 'Capital Flat Share' list, 'Help a London Child' appeal and many impressive interminable charity Christmas appeals.

Rather like travel news shifts in later years, these carelines also served as a training ground for the broadcasters of tomorrow, not least the gifted Anne-Marie Minhall at Trent, now performing excellently at Classic FM. Anne-Marie taught the innocent me the delights of wine in a box. I was beginning to enjoy life, having identified that David was the real person inside Tony, waiting to get out.

The challenges for the network were not just regulatory. In 1982 Trent again lost money, posting losses of £73,000. As the commercial radio network grew to just over thirty stations by the early '80s, over half were either losing money or barely breaking even.

On air, however, in capable hands, the best stations were starting to master the art of decent music radio with just the right amount of regulatory deference at a price they could afford.

At Trent, music programming was tight, with the usual hourly format 'clocks' to which you had to adhere, drawn painstakingly by hand in biro around a plate from the first-floor kitchen. Vinyl discs were selected from two plywood record boxes in the studio, which would alternate show by show to ensure the separation of song plays on air. Each box was separated into: A (hit); B (softer and lower rotation); C (not quite good enough to be A or B); and D (oddities you missed out if you possibly could).

Oldies were free choice, although their era was stipulated. By the early '80s, Trent's policy was that no show would play any song released before the early '60s, a rule only broken by specialist shows and middle management. Some presenters relished the oldies choice and drew from their immaculately catalogued personal collection. The rest of us resorted to the Trent record library, from which most hit singles had either been damaged or lost over the years. Hence, Trent listeners would always be treated to the obscure '7000 Dollars and You' by The Stylistics and rarely any of their hits.

Although selecting one's own oldies might seem a privilege to today's generation where each second of music is programmed by the station's music expert with the aid of intelligent software, it became a bind to many presenters of my generation, who played the same handful of obscure favourites every week. As computer scheduling began to be introduced, it was once said that 'my best music presenter can probably schedule his music better than my head of music and a computer, but on average across the schedule, the computer and head of music wins'.

Aside from the playlist shows, Trent, like many stations at

that time, still boasted a gamut of evening specialist music programmes: from rock to jazz, from MOR to country and even music from stage and screen. The ever-flexible, velvet-voiced Bill Bingham, who'd been part of the first day on air for Radio City in Liverpool, was called upon at Trent to host both the classical show – and the punk show.

The only one of these non-mainstream music shows which was to endure beyond this phase was the country show, which owed something to the genre's popularity and something to the fact that the show's presenter, Tim Rogers, also doubled as a high-billing sales executive who always secured a decent sponsorship once such things were permitted.

Trent's funky Saturday evening audiences, as they prepared for a night on the town, were feasted with a demanding hour-long weekly speech show devoted to the arts. This high-quality programme, *Alternatives*, was painstakingly produced by an unlikely new recruit to the commercial radio fold, Oxford University-educated John Shaw. Train- and cricket-loving John, who'd joined Trent from BBC local radio and was often compared with John Peel, was a rare individual. A tall gentlemanly chap, with professorial hair flailing, routinely wearing a gabardine mac and clutching a battered brown briefcase, he had a traditional view of life and never owned a television.

John had the knack of identifying the unconscious art in what we music presenters routinely did each day, and could accordingly offer a fascinating critique with enviable tact. Managing up was never his forte, however, and there was a great deal of grumpiness about commercial radio's ruling class, many of whom were considerably less bright than him. John's harrumphing intolerance of those whom he labelled 'widdlepots' explained why he did not rise to the heights his talents warranted.

Steeped in the skills of radio, and a producer of the old school, this perfectionist would sit at his reel-to-reel Studer tape recorder into the small hours, editing every 'err' and 'umm' from every recorded interview. He was always keen to pass on his knowledge and a generation of 1980s radio interns, many of whom now occupy senior positions across the industry, look back and thank him. I can never edit any piece of audio without bringing John's measured tones and furrowed brow to mind. Every single person in radio has an influence to thank.

John died suddenly in 2013, aged just fifty-six.

His devastatingly sad funeral was followed by an uplifting memorial service in his beloved Leicestershire village of Wymeswold, where the beautiful church overflowed with radio's good and great. His brother, Nick, was determined to ensure the event celebrated John's life and invited a selection of people to speak with good humour about various eras. I was charged with recollecting John's commercial radio years and, at Nick's insistence, prepared to speak, illustrated by a multimedia presentation featuring various audio clips of John's distinctive on-air performance.

Sadly, the show proved a little too demanding for the church's IT systems, which obstinately failed to play the excerpts at the critical moment. Although I sought to cover up valiantly, extemporisation at a funeral is more challenging than merely trying to talk rubbish up to a news bulletin. Thankfully, brother Nick, also a radio figure, rose to his feet and halted proceedings for five minutes whilst wires were tugged and PCs kicked. Oh, how John would have laughed.

9

ON AIR

Even the nation's most loved radio presenters would concede that their early on-air efforts were embarrassing and cringe on hearing a recording. In time, voices deepen, pace becomes more measured, and life experience provides a fund of useful anecdotes. Hearing old tapes of young Chris Moyles, then known as Chris Holmes, on Radio Luxembourg, it is difficult even to identify the human being, let alone the Radio 1 giant he was to become.

If my early Radio Trent shows in 1980 suggested some promise, I fear it was brilliantly hidden. Coaching, which is now a part of life for most presenters, was much rarer. I was privileged, however, to be treated to a session with former BBC announcer David Dunhill, who had been invited into Trent to offer his wisdom. Had Google existed, I would have checked on the provenance of this individual, whose clipped tones had closed down the Home Service as it became Radio 4 in 1967, and interrogated him about his fascinating life and times.

'In one sense, I suppose, we're like a bride on the eve of her wedding. We go on being the same person but we'll never again have the same name.'[5]

David left me with a half-page faded carbon copy of an A4 typed sheet, with the master copy, presumably, despatched to my superiors. In that note, this broadcasting great wrote: 'It is a pity to me that so much – if not all – of his quiet charm is lost when he is confronted by turntables, carts and a pile of records.' He continued: 'When he can remove the largely derivative gloss, he can talk tellingly and in the person to person way which a less glamorous form of radio requires.' Wise David was writing of what we now dub 'authenticity'. In less eloquent terms, as a programme director, I have delivered Mr Dunhill's message to countless young presenters.

Despite my painful early shows, I was awarded a regular weekend gig. *The David Lloyd Programme* featured typical Saturday commercial radio fare including updates on car park vacancies, weekend 'what's-ons', and overlengthy surprise phone calls to giggling brides at the hairdressers. There was an occasional contest too, with a £10 voucher as a prize, which I was not allowed to roll over to the next week in the absence of a winner.

I had replaced warm-voiced Kenny Hague, who was much more experienced, and frankly better at the time, on air than I was. Kenny accepted the move with warmth and professionalism for which I have not thanked him until now. Very recently, I was reminded of this, when Adam Wilbourn, a tall, popular, hard-working broadcaster, was substituted on the Free Radio schedule in Birmingham by the lovely Naomi Kent. Generous and genuine good luck messages were exchanged between the two. There is not quite sufficient professionalism and maturity, or human kindness, in our mad industry world. When I see it, it moves me – and it pays off in the long term in this close-knit media community.

My new Saturday shift was complemented by relief presentation duties across the schedule, albeit usually displaced, when a decent presenter would move temporarily to a key daytime show, and I would fill their shoes on an off-peak show where my damage would be minimised. Accordingly, I spent weeks on the late show *Sounds Across Midnight*, for stations still had programme titles, or on overnight duty with *A Little Night Music*, once the station had begun 24-hour broadcasting in 1980.

Round-the-clock broadcasting was a novelty, although stations like BRMB and Beacon had established the pattern relatively early in their lives. BBC Radio 2 was not to join the night-to-dawn world until 1979 and it was not until 1991 that Radio 1 stopped its nightly closedown ritual. Whilst overnight radio is good company for night owls, there was a certain odd satisfaction in ending a broadcast day properly and putting a station to bed at night – and a huge excitement in switching off the piercing tone and airing the first jingle of the day to wake it up again.

One memorable presenter through the small hours, in later years, was perfectionist and Notts County expert Brian Tansley, who'd begun his career in BBC local radio in its earliest days. Sadly, Brian died in 2013, but is fondly remembered. He loved the '60s – and comedy, not least a touch of seaside postcard innuendo. Towards the end of his overnight show, as dawn broke, he'd routinely play a sound effect of a cock crowing from a tape cart, which he'd preface with the words: 'Time to get the cock out.' All went well until the day the sound effect failed.

Many presenters across the country speak with puzzled fondness of those tentative overnight programmes. At the time, 'needle time' remained an issue for both the BBC and commercial sector, with the music copyright organisations still reluctant to allow the playing of continuous pop, lest it took away business from live musicians or provided yet more opportunities for people to record songs off the radio. Fraught exchanges over the years, which had ended up in court, were not just about the size of the bill which stations had to pay for the music they played – but also about the quantity.

Overnight programming could, therefore, only be achieved if stations did not squander much of their allotted needle time in the small hours. Solutions included lots of talk. PR companies recognised the opportunity and would send in dubious tapes of commercially inspired features, seemingly about the most obscure topics possible, maybe as an amusing wager to see which stations would carry them. I remember one half-asleep presenter at Trent quickly lacing up a tape and only grabbing the accompanying sheets of paper as he opened the mic. Halfway through reading the cue, listeners heard him wrestle with the unexpected topic of genital warts at three o'clock in the morning.

The other answer was playing music that was 'non-needle-time'. This included unsigned record labels, hence Sylvia's 'Y Viva España' echoed round the nation at four o'clock just about every morning. Other music was recorded especially, and listeners were treated to 'I'm Not in Love', played by the Radio Clyde Orchestra, or jolly random instrumentals from the Canadian Production Library.

Listeners form a close bond with late-night and overnight programme hosts, and the company of nocturnal radio serves a real purpose to this day. With fewer distractions, and more listening alone, listeners can become worryingly vigilant. As fellow presenters will concur, the later into the night one broadcasts, the odder some listeners appear to become. The crucial advice 'never eat anything given to you by a listener' was duly passed on to me within days of my joining the station.

One middle-aged woman would arrive in the reception area with tartan shopping trolleys laden with lovingly wrapped gifts. She wrote to me every other day on perfumed Basildon Bond, with the length of her letters increasing as the weeks progressed. The listener agonised in each paragraph about the state of our supposed relationship and would invite me to a meeting to talk it over, apologising the next day for not having been able to attend. She had engineered her own reality such that she would never be disillusioned.

Every song I played was supposedly chosen for her especially, laden with meaning, and she would write out the lyrics to prove the point. She would turn up everywhere I did, portraying herself as quite believably normal to everyone she bumped into as she awaited my arrival at local fêtes and galas. She even turned Hetty Wainthropp and alarmingly uncovered every detail she could about my life and family. She knew their names, and where they lived.

Her letters descended into pornographic diagrams of what she envisaged us doing. The painstakingly drawn illustrations were highly unlikely to be realised for all manner of reasons. Many presenters can relate such tales of fanaticism, and the symptoms are remarkably similar.

During the late-night songs, presenters answered their own incoming listener phone calls, lest anyone proved sufficiently interesting to provide a welcome few minutes on air. I recall answering the phone to one chap who informed me he was pleasuring himself every time I spoke.

10

THE PERSONALITIES

Not all radio stations are born equal. Trent enjoyed a reputation around the industry for being a thoroughly impressive station, and a good addition to one's CV. Unlike some, it boasted a distinctive sound and a rich character. A character fuelled by some larger than life on-air personalities who were typical of a time and place in British radio.

The daytime line-up featured gifted presenters, all very different. The ample figure of John Peters bounced around from the breakfast programme to the evening drive sequence. John, like many across the network at the time, had his roots in the presentation sound of the United Biscuits Network, a tight, well-programmed station influenced by the American sound of music radio. John's delivery, vocal styling and his almost rhythmic crafting of the sound, as opposed to the content, of radio marked him out. British radio never really enjoyed the high energy super-slick 'boss jock' style which defined a generation of US radio, but this approach was likely as close as it got.

John's warm and friendly voice was built for radio. It powered through the songs and he was the slickest of the bunch. If you thought you'd voiced tightly up to a vocal, John could still get in one more word.

Off air, John was affable company, and I picture him in those days standing in the pub with a pint of beer, telling stories to his colleagues, with the delivery, timing and expressions of a stand-up comedian.

Sensibly, yet atypically for the time, Trent adopted a policy of not adding all the chart songs routinely to the playlist as, to quote our boss, Len Groat, 'they're only bought by thirteen-year-old glue sniffers'. Accordingly, John's weekly Top 30 was the only programme of the week where certain discs were featured. I recall a locked filing cabinet coming off worse when it dared to come between him and a couple of singles he needed urgently for one weekend's rundown.

Trent had been a late purveyor of chart shows, preferring to set itself apart from other stations. When the policy was eventually reversed, the 'Trent Ten' was played in reverse order, building up to the climax of the least popular song.

The quiet gulf between John Peters and his line manager afforded a seam of rich amusement, whether in witnessing John's reaction to the stream of lengthy memos from two floors up, or the perfect banter at presenter meetings. Fortunately, he was adored by the MD, Ron, on the top floor, who relished the fame of being the lovable butt of John's humour in his make-believe breakfast show world. Trent's insurance company found it less amusing, when they phoned in to raise a query about the lack of cover for the company helicopter. A company helicopter which only existed as a sound effect.

Ambitious Dale Winton, also of UBN stock, had been twenty-four on his arrival at Trent. He came from a family beset by tragedy. His father died on the day of his bar mitzvah, when Dale was just thirteen. As the nation basked in the warm summer of '76, Dale's mother committed suicide.

Shirley 'Sheree' Winton had brought up Dale single-handedly. An actress dubbed 'the English Jayne Mansfield', it was clear from whom Dale inherited his presence. Larger than life in stature, he filled the room the way Geminis tend to. His move to Nottingham and a decent-sized radio station was but a necessary stepping stone in his carefully planned career path. Whilst he had secured a pied-à-terre locally, for a time he retained his London abode at Hatch End and journeyed back at weekends. Dale developed a fondness for Nottingham, but was not the provincial type and his magnetic pole was always London.

Any weekend shows he presented on the schedule were, accordingly, recorded for convenience. Dale had a way of getting what he wanted in all areas; his charm was presumptive but never rude. He played the star deliciously from arrival, and if he could have people look after his every need he did. You wanted to.

Long-suffering programming secretary Jean served Dale and the whole presentation team. A grandmotherly lady with large glasses, permed grey hair and tartan skirt, she'd enter on the stroke of nine, and take off her furry coat and pillbox hat. These garments would be draped on the leaning office hat-stand, ill at ease amongst the branded silky presenter jackets with presenter names on them. Jean tolerated the immature behaviour from the team and was a calm voice of normality in a mad world.

'Jean, darling,' Dale would say, 'can you open my letters – and we really must write back to those other lovely ladies.' Jean would sit dutifully on her threadbare swivel chair, taking down Dale's latest notes of apologies in perfect shorthand: 'Dear Julie. Thank you so much for the note. You must think I'm awful, but your letter fell behind a desk and I missed mentioning your birthday. Do write in again. Love, Dale.'

Listeners adored him – and he was a gifted and instinctive music radio entertainer. Looking back, I appreciate the skill of his craft better now than I did then. The excellence owed little to preparation; Dale would screech up to the station just before nine and run down the stairs, before delivering three hours of perfect feel-good radio.

The show would include guest appearances from the stars of music, stage and screen, on the slightest pretext. Dale greeted them with a kiss on each cheek like the old friends he wanted them to be, which in time they became.

At ten o' clock, *Dial Dale* debuted, with the then podgier presenter holding court with his listeners, who called in for what they seemed to consider the privilege of speaking with him. This preceded 'Dale's coffee break', comprising three random songs segued together. Dale, always a late riser, needed this brief repose for ablutions. At this stage of the programme, in those days before automation was possible, I'd be summoned from upstairs with a 'David, darling' to man the controls. Sitting at a mixer during someone else's show is like driving another person's car. His chair would be wound high, the ash tray brimming with cigarette ends, and his inhaler, puffed before almost every link, lying ready. This was Dale's world.

11

TROUBLE AT T'MILL

A grumpy union member walked past as he left the Trent building during yet another of the station's famous industrial disputes. Looking sniffily at me as I remained inside, he informed me that no one would ever work with me again and my days in radio were over.

Next day, as I sat at home petrified, wondering what to do, MD Ron Coles called and suggested that I should either turn up or join the union. 'One or the other,' he said, in his direct yet polite way. I turned up.

The shiny entertainment world was still beset by industrial action in the '80s, with the Association of Broadcasting Staff and the National Union of Journalists very active in commercial radio. Whilst nowadays, unions still attract appreciable membership at the BBC, it is no longer the case at the commercial stations.

Dale was an Equity member, so he also worked through the industrial unrest. The morning of the strike, he arrived in a one-piece army jump suit, one of the favourite pieces from his wardrobe, and marched through the pickets outside the main door flicking his head theatrically. Once in the safety of the quiet presenter-less presenters' office, he crumbled. 'I can't go on,' he screeched tearily. Then he went on. And put in a determined extra ten per cent. Dale and drama went hand in glove.

Other on-air shifts in that troubled spell were covered memorably by management. In any industry, it is always fascinating when the bosses hold the fort. I recall MD Ron agonising for some time over whether it was twenty-two or twenty-three minutes past eight, and programme controller Chris playing a long track before which he had informed listeners he was off out for a pizza, which he was. Notably, one news bulletin comprised simply an announcement saying that the emergency services had been called – and there was no news. It was an echo of the famous, potentially apocryphal, Easter BBC news bulletin in 1930 which had announced 'There is no news today' and fifteen minutes of piano music ensued.

ITV too was hit by strike action which blacked out screens for three months in 1979: the longest blackout in its history. Displaced advertising monies flew through the doors of commercial radio and provided a welcome boost, some of which was sustained even after the Muppets marked the eventual return of the nation's third TV channel.

It was clear, however, that the staffing levels on which commercial radio had been established could not be sustained. Production supremo Steve England recalls: 'When I got to Piccadilly, there were twenty-two people in the newsroom.' At Newcastle's Metro Radio, programmer Giles Squire observed: 'We had a staff way too big – sixty or more – that was bonkers for a station that was losing money hand over fist.'[6]

Presenters had been blissfully unaware – until recession bit and jobs were lost. Redundancies loomed across the network and Trent prepared an appropriate package of cost savings. The station boasted fifteen journalists at the outset and, when I had joined, the features department had numbered around six. A whole floor of engineers was in residence, serving the needs of this single music radio station. Sadly, for those whose livelihoods were at risk, a cannier schedule, less reliance on 'built' features and fewer random outside broadcasts meant the cuts were borne with ease.

I benefited too, being asked to present a daily three-hour weekday afternoon show which replaced two programmes. *David Lloyd in the Afternoon*, or DLITA as the self-purchased American jingles chorused, was to last a few years. My three hours of music and chat were charged with absorbing what had been a full hour of lunchtime speech between the songs across the longer programme. The 'meaningful speech' was being diluted to the point where it could no longer be tasted.

The speech quotient was easily reached. Friday was expert day, with the Trent Doctor, the Trent Vet or the Trent Lawyer visiting week by week to answer mundane listener queries. Monday meant DHSS matters with silver-haired Bill, who managed to make talk of unemployment benefits and the Youth Opportunities Programme warm, cuddly and even vaguely interesting. Our gardening experts popped up now and again, as did other random interviewees, job spots, the daily toddler and playgroup spot and, of course, a lengthy list of lost-and-founds.

The programme was wholly self-produced. I would research, arrange and deliver every item, no mean feat without the internet for sourcing topics and content. Without any support, I would often run upstairs during the songs to collect my invited guests from reception, make them tea and then breathlessly return to the studio to commence each interview.

One exception was '60s Eurovision winner Sandie Shaw. A thoughtful Trent staff member had heard the myth that it was blindness that prompted her to sing barefoot so that her toes might feel the end of the stage. A puzzled Sandie was therefore led by the arm down the stairs by my helpful colleague and pushed into a studio seat.

I'd been warned by Sandie's acolytes not to mention Eurovision, given that she'd made no secret of how she despised both the song and the contest. We got on instantly, however, maybe thanks to sharing the same birthday, and conversation drifted effortlessly to accounts of that night in Vienna in 1967 when the UK enjoyed one of the largest margins of victory in the contest's history.

Kenneth Williams was booked as a phone interviewee. I feared I had the wrong number as it was answered by a hostile unfamiliar voice. This, it became clear, was the private Kenneth. Once on air, the familiar nasal tones proved as entertaining as ever.

Having hosted a similar morning programme on BBC local radio since, puzzlingly blessed with three producers plus hands-on management support, I believe the appropriate resource solution to be some way in between that and my own commercial radio experience – as I anticipate the BBC will shortly discover.

12

TRAGEDY

Trent presenter Graham Neale was not one of us. Despite the huge differences in character between, and competition amongst, the daytime team at Trent, we lived together on the same floor like a dysfunctional family. Graham, who'd been recruited in 1980 from BBC Radio Nottingham to bring further franchise-retaining depth to the evening schedule, chose instead to create a kingdom for his nightly rock show elsewhere in the building.

On the second floor, his huge desk was organised with military precision, with tape boxes labelled in thick black marker pen stacked neatly around. For some reason, a notice from the Civil Aviation Authority was proudly affixed to the wall above the desk of this amateur pilot, reprimanding him for flying into the wrong airspace.

Whilst we each possessed a powder blue silk jacket trimmed with dark Trent blue, our name embroidered on the chest, only Graham wore his every day, together with his embarrassingly tight jeans.

Graham was sufficiently polite, however, and professional relations were reasonably cordial with all. He sought to be part of the team, but there was a division. Was it because he was the only recruit from the BBC, or was there something else?

Lynn Goldingay was Graham's on–off girlfriend. We all knew Lynn and liked her; she often worked part time on reception when evening opening was necessary to greet guests. This hugely attractive, popular girl had chosen a lengthy relationship with a diminutive presenter with a face for radio. When that relationship went awry, and Lynn went on to find much-deserved love with another, trainee accountant Duncan McCracken, Graham was emotionally bruised.

In March 1985, Graham arrived at work, seemingly distraught. Lynn was missing. After she'd been persuaded to attend a Q-Tips gig with him in the evening, she had reportedly left for work in the morning and never returned.

Halfway through my afternoon show, before learning of the disappearance, I ran upstairs during a song to grab a cup of tea and bumped into Graham waiting for the lift on the ground floor. Ashen-faced, he carried a vacuum cleaner and cloth bag, and wore no shoes. As I returned breathlessly to the studio just as the song faded, I thought I might preview his show that evening. I related on air what I had just witnessed with Graham.

The police were informed of Lynn's absence and, in time, the familiar press conference was convened, where regional TV cameras focused on Graham's face as he uttered the familiar pleas for her to return.

Just days afterwards, the police paid a businesslike visit to the station to question Graham once more; this time, to management's horror, they simply demanded to know where he'd hidden the body. What I did not know was that I had given live commentary of him storing the evidence of how he had killed Lynn.

Graham confessed that the crime had happened at his bungalow after the concert. He was duly arrested and imprisoned.

Detectives were led to Lynn's body, secreted near the Ratcliffe-on-Soar power station. To this day, I never see those mighty grey towers without thinking of this bloody episode.

A few Trent staff visited Graham behind bars in Lincoln prison, some out of genuine care for a fellow human being, whatever the circumstances, or a feeling of professional responsibility; others out of morbid curiosity. I did not go, and to my knowledge, nor did any of the presenters. I heard that Graham had suggested he was hoping to make a new life after all had been resolved; that he was trying to get through the ordeal by treating the experience as if it were a documentary.

Lynn's new partner, Duncan, was inconsolable. He chose to take his own life.

Whether this was the final blow for Graham, or whether it was self-pity, we shall never know, but days later, Graham also took his own life in prison.

Three people had died.

Life on air at happy, jolly Trent had to continue as best it could. Ron Coles called a typically fitting and statesmanlike staff meeting to bring the staff together, allow for a moment of communal grief and try to return the business slowly to a sense of normality. He wisely warned us of the perils of tabloid journalists who would likely be sat in the pub opposite, ears pricked.

No presenter acknowledged on air what had happened, apart from the 'dad' of the team, John Peters. John, not one usually to talk much about himself or real life in his programmes, faced the microphone between a couple of songs and chose just the right, measured words. He acknowledged what the families were going through, and how we were all trying to carry on as best we could.

On the Saturday when Graham killed himself, I was on air covering his lunchtime show. Graham's death predictably led the midday bulletin, as it did on Radio Nottingham. The news was delivered impeccably on Trent by the booming voice of Steve Kyte. I wondered whether I should say something during the show that followed, but wisely decided my presentation skills simply were not yet up to the job. Following the bulletin, I segued twenty minutes of music before delivering a hesitant functional link.

Tragically, almost thirty years later, another ex-Trent presenter would be convicted of murdering his partner. Two unrelated, chilling cases of a particularly disturbing crime which is committed around a hundred times each year in the UK, predominantly by the male partner.

13

BIG SHOWS

In the mid-'80s, Radio Trent without Dale Winton seemed unthinkable. Without doubt, he was the station's biggest star. His reign was to end abruptly, however, with some acrimony in 1986 after his contract was not renewed.

Shortly after his departure, he spotted me in a busy Nottingham restaurant with friends. Popping over to our table, proud and confident, he introduced himself to the group with the classic one-liner: 'Hello, I used to be Dale Winton.'

Whilst Dale would never lack the presence of a star, he was to endure a penniless and challenging spell before TV fame graced him. Some years later, I bumped into him again climbing the stairs at Tottenham Court Road Tube station. Dressed in tight shorts and looking on top of the world, he waved a videotape he was clutching. 'This is it,' he said.

It was. The recording was of *Supermarket Sweep*, the daytime TV quiz show which started him on a journey to becoming a national treasure, 'our Dale'. He was to become an instantly recognisable TV face, hosting other peak-time game shows and the National Lottery, and acquiring the stardom he'd described to me many years before. Whilst holding down a daily show on a provincial radio station, I recall him explaining his ambition in intricate detail, from the sort of programmes he wanted to be famous for, to the personalities he wanted to count as friends. Dale visualised his dream – and brought it to colourful reality.

I was surprised to be invited to take over the reins of Dale's huge Radio Trent morning show. No radio presenter ever wants to follow success, given that listeners are very likely to have loved the predecessor and are thoroughly likely to hate the new intruder. Following Terry Wogan on the Radio 2 breakfast show in 1984 was a tough call for Ken Bruce; as was following Chris Tarrant on Capital's breakfast show in 2004 for Johnny Vaughan. The wonderful thing about radio is that listeners regard you as a friend; although that very quality means they are rudely intolerant when their close friend moves out.

For me, aged twenty-four, the morning show was a welcome recipe for success, not least because of the welcome absence of compulsory dull conversation with random vets, lawyers and dentists in Dale's programme format.

There was also still little competition: Radio 1 remained marooned on AM only, albeit it had moved slightly up the dial from 247m to the better 275m and 285m wavelengths. Radio 2 was focusing on sweet music, and we had as yet no commercial competition. Given that more radio listeners were now, at last, looking to FM for their music entertainment, we were the sole choice. These factors, rather than any excellence on my part, were the reasons for the programme's impressive listener ratings.

Audience figures at that stage, from 1977 to 1992, were registered by JICRAR (Joint Industry Committee for Radio Audience Research), the uncle of today's RAJAR. The methodology was similar, with determined grey-haired researchers knocking on doors to leave listening diaries for people with nothing better to do.

The key difference between the two systems was that the BBC did not subscribe to JICRAR, preferring to conduct its own research. Given that the BBC and commercial radio published figures both for themselves and for their competitors, a merry scrap usually ensued about who was right. The two sides were accustomed to arguing. In the early days of commercial radio, before any official audience figures for the network, the MD of the successful Radio Clyde, Jimmy Gordon (now Lord Gordon of Strathblane) had fired off an irate letter to *The Times*. He pointed out that an NOP poll had suggested that Radio Clyde alone enjoyed more listeners than the BBC had attributed to the whole of UK commercial radio.

A daytime presenter on a commercial station like Trent could expect to be well known. As you bought a pack of Opal Fruits from your local Spar or phoned the local electricity board, your voice would be recognised. Random listeners would stop you in the street for a chat, knowing everything about you, yet you knew nothing about them.

Presenters were invited to be the 'star' turn at all manner of local events. I duly hopped on the green corporation bus to attend gala and coffee morning openings. We'd sign autographs, pose for photographs and draw the inevitable interminable raffle, whilst giving away singles from unheard-of artists and shaking hands. I recall one baby contest I helped to judge on a stifling summer's day, where I was quietly asked to pick a racial balance of finalists.

My Long Eaton Carnival appearance was another memorable day. The organisers suggested they would fly me in by helicopter. This was exciting. This was the big time, I thought, after being told I would touch down in the centre of the main arena with crowds applauding. Only it didn't happen quite that way. On this grey and windy day, after landing, I emerged from the helicopter, swaying and spewing.

The expenses fee for attending such activities was supposed to be £30, which I usually felt I just couldn't accept, on seeing the likely scale of event profits. Fellow presenter Peter Tait used to tell of the day he was thanked on stage by the organiser for his attendance – and the money was then counted out to him on mic, fiver by fiver, as the assembled crowd watched and cheered.

There were fewer distractions in the mid-'80s: no PCs or smartphones, whilst the few TV channels boasted little by way of daytime entertainment. Radio sets, meanwhile, had graduated from being an expensive luxury to becoming eminently affordable. The bulky, polished oak radiogram in the front room had given way to a more compact music centre. This multi-purpose gadget allowed the choice of a cassette, a vinyl record – or the radio.

If the radio did not meet your appetite for musical discovery, there was still 'dial a disc', where you could dial sixteen to hear a selection of crackly favourites in appalling audio quality down the phone. This early primitive music streaming was rendered particularly unattractive as domestic phones were installed by a grumpy, nationalised GPO who turned up when they felt like it and insisted on installing the phone in your cold hallway. Sat shivering on the stairs listening to Mac and Katie Kissoon was not an attractive prospect.

Attention levels to the radio medium were high, so listeners did not just hear you, they remembered what you said. Even now, those of a certain generation who listened to me through the '80s smile wistfully and say: 'Do you remember talking to that woman who…' Radio was treasured by its audience.

By day, I was the bleached blond disc jockey, commanding huge audiences. By night, I'd manage to scrape a bus fare home to Mum and Dad's. Mum seemed OK about my chosen career, although she was not much impressed about missing *Waggoners' Walk* just to listen to me. She was decidedly more impressed when I was given the job as the voice of the Co-op for in-store announcements. When out shopping with her bosom buddy, Joy, she'd linger deliberately under a convenient ceiling speaker and smile proudly. Mothers derive vicarious pleasure from the strangest things.

Listening to muffled cassette recordings of my radio programmes from those days, my audience adulation was not deserved. Overlong rambling links butted into successive unrecognisable songs, 'what's ons' and 'lost and founds'. Music flow had yet to be invented. Indeed, as a fellow presenter once pointed out, if you played two songs without speaking in between, someone would pop down the studio to ask if you were ill.

The first new competition for the sector came from a familiar foe in the North Sea.

Just as the offshore pirates had challenged the BBC in the '60s, it was the offshore station Laser 558 which caused furrowed brows in the '80s. This slick operation was technically lawful, broadcasting from the Panama-registered ship the MV *Communicator*, using American presenters and apparently serviced from outside the UK. It gave Britons back-to-back familiar music punctuated by laser sound effect imaging – without the lengthy news bulletins, long feature material and puzzling music selections found on many UK commercial stations. Their promise: 'We're never more than a minute away from music.'

Whilst music predominated on Laser, the American 'jocks' reminded British presenters that you could deliver personality and impact without five-minute links. Favourites of mine on board included the creative Charlie Wolf, now often heard as a pundit on American politics and news stories, and the remarkable Jessie Brandon. At a time when women's voices were still rare on British radio, Jessie powered through the music with enviable skill.

Just as Radio Caroline had proved a port in a storm in the '60s for a generation starved of its music, Laser offered respite to the young of the '80s who were bored by lists of lost pets.

The impact of the station was quickly felt on British audiences. Seasoned broadcaster Roger Day relates with a smile the tale of how the then deputy director of radio at the regulator, military man Peter Baldwin, invited his views on Laser. After Roger had offered a sensibly deferential response, Peter punched the button on the radio on his large desk gleefully and an energetic burst of hot Laser presentation blared out. 'They are rather splendid, aren't they,' observed the regulator with a chuckle.

Sensible UK stations responded to the surprise competitor. Trent launched an hour of back-to-back music in twice-daily programmes called *Music Jam*. The programmes did have presenters, but the links were tight by design, with segues and crunch and rolls. Thus began the sound of the tighter daytime music radio we know today.

14

BUTTONS AND FADERS

History has been unkind to the '80s. The fashions have not stood the test of time, and I prefer to hide the blurry photographs of me with permed hair, wearing alternative black trousers with huge buckles down the side, dancing to Limahl in dark Nottingham clubs.

At home, we still rented a TV from Rediffusion. For some unknown reason, it had slatted doors which would slide and close to disguise the set as a sideboard. It was likely the most technologically advanced gadget in our house. Radio studios were not much further ahead in those analogue days, with turntables, a stopwatch, no computer screens – and a telephone with a dial.

The complex matter of scheduling the commercials in accordance with advertisers' wishes and budgets was carried out manually with a cardboard strip representing each 'spot', juggled round on a slatted board depending on the booking. The audio for each commercial lived on a single tape cartridge which had to be found, played and returned to its position on the large wire Lazy Susan rack. Life in radio was manual work.

Audio production called upon sturdy Revox or Studer tape recorders. These chunky beasts were laced with a huge heavy metal spool, almost a foot in diameter, bulging with quarter-inch tape. To log an hour of output demanded an entire reel. I was reminded recently by a former commercial radio head of sport Tom Ross that sports programmes would often be recorded on these – and each time a goal was scored, a scrap of paper would be inserted at the appropriate point in the tape take-up spool, so one could swiftly rewind at the end of the show and identify match highlights. The speedy process risked slicing off one's finger when trying to stop the spool too quickly. I am not the only person to have operated a show with blood dripping from my fingers onto the Formica.

Each edit was painful. An individual cut of the tape with a razor blade and the elements repaired with white splicing tape. An early tip was to keep the bits you'd chopped out, just in case you needed to rescue them later. Someone assembling a long production piece would have pieces of tape draped all over the studio.

Complex production necessitated mastering on one tape machine, playing back from another, and adding in other sound ingredients during the dubbing in real time. Lucky studios were equipped with a third tape machine or you could, as I often did, open the fader to the studio next door and run between the two to play in extra effects. One could also play a spot effect off vinyl, from a cart machine or cassette. Your own voice could supply the second or subsequent track, mixed in live. Using your own 'multi voice' meant counting yourself in and trying to speak with, or to, yourself. Whilst nowadays digital recording and motorised faders make complex mixing a relatively simple task, back then each 'take' was an exhausting ballet.

To achieve further effects beyond this exhausting performance, the whole thing would be copied off again, affording a further opportunity to add ingredients, sacrificing audio quality for complexity, remembering that in those analogue days, quality deteriorated on each dub.

The familiar 'phasing' or flanging effect, now available at the touch of a button, entailed two copies of the audio, played simultaneously and recorded on a third, with a finger placed on one of the spools every now and again just to slow it down slightly. The waveforms of the two sounds would interact and the effect resulted. Echo was achieved by putting up the fader on the machine that was recording. Playing the item at half speed resulted in a better echo and reverse echo entailed the same process with the item played backwards.

Kenny Everett was the master of his generation in terms of production techniques. Would digital facilities have made him any better? Or would they have diverted his time and provoked a relentless pursuit of 'perfection'?

As an added burden, the whole production ritual was often conducted at midnight, given studio time was in short supply and audio production, by necessity, was confined to the studio. Rows about studio time would come to blows, followed by typed memos and new booking systems, followed by more anger when the procedures were ignored.

As proven by *Pet Sounds* and *Sergeant Pepper*, you could achieve marvellous things with primitive audio technology. Agility was essential, as well as a knowledge of tricks that are now are about as useful as being able to thatch a roof.

15

NEIGHBOURS

A wise friend once suggested to me that nothing great was ever achieved by committee. Given how political the matter of broadcasting policy can be, it's little wonder that it has enjoyed rather more than its fair share of studious committee scrutiny.

The Pilkington Committee report of 1962 concluded that local radio was incompatible with commercial funding, and agreed that local radio could begin, but only under the auspices of the trusted BBC. The Annan Committee, established in 1974 by the new Labour government, reported in 1977 that all local stations, including the BBC, should be handed over to a new 'local broadcasting authority'. The three-year wait for that report was cause for pause in commercial radio growth, but as the Thatcher years began, commercial radio development geared up once again in the UK, with the network growing at a rate of up to eight new stations a year.

For experienced staff, it was an appropriate time to brush up the CV and look for bigger opportunities. At twenty-seven, I was becoming impatient. David Lloyd became the sort of awkward presenter I was to witness so often in later life. Hungry for change, I sent out numerous audition tapes, this time supported by audience figures and the Trent credentials.

Part of me, however, simply wanted to run the Trent operation. I had become a little impatient with what I believed was poor management and judgement. In later years, I was to discover that programmers, and radio managers in general, face all manner of challenges and conflicting pressures and considerations that are not always evident to the mid-morning show presenter.

On one occasion, I ran up the historic staircase, which runs through the heart of the Trent building, protesting loudly and rudely that the programme controller could not 'organise a piss-up in a brewery'. Sage Chris did not baulk. I was simply escorted to the Farmhouse Kitchen down the road, in the bowels of our local WHSmith, treated to a coffee and a bite to eat, and asked what was wrong.

The solution offered by my over-tolerant boss to cheer me up was to 'play a few of your favourite songs on the show'. I cannot imagine the solution being recommended to boost the morale of today's presenters. Former Capital and Magic presenter Neil Fox shared with me the story of how his PD, the famous programmer Richard Park, had shouted at a colleague: 'If you really want to play that song, play it at home. Don't play it on my radio station.'

Competition arrived close to home, which would eventually lead to new opportunities. Down the road in Leicester, a new neighbour debuted – Centre Radio came on air in 1981. Trent geared itself for a battle on its fringes and it realised it could no longer claim the entire East Midlands region as its own.

'We are a commercial station and we'll have a bright popular image, but this doesn't mean any lack of information, news and features,' claimed launch MD Ken Warburton.[7]

Many talents walked through the Centre Radio door, including breakfast show presenter 'zany' Timmy Mallett, as 'Timmy on the Tranny' replete with multi-coloured hair and bowtie. A host of now well-known journalists also made their mark and the station was confident of success.

Centre, however, was overambitious in a challenging economic climate. In 1982, the chairman walked out during a board meeting, citing 'irreconcilable differences'. The station became the first UK commercial station to fail, closing after just two years on air. Trent sought to save the station by proposing a rescue bid, and its MD Ron Coles recalls that the plan had been accepted by the regulator and the unions. To his surprise, the life-jacket was rejected by Centre's employees.

On 6 October 1983, Paul Young's 'Come Back and Stay' faded away and the station prepared for death. Memorably, despite the pressure of the closing moment, the presenter joined in with the song's final chorus, rapping the words 'rinky dinky', proving once again that if you surprise the audience, it'll be remembered. Newsman Tony Cook delivered the last rites and the station closed. The city which had produced the first local station, Radio Leicester, had produced the first commercial radio casualty.

Such had been the confidence that staff might vote to keep the station on air and retain their jobs that Len Groat had been despatched to re-record his Trent jingles with its proposed new sister station's name, Leicester Sound. As he arrived back from Manchester, eagerly clutching a couple of large spools of tape bearing the fresh station name sung repeatedly by gifted singers, Len wrinkled his nose at the news that the station identifications wouldn't be used any time soon on the radio, if at all.

The regulator duly readvertised the Leicester franchise and Trent prepared to submit a formal bid to start the venture afresh. Trent sought growth, but also wanted to ensure, commented MD Ron Coles, that commercial radio should appear a secure business so that confidence remained in its Nottingham operation.

During the process, Centre Radio's impressive stately home next to Victoria Park was disposed of by liquidators. Who would want the lovely Granville House, boasting a built-in set of barely used studios in what had been the building's stable block?

Trent decided on a brief foray into the property business, when Ron Coles presciently concluded that, if successful in its licence application to run the station, Granville House would be an economically sensible and timely solution for the new station's accommodation.

An engineer and I were despatched to Leicester in a dirty, marked car, armed with a large bundle of keys. Parking across the road on the edges of Victoria Park, we gazed across at the 1876 pale-bricked Downton Abbey-esque building with its stained-glass windows. Up the drive and behind the two pairs of double glass doors lay the ghost of a radio station, its contents untouched for a year.

I switched on the lights to studio one, its walls covered in dusty green baize. On the black mixing desk lay the weather forecast for the day the music died. By its side, a coffee cup and a scrap of paper on which the words 'Centre Radio lives' were doodled in red pen in determined red oblongs. A memorial to Britain's first commercial radio death.

Leicester Sound was successful in its licence bid, and the new station took to the air in September 1984. The former Centre Radio receptionist was reappointed, and arrived clutching a bunch of rusty desk keys, as she'd been off work on the day of its death. She found her drawers still replete with paper clips, pens and tardy telephone messages.

I had little input into the launch and Trent's programme controller hired Leicester's daytime line-up, poised to broadcast live for twelve hours a day, with specialist music programmes and the late show filling the remaining hours, piped from Nottingham.

The new team of local presenters resided in a magnolia woodchip office, cheered by painted coving. The messy room was strewn with cardboard 7-inch single covers addressed to ex-presenters and a model of *Thunderbird 2* dangled from the high ceiling, adjacent to the desk of one notable presenter, the avuncular Andy Marriott.

My Trent colleagues and I observed critically, from down the road at the mother ship in Nottingham, and the rivalry which always exists in any multi-site operation began. The people in the other place really don't know what they are doing quite as well as we do.

Leicester Sound launched cautiously, as suggested by its geometric logo in corporation green set in anaemic caramel. That was best showcased on the radio car, a lop-sided, converted Ford Cortina with questionable suspension and a retractable mast as high as Droitwich. The vehicle and the studios overall were duly maintained by the station's three committed engineers, who lived in the station's engineering workshop from which the delicious smell of flux would waft.

My dad once said that if you can sell something in Leicester, you can sell it anywhere. The station was a decent offering on air but struggled commercially. I recall it once being suggested, probably accurately, that the station made more money from running the Coke machine than the radio business. Client suspicion of a second failure added to all the difficulties its predecessor had faced in getting local advertisers to commit to spending. Sales directors came and went, including the familiar British error in thinking that a brilliant high-billing sales executive will be similarly gifted in management. Let's just celebrate exceptional sales executives, without feeling the need to attach a manager title to their lapel to show how brilliant they are.

After seven years on air at Trent, my management pretensions were clear. I'd assumed responsibility for all manner of operational matters in Nottingham and had become an established part of the line-up. The company apparently felt that my abilities in generating local noise and relevance on and off air might help to build audiences in Leicester – and I imagine they wanted to shut me up. Leicester Sound had hitherto been run part time by Trent executives, and I gathered they now sought someone on the ground to lead this challenging station to audiences which more closely resembled its successful sister.

It was announced that I would leave Trent and move to a management post in Leicester. The startling news appeared to be sufficient for the *Nottingham Post* to carry a generous spread. Like so much press coverage of radio matters, the journal staged a pointy photograph with me showing my replacement, the new morning presenter, 'how to do it'. The fact that Tony Lyman been doing it longer than I had seemed irrelevant to the donkey-jacketed photographer.

You never forget your first station and there will for ever be a huge part of my heart bathed in Trent memories. I'd turned from boy to man behind its doors. The valedictory morning show was thoroughly emotional and utterly self-indulgent. As the recordings sadly illustrate, when I tried to announce my last song, the immaculate 'Goodbye to Love' by The Carpenters, I sobbed instead. As Tony Peluso's famous fuzz guitar solo faded four minutes later, I was inconsolable. Who on earth would volunteer to leave Nottingham for Leicester?

After seven years on air, some listeners did miss me, I hope, not least the chap who left a message with the receptionist to say: 'I thought he was a twat at first, but sort of liked him by the end.'

16

OFF TO LEICESTER

Rolling up at Leicester Sound on day one in my new post, clad in smart, baggy chinos, white shirt and showbiz tie, I tried to do the things I thought bosses did. Like many fresh managers, I wasn't very good. Unable to persuade or influence a team older and more experienced than me, I relied purely on the authority vested in me by my title to get anyone to do what I felt was needed. Blessed with neither management experience nor training, I could draw upon very few influences of style.

The role was general manager, effectively responsible for everything, but in charge of nothing. I became programme director, marketing director, facilities manager and still hosted the morning show. When an outside broadcast was organised at the city's annual show, I'd talk about it on air; record a promotional trail; book the large drop-down stage; beckon it into position at the crack of dawn as it reversed on site; help to crank down the legs and set up the merchandising stall; jump on stage to entertain and broadcast live; before then helping to de-rig, pick up litter and disappear back to base to consider strategically whether such an outside broadcast was a good way to be spending our time and money.

Whilst line management responsibility for the commercial team lay elsewhere, I had to suffer the day-to-day fallout of their efforts in the building. The advertising sales executives were an interesting bunch, including one delightful woman who chose to throw a glass of red wine over me during some celebration in the department's top floor attic office. I recall standing there, feeling humiliated, reminding me of when a girl in the fourth year at school had spat her Mars bar at me. I learned later that the sales executive was to develop more problems with alcohol than the single glass she poured over my shirt.

The theme was to recur. In the early days of my reign, news quietly reached me that the breakfast presenter, Nick Murden, was frequently a little late. His colleagues had, apparently, become quite accustomed to this. In my new capacity, I felt I had to be seen to act. On a chosen morning, my alarm was duly set, and I hurried to the main studio to witness his likely tardiness.

As six o'clock came and went, no one else arrived at the door. I fired a torrent of station jingles, introduced the news in a 'just got up' voice and got the station underway. When a crestfallen Nick eventually meandered in, I sent him home and continued presenting the programme myself. Utterly firm and decisive action from this capable new manager.

As nine o'clock came, I quickly phoned head office in a wild panic and asked what on earth I should do next.

Sadly, Nick was not to return. A hugely popular chap, he had his own demons that had led to the end of his career that day, and ultimately claimed his life at the tragically young age of thirty. The station's first voice is remembered with fondness by former colleagues and many listeners. I reflect on my actions that day.

In those days, radio stations were where the stars were. With little daytime TV and no online coverage or social media, radio was the place to be seen and heard. The boyband Bros, who were to become hugely popular heartthrobs in time, visited Leicester Sound just before their career took off. The day of their visit coincided with their first TV performance and they didn't want to miss seeing themselves on the famous *Pebble Mill at One* just because they were on the road doing a radio interview. Whilst there was ample time for the boys to watch the programme, Leicester Sound, sadly, did not possess a TV set. I ran back to my flat nearby to grab a heavy portable one and returned breathlessly, just in time to twist the wire aerial to get a fuzzy picture of their three young, smiling faces.

The newsroom was housed across the corridor in a draughty conservatory, with the compulsory aged car stickers from other stations peeling off the cracked window panes. Newsroom staff, now using electric typewriters, were supervised by the gentlemanly news editor Peter Butler, as the religious programmes duo bickered in the corner. This was another station brimming with character.

I remember tackling one of the news team, probably poorly, about a story treatment, to be greeted with an indignant response from the talented Jackie Leonard, now at the BBC World Service. Although she might not actually have said 'what on earth do you know?', I recall her face suggested just that.

The reception area at Leicester Sound was unusually impressive, owing to lavish investment by its predecessors. With soaring ceilings, intricate coving, a huge marble fireplace and a couple of large brown leather Chesterfield sofas, it was one of commercial radio's more welcoming vestibules. One programme guest made herself so comfortable as she waited for her appearance that she fell asleep.

Brilliant cartoons dangled from the elegant mahogany picture rail, donated by a local artist who was a loyal listener. Every presenter was gifted a personal design, inspired by their on-air character, and the observational detail on each was frighteningly accurate. Just by committed listening, the gifted designer had identified not only who we were but the friendly and not so friendly rivalries and sensitivities.

At the desk on reception duty was Wendy Staples. Every great company needs a Wendy: an individual who instinctively unites the building, whatever their title.

Wendy understood her job was to meet – and then exceed – listeners' needs, not to answer phones. She also knew everything and everybody in the business. She listened; and said the right things to the right people to ensure the most positive outcomes. She defended vacillating management decisions with serial professionalism and loyalty, and supported managers less able than she was. She both looked after her 'boys', and told them off. People both hugged her and cried on her shoulder. She danced to the Bee Gees as you played them and made the sort of encouraging faces through the glass to the studio that every presenter needs to see when they are on air. She understood. I met other Wendys in my career, and radio owes them a debt.

On air, the station was fun. The imagination and freedom of the early 1980s was evolving into a slightly more considered approach. Oldies were still selected from the huge walls of vinyl in the record library, overseen by a character known on air as 'Bubbles Goodbody'. Playing something 'off CD' was a major event and thoroughly trumpeted on air. The CD albums we chose, however, rather depended on which ones our friendly local hi-fi store had lent us.

By the second half of the decade, music was being programmed at several stations in the growing network 'by computer', a fact which caused some lively division of opinion.

The computerisation depended on Selector: sophisticated American software, which, in the case of well-programmed radio stations, was simply a convenient way of doing what had always been done. The secret of its excellence to this day – and of its adoption in radio markets around the world – is that it was developed and supported by those who understood music radio programming.

In the UK, Selector training and support was offered initially by the redoubtable Angela Bond and her daughter Sue. Angela, who died in 2013, was a dame, renowned for her music programming ability from her Radio 1 days, and for having been Kenny Everett's favourite producer. Like the greatest producers, wonderful Angela had become mother-confessor to this complex soul. She was the right character to deal with the sometimes prickly presenters and programmers she would meet, as she helped drag British radio into a more sophisticated approach to music radio.

No longer would we arrive in the studio with a pile of random records; instead we'd clutch a carefully assembled programme song listing log, printed laboriously on a noisy dot matrix printer. I recall that the font could not be changed and thus the titles of songs would not be printed in their entirety. Much mirth ensued as one enthusiastic presenter announced Paul Simon's hit '50 Ways to Leave Your Lo...'

From the outset, there was a worry that Leicester Sound was being confused with the hugely successful, and first ever, BBC local station, Radio Leicester. We experimented, puzzlingly in retrospect, with declaring that we were 'the commercial sound of Leicestershire' and 'after-the-break radio' to highlight the distinction that we were the station with the ads on. It's not a strategy I'm proud of. Then, as a last resort, we discarded the element of our names that we shared: Leicester. Hence 'Sound FM' was born, possibly the worst station name ever. It was another wholly imperfect solution, and, wisely, the 'Leicester' returned after my departure.

Like at Trent, a careline was installed, albeit even more politically correct than its Nottingham equivalent, with Christmas trees dubbed 'inter-denominational winter trees'. One never quite knew what would follow the acapella jingle. There was once some sort of military coup amongst the careline's complex management factions so, whilst on air, on went my management hat halfway through a long song and I dashed out to the pavement of London Road opposite, to arbitrate a tug of love over custody of the desks.

Radio stations are renowned for their merchandising, albeit many BBC local stations seemed to miss out the vital stage where a qualified designer and copywriter are involved. Leicester Sound boasted an impressive array of merchandising, from the usual T-shirts and mugs to branded, cuddly teddy bears and a selection of boxer shorts. Given there were male and female versions of this fetching green and white logoed underwear, it was Wendy's critical job on reception to ensure that those who needed a pair with a useful opening received just that.

One piece of inspired marketing made use of the thousands of old Centre Radio T-shirts that had been uncovered in the basement. The Centre logos were splashed across with a Leicester Sound logo, above the words 'Recycled T-shirt' in bold print.

The station took its place in the fabric of the city, and rallied round in times of crisis. In the terrible February snow of 1991, young presenter Mark Hayman and I launched emergency programming with non-stop information on power cuts, proposed school closures, travel news and road conditions. That double-header Sunday show continued for eight hours, receiving special dispensation to barge right through the Pepsi Chart.

One valiant listener parked his car just outside and slid up the icy path to bang on the reception door, only to ask for a wire coat hanger with which he could fashion a makeshift aerial for his car. Back then, before the days of social media and online information, you just couldn't live without radio.

17

JINGLES

Some people collect stamps; others are trainspotters. In the UK, more so than another country, I gather that there are a sizeable number of puzzling people who obsess over radio station jingles. Like the other two hobbies, most jingle collectors are male.

The short lush bursts of close harmony performance are impressive, not least because of their brevity, their clarity and the way in which the best sew programme content together. They serve to 'image' the on-air environment with audio colour and, in the words of John Evington, long-serving Signal Radio programme controller, are like 'the decor in a nightclub'. Like many art forms, they sound considerably easier to create than they are.

In our younger days, like-minded anoraks and I would patiently capture these treasures off air like rare butterflies, the allegiance with a favourite jingle company resembling that of a football club supporter.

Even in my teens, I observed a difference between the thoroughly decent early Trent jingles and the immaculate Radio 1 identifications. Unwittingly, I had detected the difference between the product emanating from the UK, where radio jingles were a new industry, and the US, where hundreds of fast-moving rock 'n' roll stations had been demanding them for years from companies like PAMS and, subsequently, JAM in Dallas. Dallas was to jingles what Detroit was to cars.

'It's a merry-go-round of musical fun. Radio 1 funderful – Bee Bee Cee. Funnnn.'[8]

Whilst BBC Radio 1 had been permitted to use American jingles from its first breaths in 1967, inspired by the best of the offshore pirate stations, the approach was frowned upon for commercial radio, owing to the complexities of the relationships with the copyright bodies. Some stations accordingly resorted to the best that Britain could offer and launched with a memorable home-grown package; others aired more puzzling material.

'Pennine 235 – that's the sound going into your ear-'oles.'[9]

By the time Leicester Sound launched, both itself and Trent were using jingles created by a promising English company called Alfasound, based in a former school building near Manchester. The company was run by talented musician and jazz fan Alan Fawkes alongside radio brain and jingle fan Steve England. Alan recognised the big band sound underpinning some of the greatest American jingle cuts and that the harmonies resembled those of '50s vocal quartet The Hi-Los. In turn, Steve knew, from his own on-air work at the pirate station RNI and Piccadilly, just how the jingles needed to work on air. Inspired by the JAM sound, the company got closer and closer to producing something which resembled its polish.

Poetic Trent jingle packages, featuring lengthy station anthems in iambic pentameter, were caressed by Len Groat, another knowledgeable jingle fan who was afforded a generous annual budget to spend, given the company was obliged to spend money on British musicians. Knowing of my interest, he indulged me, and I contributed a few corny couplets from time to time.

'Listen (whisper). Discover the secret! The magic – of Radio Trent!'[10]

The arrival of a freshly baked package was a Christmas Day feast for those with the jingle gene. We'd play through the tapes repeatedly at top volume before beginning the labour of love of naming each 'cut' and planting it on a pristine tape cartridge. Each 'cart' lovingly labelled, colour coded and ready for use.

The next day, using the new jingles on air for the first time, all programmes were discernibly impaired both by their over-use and by the fact we were listening to them during the songs rather than concentrating on more important matters.

Once in charge at Leicester Sound, I was authorised to commission my own station identifiers, and we wasted no time in devising over-wordy localised versions of the famous Trent jingles. Off I drove across the Snake Pass to Manchester for the recording sessions, watching and listening as each seven-second cut was lovingly sung, syllable by syllable, layer by layer, hour by hour, cut by cut until the lush harmony was mixed to perfection.

Daringly, in 1987, Len chose to invite one of the perfect American singers who did a lot of work for JAM to join one of our recording sessions in Blighty. Jackie Dickson probably sang Abraham Lincoln's namecheck, and her breathtakingly pure voice had been heard on jingles coast to coast on all formats in the United States for generations. Injecting her talents into a recording session in rainy Manchester was a treasured experience.

The American singers sight-read music and perfected their parts in seconds; they'd been doing it all their lives. Whilst the British singers continued rehearsing, Jackie would sit casually knitting a cardigan on her high stool by the microphone. Every so often, she'd put down her needles and sing the requisite half a dozen notes – perfectly. The British singers were quick learners and wasted no time in acquiring Jackie's skills, to the extent that some of them are now working in America.

In due course, we were permitted to buy jingles from whomsoever we wished. In 1988, to my surprise, I was designated the company representative for our first imported project and was flown via New York to Dallas to witness the creation of our great American dream.

Accompanied by Steve and Alan from Alfasound, this was my first ever US trip and we were well looked after during our December days in Texas. From being driven from the airport by Jackie Dickson; dinner at vocalist Johnny Hooper's house, replete with an unforgettably large, American-sized Christmas tree; to being shown round the set of the popular soap *Dallas*.

As Christmas loomed, we wide-eyed Brits were also invited out by the locals to attend a festive concert at a local theatre. What our hosts had failed to explain was that many of the vocalists involved in the performance were jingle singers. This was Dallas, after all. If you were a good singer, you'd likely be earning your crust in the trade for which the city was renowned.

The Dallas auditorium fell silent. The curtains opened, to reveal the sight of Santa's twinkling red and green grotto. As the orchestra struck up, the ruddy elves burst into song, delivering familiar Christmas melodies with the multi-layered JAM jingle excellence emanating from the cheeky little red faces. For a jingle enthusiast, it was as if all my Christmases had come at once.

In almost Shakespearean contrast, we flew home by Pan Am. It was the same plane, the same carrier, on the same day, on the same route which would be bombed over Lockerbie just hours later with the death of 243 passengers and sixteen crew.

As the style of radio changed, pretty sung jingles suffered the fate of bell-bottom trousers. In Britain, they were to be replaced on many stations by voice-over 'liners' buried in explosive whooshes and bangs. Where vocal jingles were retained, their style was less glossy, in keeping with the prevalent music styles. In the words of Steve England, whose brilliant business suffered from the changing fashions, his jingles were viewed as 'too good... too polished'.

For those of us who get a high from cranking up the volume on a set of quality jingles, and for whom listening back to a favourite old package is like flicking through a photograph album of happy times, the fall from grace of these perfect lush harmony pieces is sad, although station name recall and ensuring a station's sound fits its brand are the genuinely important matters, howsoever they are achieved.

Average listeners did recall the station jingles and would sing them as they walked past your premises, albeit the melody yelled across the cobbles usually resembled nothing which had ever been recorded.

18

DOING THE SPLITS

Commercial radio's earliest stations proudly defined themselves by their AM wavelength, as had Radio 1 and Luxembourg.

'Metro 261 – the North East sound.'

Although each commercial station was awarded a principal FM frequency, on which it broadcast excitedly 'in stereo', AM listening was still predominant through the 1970s. Even midway through the decade, your Austin Allegro was as likely not to have an FM radio as it was to have one. The burst of new stations, however, helped FM to grow, and soon most of the radio sets in homes and cars purveyed both wavebands. Similarities are clear between FM's trajectory and the growth of digital audio broadcasting (DAB).

Leicester Sound was one of the first stations in the country to put its AM and FM frequencies to different uses rather than simulcasting the entire output, and it formed one of the six stations in a 1986 IBA experiment. Clyde tried out a weekend 'Clyde FM' alternative to Radio Clyde and Capital launched a weekend 'CFM'.

In Leicester, evening Asian programming on AM proved hugely successful. 'Sabras' (all tastes) – run by the impressive and gentlemanly Don Kotak, a Leicester businessman with a passion for radio – expanded from a programme into a full night-time Asian radio station, lodging at Leicester Sound.

Its dedicated team became part of the building's rich character, from the wonderful curries delivered by the team to rather large overseas phone bills. I was also called upon by the hard-working Asian commercial producer, Anwar, to read commercials for '30 per cent off all saris, Belgrave Road, Leicester', which would be liberally spiced with tape echo. Anwar worked literally through the night at busy times and was always puzzled with English work patterns: 'Why do you work 9–5 when there's nothing to do, and yet go home at 5 when you're busy?' He made a fair point.

Sabras became huge in this cosmopolitan city where, in 1972, 10,000 Asians had arrived to start new lives after being expelled from Uganda by dictator Idi Amin. Audiences were impressive, response was enthusiastic and the building throbbed with visitors on 'open days'.

One afternoon, Don wandered considerately into my office to alert me to a special guest who might draw crowds on the programme that evening. Knowing I'd be unfamiliar with the Bollywood star's name, Don volunteered that he was the equivalent of the Bay City Rollers, although, if we had been discussing this more recently, he'd likely have said One Direction. In common with most companies of the time, I'd been given no health and safety training and was unsure quite how to prepare for the visit. I did take the precaution of phoning the police and alerting them, ignoring the fact that any fallout was likely to be within our leafy curtilage rather than on public property. The patient police officer I spoke to shared my lack of understanding of the star's likely appeal and spoke to me as if I were a man calling about having seen a flying saucer.

Later that evening, as Don had predicted, the crowds grew and grew. As the broadcast began, they grew further, as thousands of fans made the pilgrimage to our building. By the time the interview was over, the car park was packed solid, as was the frontage into neighbouring Victoria Park. Feasting off the adulation, the star then chose to address the crowd in a Pope-like manner from my first-floor office window, whipping up even more excitement.

His acolytes concluded correctly that the personality's exit would be problematic. I don't recall being involved in the conversations which resulted in his leaving through a side door; a door, however, which also opened into the baying crowd. As the star left, jumping into the large vehicle with blacked-out windows, the crowds followed; wailing teenagers jumped on the bonnet and clung to the car's doors as it revved to escape.

As the crowds dispersed, I surveyed the car park; it was littered with detritus. A lone, late constable ambled up the drive. 'Everything all right?' asked PC Plod. I was shivering and shaking – and could barely respond. A serious injury or fatality could have occurred that night, and I learned a quick lesson on health and safety which was to stay with me throughout my career.

In later life, when organising things such as clandestine visits from One Direction, The Wanted or The Vamps to our Birmingham radio station, record companies would comment on our immaculate procedures. The night in Leicester helped me learn the hard way; just as the West Midlands station BRMB had in 2001, when it was fined for a competition where the backsides of listeners were damaged when they sat on dry ice to win 'the coolest sets in town'.

19

GOLD IN THOSE HILLS

Listeners know the answers when you trouble to ask them. Puzzled as to the extent to which FM had been adopted by our audience, a cheap experiment was devised by Radio Trent. A recorded contest was played out simultaneously on AM and FM, but with the answer options labelled differently on the two wavebands. As we counted the numbers of each response, the conclusion was overwhelming. By 1987, for us at least, FM ruled at last.

Buoyed by such results and the success of 'split frequency' experiments like Sabras, a 'use it or lose it' mantra was proclaimed by the regulator, whereby stations were strongly urged to create two distinct services on their allotted frequencies or risk losing one.

Most reached for The Beatles, Cliff and Elvis CDs, and chose to run freshly branded 'gold' oldies stations. Capital Gold is often cited by those who should know better as having been the first AM oldies station. It was not. County Sound, which served Surrey and north-east Hampshire, launched County Sound Gold in June 1988. Capital Gold was not to enter the fray until November 1988, proving an excellent home for a whole host of familiar talent including Tony Blackburn, Paul Burnett and Kenny Everett.

Some stations initially swerved the gold rush. Liverpool's

Radio City launched City Talk on AM; and in Manchester, the Piccadilly brand moved to AM, creating a new upmarket ABC1-focused service on FM called Key 103 – under a slogan which puzzles to this day: 'Music, not music'. Were it not for this unusual strategy in September 1988, Manchester's local FM service would probably still be called Piccadilly.

In the absence of a rational conclusion, which is puzzlingly often the case with life's major decisions, instinct usually takes over. When the plum job of running the Manchester station was offered to me by owners TransWorld in 1988, I was utterly unsure of what decision to take. I heard myself saying no to this influential gig running a station in one of the UK's biggest markets. Shortly afterwards, the station was acquired by EMAP. It's good not to be newly appointed when ownership changes.

The East Midlands also beat Capital to the gold format, launching the UK's first 24-hour stand-alone oldies station, dubbed GEM AM, in October 1988. It was to commandeer the medium wave frequencies of the three FM stations in Nottinghamshire, Leicestershire and Derbyshire, although evening programming on the Leicestershire transmitter was still provided by the Sabras team.

To launch GEM AM, an idea had been hatched to cash in on Seoul Olympic fever by means of a team of runners carrying our own 'Olympic Torch' from Leicester Sound to the Derby premises, and then to Radio Trent HQ in Nottingham, from where this new regional service would launch at midday. What better way to unite this region, which refuses to be a region, than showing you can run all the way around it.

At six o'clock on the morning of the launch day, we duly gathered outside Leicester Sound: shivering station staff, a few accomplished marathon runners including Olympic medallist

Duncan Goodhew, and smiling MD Ron, who was in celebratory yellow trousers. The dedicated runners were accompanied by our battered radio cars, crawling along the route. I broadcast from one, linking live into the separate programmes on the stations in Nottingham, Leicester and Derby to provide coverage of the six-hour journey to Robin Hood's city, at the end of which, we would steal their AM frequencies.

I had anticipated a memorable finale in Nottingham's Old Market Square with throbbing crowds, cheers and bunting. As it transpired, the designated finish line was a deserted car park behind Nottingham's less illustrious, concrete Broad Marsh shopping centre. The runners and I arrived duly on time to be greeted by a small group of smiling station staff in sweatshirts, two odd-looking listeners armed with carrier bags and a puzzled, lone client with a dog.

As the clock struck twelve, I shouted a garbled commentary of the lighting of a large celebratory firework, marking the start of transmissions. John Peters fired in a few extra sound effects of fizzes and bangs on air for good measure – and then took over with his perfectly polished opening. He fired the first jingle and GEM was live and sounding like a million dollars as 'All You Need is Love' pulsed out of three highly processed AM transmitters.

Like many of the proficient gold format stations around the country, GEM, like Magic 828 in Leeds and Xtra AM in Birmingham and Coventry, commanded huge audiences, despite only being available on crackly AM. They were likely some of Britain's most focused radio offerings to date, being, for the first time, targeted radio brands. Some even outshone their FM partners in audience scale. Stations were now facing the first icy wind of competition, albeit self-induced.

Many AM operators pleaded for access to additional FM spectrum to upgrade their stations, but such requests fell on deaf ears. Some daring companies even applied formally for additional FM licences in their areas, but the regulator was in no mood to give additional advantage to those who already ruled their markets. Indeed, as the former bosses of the major GWR and Capital groups, Ralph Bernard and David Mansfield, reminded me, despite best efforts and proven ability, they were never to win a new licence, in their own right, for any format.

What missed the attention of programmers of the age is perhaps that, on the day they were cooing excitedly over their new AM babies, they failed to pay due attention to their jealous older FM sisters. Not least because the new arrivals had sucked away the most familiar music and presenters.

In many markets, FM stations started to lose direction, leaping off into a grey, overstrident world, and leaving an adult contemporary gap which other stations would fill, in time. This moment was the beginning of the challenge for the original tier of FM stations and, in markets more competitive than the East Midlands, a challenge from which recovery was never to occur.

20

MERGERS

As Pac-Man advanced across Britain's amusement arcades, commercial radio stations were also starting to devour one another. These small 'corner shop' companies were being gobbled up, not least when shareholders realised that their tentative risky investment in the crazy new commercial radio world had achieved more value than they'd ever dreamed.

Just as I had grown up and invested in my first property, a draughty, odd flat on the top floor of a rambling old Leicester house, my industry had grown up too. Pioneering spirit and the ambition of creating great independent local radio stations had given way to the necessary business of making money, or at least not losing it. This day was always going to come. Shareholders wanted to see the fruits of their investment, struggling stations knew they could only survive with some shared overheads and selling larger volume to advertisers in a cohesive way brought real advantages.

Around the country, station bosses were doing the courtship dance over discreet dinners, chewing over how a merger or an acquisition might work. Having left another suitor at the altar, the East Midlands stations in Nottingham, Derby and Leicester, married BRMB, Mercia and the AM service, Xtra, in the West Midlands, to form a union called Midlands Radio. The merger was sensible, as the Midlands was a 'must-buy' region for national advertisers, and an easy offering encompassing its major cities would benefit all.

My Leicester Sound was no longer one of the legs of Trent, it had become one of the smaller stations in a major UK radio group, which had become a plc by 1990. The suits of management got sharper and increasingly distracted by the demands of the new corporate structure. Across the country, stations were owned increasingly by a variety of stock market-listed companies, with all the complexity that brings.

Humble disc jockey and green manager David was suddenly around a senior managers' table, pretending he knew what he was talking about. The relationships were fascinating to watch as we met in the new head office carved out hastily in plasterboard upstairs in the Nottingham premises. Despite the existence of a small drinks cabinet in the corner, a throwback to BBC local radio tradition, meetings did not resemble the jollity of *Abigail's Party*.

At the outset, chairing the new conjoined Midlands Radio from the head of the table was not Ian Rufus, who had run the larger West Midlands operation, but Ron, the East Midlands head. Alongside the Midlands station representatives sat Joe Douglas, who represented London station WNK (wicked, neutral and kicking). In a puzzling IBA experiment of 'incremental radio', this station shared a frequency with a Greek radio station, swapping format every four hours. The investment in WNK was a route for Midlands Radio to grow a valuable London presence. It was a sound strategic objective but a challenging solution – and a questionable station name.

By day, I continued running Leicester Sound, both hosting my three-hour morning show and dealing with all other day-to-day demands of the company with ever less moral support and increasing burdens from the new corporate world. In a cost-saving round, I was asked to share evening programmes with Trent at a time when I was ill positioned to stamp my feet and say no. Hearing that it was 'busy on Nottingham's Maid Marian Way' on my Leicester station was annoying, especially as we were seeking to carve out a reputation as the local station. Those who tut at today's regionalisation easily forget the quiet economy measures of earlier eras.

I also recall the occasion when all Midlands Radio stations were each asked to make two redundancies. This downsizing hit harder in Leicester than it did in the large Birmingham operation; and I cringe as I reflect on my first ever round of redundancies. As a manager, you remember vividly and painfully the first person you make redundant, not least if you disagree with the process. We saved £8,000 and made Gina very unhappy.

My morning show was going well. I'd got to know the city and its people and had acquired the knack of translating links from Nottingham to Leicester with the help of Wendy through the glass on reception duties. I'd buzz through and mouth 'give me the name of a '70s nightclub in Leicester', and she'd oblige, providing me with suitably relatable content.

I recall, too, when a railway bridge in the city was being demolished, we suggested that listeners keep a piece for posterity and urged them to bring it in. They did. This was true interactivity, not just a quick tweet; people actually jumped in their cars and drove five miles to take a random brick to a radio station for no apparent reason.

Ratings improved, suggesting we reached a record 40 per cent of all adult radio listeners weekly across our AM and FM services, prompting the commissioning of a pricey, over-wordy, celebratory spread in the *Leicester Mercury* newspaper headlined

'40 per cent' in a very large font. That must have meant a great deal to readers.

Every radio group has a challenging station in its fold that struggles for no explicable reason, and some particularly gifted individuals are often berthed there in a valiant effort to make progress, before being spat out again. The Leicester Sound diaspora is impressive.

The job was demanding as my first management post, and the change in ownership brought a flood of extra pressures. Whenever I requested an audience with my boss to chew over some of my challenges, the agenda would quickly shift, understandably in retrospect, to the latest head office matters rather than what was keeping me awake. On air, during songs, moaning staff would wander in routinely with the latest challenges, not appreciating how such things require a different part of the brain from the one required to make the next link entertaining.

One morning, as I trundled into the studio clutching my cardboard box full of the usual records, tape cartridges and notes ready for my morning show, something snapped. I couldn't go on, and handed the show over that day and went home. I should have seen the writing on the wall.

Just a few weeks later, another busy day loomed. The day's schedule meant putting on my jacket during my final Dire Straits track, then running out the studio to drive to Coventry just in time for yet another Midlands Radio summit.

Coventry was not my favourite city, nor was I familiar with its road system. Without the help of a sat nav, I tried to find the Mercia premises. Time and time again, I got tantalisingly close, before I would take a fresh new wrong turning in its silly city maze. Eventually I arrived, late and distraught. All the frustrations of this overcomplex first management gig had bubbled over and been compounded by the lunacy of this concrete city. I pulled up, ran into the office in tears and surprised myself by resigning dramatically. Ron was surprised and sympathetic and even offered me half of his prawn sandwich. He was generous in the exit – beyond the sandwich – and I departed. Looking back, I was likely close to a nervous breakdown.

After just over ten years, my dream radio career was over.

A period of bereavement began. The timing wasn't great, as I had just bought a wonderful first house in a lovely Leicestershire village with my partner, Paul Robey, aided by an eye-watering mortgage. The property went on the market immediately and, as luck would have it, it was bought by a couple down the road who wanted to upsize. We swapped and, given that they were solicitors, the transaction was unusually speedy.

I also had to say farewell to my favourite ever company car, a gunmetal grey Nissan 200SX with pop-up headlights that emerged from the bonnet like flirty eyelids at the flick of a switch. The severance arrangement did mean, however, that I inherited a battered old company Ford Fiesta with the outline of old station branding still showing. The headlights barely worked.

Loughborough was my nearest town. I wandered round on one of my new endless, free days and stared in a job centre window. It occurred to me that I was qualified for little else other than talking rubbish and playing Abba records.

21

A FRESH START

1990 – and a tetchy regulatory divorce was in the air. The Independent Broadcasting Authority was dismantled and regulatory spoils distributed. The Independent Television Commission assumed control of television; and a new dedicated regulator was created for radio, ensuring that radio licensing could proceed apace, rather than as a 'Friday afternoon job'.

The IBA, which had taken on its radio responsibilities with some caution, fought to keep them. Its chairman was clearly in no mood to be messed with as he protested to the Home Secretary: 'You should not underestimate the risks of financial disaster and chaos if the process is not handled well. Your plans seem to me to be a recipe for uncertainty, delay and dislocation'.[11]

The new Radio Authority grasped its new abilities with eagerness as it began its operations on New Year's Day 1991. Preparations began to license three national commercial stations, via a highest bid process, with the one on FM having to be 'non-pop'. The stipulation gave rise to lively debate about what pop was and wasn't, culminating in the memorable 'thump, thump, thump' definition of pop by Lord Ferrers.[12]

The UK came close to back-to-back Mary Poppins rather than Prokofiev, when Showtime Radio won the financial race for the single national FM licence. Showtime failed, however, to raise the required investment, and the licence fell to Classic

FM, which proved a worthy recipient, although its journey to air was a complex one.

With TalkRadio and Virgin winning the AM national licences, assuming frequencies offloaded by the BBC, UK commercial radio now boasted significant extra scale with which to tempt national advertising agencies. Some individuals operating local stations, however, were less pleased with these new competitors, whilst others wondered why, if we were to have an FM national licence at last, we were not allowed to play pop. There is little doubt, however, that the new tier of commercial radio contributed hugely to the profile of the medium in the '90s; and Classic FM would, in time, achieve double the audiences it had projected at launch.

The new Authority also got to grips with further local radio licensing, and one clever executive observed that Lincolnshire appeared to be the last huge white splodge on the map that did not yet enjoy the luxury of a commercial channel. An FM licence was accordingly advertised for this large agricultural county.

My former employer, via Radio Trent, applied to the regulator to run an offshoot in the patch, which seemed an efficient plan as the country faced fresh economic challenges. Bolting on Lincolnshire to the Trent operation would be an obvious safe option.

There was, however, also an outsider. An application under the name of Lincs FM was fired off by a man originally from Lincolnshire, canny Michael Betton, who had spent his early career at Radio Orwell in Ipswich and later played a key role at Power/Ocean on the south coast from launch. Michael harvested investment in Lincs FM plc from family and friends, and a local publisher.

Against the odds, in the view of many in the industry, this applicant group, which existed at this stage only on paper and in visionary minds, was to succeed in winning the licence rather than the established radio group next door. The Authority's decision was fortuitous for Michael, who'd already stepped aside from the south coast job he was not enjoying quite so much, following ownership changes.

As the ink dried on the new licence offer, I got in touch promptly with Michael and volunteered for some relief programme presentation duties on his new station. It is beyond me now why I thought that an entrepreneur just starting a radio business would already be worrying about who might fill in when the afternoon show host went on holiday. He agreed to see me, however, and suggested not relief on overnights, but senior programming responsibility at this new station.

We met for lunch in Covent Garden and he asked me how the station might sound. 'Fun,' I replied enthusiastically. 'No,' said Michael, who could vest more meaning in that single word than anyone. 'Entertaining' was the correct answer, he explained. Few in this business have the quiet confidence and intelligence of Michael. He was to need it.

22

FROM THE HUMBER TO THE WASH

Cut off from the infrastructure of any established neighbouring station and in a pre-internet world, with just a shorthand notepad and a landline phone in front of you, how do you create a radio station?

Who supplies a complete CD record library? How much should we pay for a weather forecast? How do you sort out production music? Where do you find on-air talent? Remind me about copyright again? Most critically, who sorts out printers that don't work? There is no useful paperback book which tells you how to set up a radio station for the first time. You just guess.

In the preparatory days for Lincs FM, there were but three of us, lodged in a large open-plan office whose other occupants were busying themselves with something to do with conservation. Whilst my new neighbours presumably were making critical phone calls about saving the planet, I was hiring chirpy disc jockeys. The new premises for the station were being assembled next door, on the banks of the River Witham, just feet away from the original site of the famous Ruston train and engine manufacturer.

Radio is an intangible thing at the best of times. There is something even odder about preparing to programme a radio station when it lives simply in your imagination, and when the building in which it will be housed does not yet exist. As I described the venture to those I wanted to attract to work for us, it occurred to me that all they were buying into were my words and conviction.

For the on-air programme schedule, Michael Betton's simple, but evidently persuasive, Radio Authority licence application document served as a template and I knew that the well-thumbed pages illustrated how this committed individual envisioned the station in his mind. I noted he had also kept open his right to interfere by appointing me as 'programme manager', rather than as the more familiar 'controller' or 'director'. In truth, considering that he and his family owned a considerable proportion of the affair, and given that he was also an ex-programmer, I would have expected some interference no matter what it said on my business card.

Michael was unlike any other character I had ever met in the radio world. A scientist rather than an artist, his personality was well illustrated by a willingness to serve loyally as chair of the commercial radio pension scheme, and the fact that his radio station's offices were so immaculate you could have performed open-heart surgery on the reception desk. Michael's passion was evidenced by the very creation of the station and the risks he took along the way to win the licence. He had put his whole livelihood at risk by launching a station that others said would fail in challenging economic times. But, unlike so many of his radio rivals, Michael rarely gave vent to his passion with a rabble-rousing display; it was locked deep in his heart. To an onlooker, he had the calm demeanour of an auditor.

Any doubter of graphology would easily be defeated by a study of Michael's careful signature alongside his detailed, intelligent scrutiny of each and every matter. Michael questioned everything. If the result of all this careful consideration was that we should not do something that every other station in the world happened to be doing, Michael seemed particularly happy. I have a hunch that, as a child, he never did something just because his friend did. Rarely have I encountered such unshakeable self-belief.

That calm, objective and determined demeanour, however, served the company brilliantly in the hugely challenging opening months. Being part of a stand-alone outfit in its early days, knowing that your efforts will determine whether the staff bill can be paid, focuses the mind. Michael's firm hand was on the tiller at a time when instinctive enthusiasm would have risked the ship sinking. I admired him hugely.

He did, however, insist on some strange policies; some of which I tolerated and observed; some of which I challenged; and some that I quietly forgot about. I thought that he had never noticed my quiet strategy until, as our relationship had grown after a year or so, he recited my policy back to me word by word with a wry smile.

Lincs FM law required that all presenters wore ties. Michael feared that, as we were a new station, clients and local movers and shakers might conclude we were pirate broadcasters unless we looked like Burton's sales assistants. The rule had no exceptions, not even the breakfast presenter whom only the milkman might see. Breaking the news of this formal attire diktat to my enthusiastic new young presenters was a task which required deft handling, but they did me proud and presumably chose to save any awkwardness for other matters on other days.

I was hugely proud of the quality of the launch line-up, and delighted that they'd had sufficient faith to join the venture. Nick Jackson was an old colleague from Leicester Sound and a textbook music presenter. Short-sleeved-shirted Eddie Shaw was a safe pair of hands with a traditional commercial radio background and vocal sound from down south. I found spiky young Ed Bretten in Lincoln's Our Price record store; and Veronica Capaldi, the country music presenter, ran a shop selling musical instruments. Andy Marsh was a willing loyal recruit from nearby; Simon Grundy was an eager young thing, fresh from a local grammar school; while Steve Jordan had been a postman. Most importantly, they all came in on budget: a princely £8,000–£10,000 per person.

The humour and authenticity of Simon Grundy's five-inch cheeky demo spool impressed me hugely. I knew that Simon would be the naughtiest, and that he would also be brilliant. This funky young bright-eyed character disliked most of the music this full-service adult station played, apart from Neil Sedaka's 'Laughter in the Rain'. But I had learned at a very early stage of my career not to get too distracted by presenters questioning my stations' music policies.

Many of the team remained at Lincs FM for several years; and all have gone on to enjoy success. Eddie Shaw and his wife are still settled happily in the county, a quarter of century on, having brought up a family there, all because I happened upon his demo cassette on a rainy day back in 1992.

The great benefit of audition cassettes was that they could be repurposed. I recall being stuck in an endless M1 traffic jam playing back something I'd recorded on a cassette with a scribbled-out label. As the tape neared its end, I flipped it over to hear the dying minutes of someone's impressive audition recording. On return to base, I called the cassette's owner; and it was good to be able to offer some decent early opportunities to Wes Butters, who would later become the tenth ever host of the Radio 1 chart.

Clare Carson was Lincs FM's news editor and my rock in the early days; a ginger-haired, confident and intelligent operator who could break devastating news with a smile and carry it off. We lamented frequently about how much we used to get done in the months before the staff we'd hired had joined. As any manager knows, it's staff who stop you really getting on with any work. An ex-sales manager once told me how relieved he was when he returned to a grass-roots field sales post, as no longer would he hear those words: 'Do you have a minute?'

Turning on the transmitter for any new station is always a magical moment. Like a birth, the actual timing of the first scream comes as an exciting surprise. The team were out on a bus trip familiarising themselves with Mablethorpe when the mighty 102.2 first crackled into action and test transmissions broke the silence. Mine was the first voice, played in from a CD of music and formal announcements, signalling the imminent arrival of the new service. As far as was relevant, I modelled the phrases on the ones I'd grown up to on the test transmissions of my beloved Radio Trent. It was a nod to the wise.

Not only was I in charge of programming, with the burden of devising shows, sorting jingles and hiring and coaching presenters, I was also destined to host the morning show six days a week. Thankfully, my partner popped in on a voluntary basis to help set up the music scheduling software.

As we had no marketing department, I was also tasked with organising promotional activities, including showing random mayors around the premises, co-ordinating photo shoots and writing a launch newsletter to be delivered to all Lincolnshire homes. What's more, because our commercial producer had yet to be appointed, I was also busy making ads. If you had wandered into the building back in those early days you might have appeared in a commercial, as did the sales director's wife.

Sunday was launch day. It was Michael's view that Sundays were the best days to woo the most available listeners. As the good and the great gathered and clinked wine glasses in our immaculate green and grey office, my production piece rang out at ten o'clock. Clare Carson delivered her first bulletin impeccably and Nick Jackson was live. The station was underway. Commercial radio had arrived from the Humber to the Wash and the UK network map expanded once more.

Given how much my confidence had been dented by the Leicester Sound experience, the Lincs FM project was ideal. If it went wrong, I could hardly blame anyone else.

23

A LINCOLNSHIRE LIFE

Lincs FM quickly became known and, when making phone calls, one soon did not have to preface its name by saying that it was a radio station. It made a decent start, generating impressive weekly audiences, which grew slowly but surely.

In the early days of building necessary local relationships, a civic visit was convened at the local BBC station and we were even invited to attend a local BBC management meeting. On arrival at the station's base in a lovely old former cinema, I recall committing the sin of sitting in someone else's chair, and received the glare of one who has entered a country pub and sat in the wrong place. Things there appeared to be quite settled, but I feared our arrival was about to disturb their tranquil existence.

Having wrestled with the confusion between the names of Radio Leicester and Leicester Sound, I feared the worst for Lincs FM versus the successful BBC Radio Lincolnshire. Years later, when visiting the BBC station, it was amusing to hear of their concerns about their listeners being misattributed to Lincs FM.

News editor Clare Carson and I attended the sort of local functions one does when building a reputation for a new media outlet, including a memorable trip to the impressive medieval Lincoln Cathedral, once the world's tallest building. A senior cleric poured us both a small sherry and then proceeded to bitch about all the merry goings-on in this mighty building of Christian hope and faith.

Revenues were not yet flooding in, so in the early days, I would journey to London to record voice-overs to raise extra funds. It likely made scant difference, but it was a gesture. Although I was more aware of the challenges than the staff at large, I also knew that matters were under Michael's watchful eye, and I had faith that all would be fine. Media businesses take time to grow as audiences are built and value realised. National revenues were not making a huge contribution: one of the downsides of running a station in an area that trendy London media agency buyers could barely identify on a map.

Local advertisers, however, grew to embrace the prospect of an alternative to a dull column in the corner of the pages of local press, and sales director Jeff Harwood did a decent job with his team in developing good client relations and securing repeat business. He relished any programme ideas which might be sponsored, including the memorable August Bank Holiday outside broadcast, where we pledged to bring the coast to town. A truck-load of sand was duly tipped onto the tarmac of an Asda car park and fitting seaside attractions installed. It rained. There was also the daily 'Firm Favourites' where the staff of local companies were invited to submit their song choices. In these days before social media, such suggestions were submitted by grainy illegible fax.

A weekly cooking feature was broadcast from the station's 'British Gas kitchen'. This was no radio make-believe: British Gas did indeed fund the hob. Listeners were invited to write in for copies of the recipes, which they certainly did.

Texting was rare at that stage, and few listeners had mobile phones. As a senior executive, I was afforded but a company pager, strapped to my belt. This wretched thing would bleep as I drove into work, causing me to pull up at the nearest phone box, call the station's ex-directory line and, whilst I stood shivering in the kiosk, be told that they'd already sorted the critical decision about who had won the prize for the contest for which the presenter had given the wrong answer.

24

THE NATION'S FAVOURITE

To teenage screams, the boyband Bros flew around the country in a helicopter in 1988 to herald the official BBC Radio 1 FM switch-on day – although it would be a few years before the new transmitter network fully covered the country. Radio 1 became the then trendy and explicit 1 FM. Radio listening was moving inexorably away from the old AM band, although this poor station had suffered a twenty-one-year wait for the rollout of its FM network.

Whilst FM carriage delivered Radio 1 more easily to the music radio audience, thus potentially creating a more powerful competitor for the growing commercial radio network, Radio 1's on-air approach was to change helpfully in the early '90s to the extent that its competitive impact was restrained.

As told dramatically in the BBC TV documentary *Blood on the Carpet*, a new Radio 1 controller, 36-year-old Matthew Bannister, was installed at Broadcasting House in 1993. The youngest ever BBC radio station controller, Matthew was charged with reinvigorating this once spunky station, which in a quarter of a century had matured from a youthful pirate echo to a service mum and dad would find eminently tolerable.

'Smashy and Nicey' had gained popularity on *Harry Enfield's Television Programme*. These ageing 'presenters', with their stereotypical disc jockey voices and silk jackets, illustrated just how out of touch Radio 1 could seem to be. As with all comedy, however, they were exaggerated characters, and to suggest that Radio 1 had failed to move with the times would be oversimplification.

During the reign of outgoing Radio 1 controller Johnny Beerling, the station had successfully attracted large audiences, in keeping with the steer from the then managing director of BBC radio, David Hatch, who needed to demonstrate that the BBC was giving value to all from the licence fee. As Johnny pointed out to me as we chatted in later years, however, he did tune the station sound to the age, adding new presenters to the line-up, extending the *Newsbeat* programme, developing social action broadcasting and introducing daring comedy content and concerts with enviable line-ups.

Listeners, however, can sometimes remain too loyal, staying with a familiar station even though they have aged beyond its desired audience target. Despite a demonstrable evolution of approach on air, therefore, the listener profile suggested by audience research still failed to meet the changing demands of the BBC's fresh top management.

Matthew Bannister explained that BBC director general John Birt saw radio as the most recalcitrant and old-fashioned part of the BBC in its working practices. As Matthew arrived, there was even external pressure for the station to be privatised. It was against this political backdrop, therefore, that the Radio 1 changes had to be made promptly. For the BBC's overall ambition of ensuring it served all demographics well, a renewed focus on younger audiences through a fresher Radio 1 brand was an eminently sensible move; the problem for the BBC lay in the pace of change it demanded.

Matthew felt that Radio 1 needed to be more distinctive, with true innovation in both music choice and presentation style. But he believed also that distinctive output could also be popular. To achieve his aims by the deadlines that had been set would require swift action, and the team he inherited were all well aware of this: 'On the first day, I walked in to meet the assembled staff ... and they weren't looking at me welcomingly – they were looking at best, expectant; at worst, as if I was something they'd trodden in.'[13]

It was pointed out that some of the Radio 1 presenters at the time were older than the BBC director general, the Prime Minister and the Archbishop of Canterbury. Some familiar names would need to be displaced from the schedule. Some chose to jump before they could be pushed.

Resigning on air is tempting for many presenters. Feeling buoyed by huge audiences, it's easy from the isolation of your studio to feel that you are in charge and reason is on your side. It's also a very damaging strategy and, once you're out in the cold, public interest quickly wanes and potential employers are only too aware that you have behaved unreasonably. Whatever you feel about the size of your contribution to a station's success, you are but a temporary tenant.

As Matthew took a holiday in Majorca in 1993, and prepared to execute his strategy, Dave Lee Travis, a former breakfast show host but now one of the old guard enjoying comfortable weekend programmes, acted pre-emptively and read out his famous suicide note on air: 'Changes are being made here that go against my principles and I just cannot agree with them.'

DLT was fired, not by Matthew, but by the outgoing controller, Johnny Beerling, who told me that he wasn't fired for what he had said, but for selling his story to *The Sun*: 'He'd had some sort of sound-off a couple of days before and I'd given him a fairly heavy warning that if he were to do it again he'd have to go ... then he went and gave an interview to Piers Morgan.'[14]

Popular accounts suggest that rather more presenters were displaced by Matthew than was actually the case. Nevertheless, significant voices who had defined the station for a generation were suddenly and very publicly absent from the airwaves. Many aspired to a neat transition to Radio 2, but that station's controller was unwilling to countenance their appearance on her cautious schedule, despite Matthew asserting 'that [it] would have been the sensible thing to do'. Johnny Beerling was also puzzled by the lack of intervention from the overall head of BBC radio: 'She had a very strange approach ... [it was the] controller's job to control – and it's not my business. She wouldn't dictate to Frances Line that she should take DLT.'

The presenters were thus silenced and a proportion of their 19 million listeners alienated. As Matthew appointed replacements with a 'passion for music and an intelligent engagement with the audience', listenership fell and the press sought a scapegoat. Matthew's name was convenient and the tabloids gleefully depicted his audience sliding down a bannister. He'd been alerted to the likely response by a question from BBC chairman Marmaduke Hussey at his interview when 'Dukey' asked 'how do you feel about being Mister Nasty in the newspapers?'

Matthew was supported in his changes to management by another former BBC Radio Nottingham colleague, Radio 1 head of production Trevor Dann – dubbed 'Dann, Dann, the hatchet man' by the press. It was reported that Trevor had chosen not to play a new Status Quo song, prompting outrage from the 'rockers', resulting in press coverage which was to prove useful as the station sought to reach out to its new audience.

Trevor reinforced the importance of what he called 'continuous revolution' for Radio 1: 'It's not great being unpopular – but if you're unpopular doing something that needs doing – you do sleep nights'; although he conceded to me: 'I probably made some enemies I didn't need to make.'

Matthew was certainly seen as being far from 'Mister Nasty' in my commercial radio world. His changes were greeted with an excited rubbing of hands, alongside a shaking of heads in disbelief that the BBC should choose to throw away its mainstream audiences. As a listener in my early thirties, I'd fallen out of love with listening to the station, and it was utterly correct that I should have.

Whilst the pace of change and overall management of displaced listeners was evidently not well co-ordinated by the BBC as a whole, I recall voicing the unpopular view at the time that the readjustment at Radio 1 was wise and necessary. I believe history will be kinder and that the enviably credible Radio 1 of the twenty-first century owes something to the decisive, visionary programming strategy of the 1990s.

25

SPREADING WINGS

'Radio is a kind of television perfected to the point that only sound need be transmitted'
Bob Monkhouse

Comedian Bob Monkhouse was someone I grew to appreciate too late in life. If ever one needed an example of a time-served professional who understood the need to prepare conscientiously for any performance, it was Bob. I recall him appearing as the post-prandial act at a Radio Festival. He welcomed those from the GWR commercial radio group on table eleven, before observing that the company was likely, by now, to also be occupying tables twelve and thirteen. The topical gag attracted much laughter about the hungriest of the new industry consolidators.

GWR, which had floated on the stock market in 1988, acquired such stations as my former Trent group plus Mercia and Beacon. It also snapped up East Anglian Radio Group, Marcher Radio Group, Mid Anglia Radio Group and Chiltern Radio Group. For a while, the group became a bête noire in some radio circles, charged with eviscerating the once proud, very individual, local stations.

The face of GWR's chief executive, Ralph Bernard, a confident and engaging moustached figure with curly black hair who'd risen from a post as a journalist to leading the country's biggest radio group, defined the era. He told me of those heady times, when the company would make use of an executive bus, replete with board table inside: 'The three of us … plus support team … and we would literally go around the country to where our new acquisition targets were. I would do the deals, Steve would talk about how he would change the programmes … it was formulaic, there's no getting away from it.'[15] In truth, several of the original valiant FM commercial pioneers had lost their way and were starting to suffer from the impact of new competitors. As GWR acquired stations, it brought research-driven, refreshing, clear thinking, challenging some of the radio wisdom on presentation style, news and music – and adopted a more targeted approach. The original stations were 'closed down', one by one, and then relaunched as 'the new (station)', with resulting audience growth, in many cases.

Ralph admits he became a 'hate figure', and now concedes that some of the more successful stations possibly required a less dramatic approach: 'I did … what I thought was the right thing for radio as a medium but also the people who worked within it.'[16]

Freed from the shackles of the cautious IBA, the new Radio Authority wasted no time in scattering new commercial radio licences across the country in areas large and small. The '90s were a great decade if you fancied running a new radio station in a town near you.

The earliest stations were undergoing a painful licence renewal process where incumbents could be challenged by alternative hungry new operators. Whilst there was always some degree of risk, as proven by the termination of the original LBC and DevonAir, the existing stations usually had their licences re-awarded, sometimes through gritted teeth. When Capital's London FM and AM licences were renewed in 1994, the Members of the Radio Authority asked their chairman, Lord Chalfont, to 'convey the Authority's disquiet about Capital's complacency'. Whilst licence security would be a comfort to us at the end of our own term, it did not make for ready expansion.[17]

Lincs FM sought to grow by winning licences to broadcast in adjacent areas and Leicester held some interest for us, not least being an area painfully familiar to me. At the point its licence to broadcast faced scrutiny at renewal, my old station Leicester Sound was at a nadir, with weekly audiences slumping to worryingly low levels. It had also just been acquired by GWR, which, we anticipated, would introduce its eminently sensible format. Whilst I had no doubt that the GWR approach would boost audience numbers, I felt the programming proposition would seem less appealing to the regulators as they appointed the next licensee, and hoped the Radio Authority might favour our plans instead.

The future of the AM licence was also being determined, and my former Sabras Radio colleague Don Kotak was planning to apply, to reclaim the frequency for a full-time Sabras Asian station. We felt we could be a dream-team partnership of real interest to the regulator. Two new, yet proven, locally driven operators entering the fray would be a shot across the bows for any other complacent licensees in the country.

I felt I had something to prove. The licence had to be won so that I might go back and achieve what I'd failed to achieve before. With the support of the Lincs FM board, I began the lengthy application process, with all the painful drafting and redrafting of the necessary documents. I dashed down the Fosse

Way any spare moment I had, during evenings and weekends, to garner support from the good and the great. We sought press coverage, convened public meetings, lobbied MPs and assembled an enthusiastic board of directors. I felt the tide move in our favour. Nothing could stop us.

Our new 'Jupiter Radio' for Leicestershire was almost a certainty – and a demonstration jingle was even recorded. Our parent company would more than double in size and reap the revenues a big city could offer. I should have anticipated that recording a jingle would tempt fate.

A familiar character was to ruin our plans. GWR's chief executive Ralph Bernard was an old associate of Ron Coles, who had significant Leicester heritage, not only from the time we spent working together at Leicester Sound, but from having been part of a fledgling BBC Radio Leicester. By this stage, Ron had fallen out of Midlands Radio in an earlier putsch.

In a stroke of annoying genius, Ralph hired Ron to assemble the GWR bid to retain its Leicester Sound licence. Ron was a formidable opponent in licence battles. He liked local radio, he knew what the regulator wanted, he boasted deep roots and contacts in the area, he knew the business of radio and he could write like Shakespeare.

The licensing process was arduous, particularly the necessary harvesting of letters to prove local support. Ron and I would squabble over significant supporters, and I remember one Leicester City football club executive promising to support us, just before turning up on our rival's board. Dirty tricks surfaced too. One of our directors even had an anonymous letter pushed through her door warning her she 'must not get involved with Jupiter'. I spoke to Ron at the time about that, and I am confident the note was not of his doing. He was a rival, but a gentleman.

The Radio Authority routinely felt a need to phone licence applicants about their written proposals before making a decision. I sat nervously in my office waiting for the call at the appointed hour from the Authority's frighteningly capable head of development. Nothing escaped David Vick, and I expected, and received, a full interrogation. I got the feeling that David had been informed about my tearful exit from the city's station five years earlier.

Licence decision days make O-Level results days seem like a walk in the park. Folklore suggested that the later your phone rang after the designated decision time, the greater the likelihood of you not having won. Our moment ticked by – and the news was indeed disappointing. The Authority told us GWR would be running Leicester Sound FM. The AM licence was, however, won by newcomer Sabras. Our dream plan had half come true – but it wasn't our half.

I was furious and emotional. I felt the regulator had not considered what GWR would do in practice, once the poetic licence pledges had been summarised into a prosaic Radio Authority 'Promise of Performance'. I did not blame Ron; he'd done his job annoyingly well, and GWR had played a clever move and would programme the station successfully. I simply felt the licensing process was unfit for purpose and had wasted everybody's time.

No one applied for a radio licence without a fervent belief that they could and should win. The disappointment was painful.

Michael was typically stoic, although he did confess that he'd eaten a very old yoghurt, way past its best before date, which he'd taken from the station fridge in a momentary delirium. Knowing that nothing could be done, he allowed himself a brief period of annoyance before planning the next move, an approach typical of good leaders. He gave me the next day off on compassionate grounds for my loss, which I spent wandering around Leicester's Abbey Park, kicking the leaves and scuffing my shoes on the tarmac path, mulling over what night have been.

26

MAKING A DIFFERENCE

When your boss is talking to you and the phone rings, you are never quite sure whether to answer it or not.

As Michael Betton walked out of my Lincs FM office door one day, possibly having had a quiet word with me about the use of the word 'kids' on air rather than 'children' or a presenter having referred to Mothering Sunday as 'Mother's Day', the phone rang. The frantic waving from a silhouette in reception suggested the call was of some importance. So, I excused myself with apologetic gesticulation and picked up the receiver.

It turned out to be a call from the Radio Authority. I mouthed the name of the regulator to Michael, who disappeared deferentially with furrowed brow, wondering what we'd done wrong. Surely there was nothing actually in the Authority compliance code of broadcasting conduct about calling children 'kids'?

A familiar military voice boomed down the phone: 'Ever fancied a career in regulation?' It was Paul Brown, a senior executive at the Radio Authority. He was about to leave and suggested I should apply for his job, a key post in British radio regulation at a critical time for the industry. I did not answer his question directly, for surely no one dreams of being a regulator when they grow up. Kids who did probably lunched on regulatory fudge and ran around their grey playgrounds just screaming 'no', 'don't' and 'stop it'.

As I later recounted to a curious Michael, the potential job did have its appeal, specifically because I felt it was a chance to make a difference. How can one be wholly disillusioned with a body that's ruined your plans and yet choose to turn down the chance to help mould it? I'll concede that the opportunity to make a mark on the national stage in London and double my salary were additional incentives.

A summons for interview arrived, and the Radio Authority glitterati gathered round chief executive Tony Stoller's round table, on the hallowed eighth floor of the towering Holbrook House in Holborn, to interrogate me. It had been a long time since my last job interview, although I remembered to dress appropriately this time.

As he thumbed through my CV, Tony suggested the page listing my academic record was absent. I pointed out to the assembled highly qualified throng that no such page existed. I had no such academic record. Evidence of my achievements amounted purely to some dog-eared O-Level certificates and a lonely General Studies A-Level. I doubt many conversations in that office had ever occurred with someone as ill qualified as me, let alone job interviews. As the questioning came to an end, I was asked to write a paper on some meaty regulatory subject. I hoped this was a routine request and not because they doubted my literacy.

Presumably I impressed them, or someone better qualified turned down the job, because my phone rang days later and the post was offered. I showed the original press cutting of the job ad to my mother to help her understand the role, which appeared even more confusing to her than my old one. If one does not work on air in radio, the answer to the question 'what do you do?' is always challenging. 'I'm just behind the scenes' usually suffices.

Mum stared at the part of the ad that quoted my salary and beckoned Dad over to put on his spectacles and do the same thing. They had no idea what I'd be doing, but they felt it must be something impressive. The boast 'My son works in London now' seemed to nudge my mother up the league table when chatting to her friends in the British Legion Women's Section.

London beckoned and I rented a studio flat from a friend in a fascinating complex in east London, which according to the BBC's *Who Do You Think You Are?* had been the Bryant and May match factory where Barbara Windsor's relatives once worked. The London life, which is so puzzling to non-Londoners, became my life. The hot and cramped Central line in the morning. The timers on the platform that suggest a train will arrive in two minutes – two minutes after a previous announcement said exactly the same thing. And the cost. My small flat, whose foundations were shaken by Tube trains every few minutes, was almost as expensive as a whole East Midlands village.

The difference between the atmosphere of the regulator's offices, and that of a radio station premises, was stark. The Radio Authority's large, quiet floor was filled with calm, frighteningly intelligent people, scrutinising lengthy reports, stroking their chins and poring over spreadsheets.

The silence was disturbed from time to time as one of my new team played through the tape of a piece of programming about which angry listener complaints had been received. 'David, can you pop over and give a second view here, does this sound like "fuck" in this song or not?' The tape was rewound. 'Fuck.' And again. 'Fuck.' This was turning out to be a very odd fucking job.

I reported to the chief executive as head of programming and advertising. My role was to ensure we judged complaints about advertising or programming fairly; updated the programme codes by which stations are bound, where necessary; monitored stations, when appropriate; helped to assess the programme proposals from licence applicant groups; and held them to their programme promises.

Disgruntled listeners who were annoyed at something they'd heard would phone in and let off steam. When they eventually paused for breath, we would sympathetically grunt and ask them to list their concerns in a letter. In those days before email, we surmised that half the concerned folk probably calmed down and never bothered writing to us. There is something to be said for the reinstatement of such a hurdle, maybe requiring complainants to run around the block before pressing 'send' on an irate note to Ofcom.

At the time, we investigated every complaint, no matter how trivial. One chap wrote in every other day. A computer program was even designed to handle the administration, with drop-down menus offering a range of choices depending on just how annoyed we felt. Recordings were requested from stations of the offending item and we'd listen through with furrowed brows. After a human, instinctive response, we'd pause, rightly, to consider audience expectations of that station and that programme at that time of day; and the requirements of the relevant Code rule.

Some stations failed to send in recordings when instructed. They either believed that the penalty for such failure was likely to be less than for the alleged offence; or they had genuinely not kept tapes for the requisite forty-two days, which was quite likely in the days before digital recordings. More than one foolish licensee supplied tapes of a different day from the one requested, only to be caught out by the content of the news bulletins.

Some matters were trivial. Others proved more substantive, relating to political controversy or accuracy, highly misleading advertising or appalling lapses of judgement. I still recall the radio station which staged an intolerable prank call to a poor chap who'd had a run of awful luck, losing his job, house and partner – the list went on. His friends had suggested the radio station call him to say his replacement car needed to be taken off the road, for whatever reason. Already at the end of his tether, this last piece of news, delivered by the station's presenter with great authenticity, was the straw which broke the camel's back. The man was audibly upset and could have taken radical action in the seconds following the call. It made for highly uncomfortable listening, and I wondered why any station would ever consider such bullying entertainment.

Another memorable complainant was a cocky MP, suggesting a station had misrepresented him. He'd been interviewed live by phone and had not come off well. He alleged the station had edited the interview, which it quite clearly had not, and insisted on visiting us to discuss the matter. We duly listened back to the programme in silence. The evidence spoke for itself and my view of him remained as it had been when he had behaved rudely to me some years before in different circumstances. I don't think he recognised me in this different world, but I remembered him vividly. Such characters do little to build faith in our treasured democracy and serve to diminish trust in MPs, which is wholly unfair to the many who enter Parliament, often at great sacrifice, to play their part.

The Authority was a non-departmental government body, established under statute. Its approach was accordingly formal, and very much like Parliament, with the Authority Members being the MPs – and we were the Sir Humphrey Applebys. As I was summoned to my first full Authority meeting, my helpful deputy, flaxen-haired Janet Lee, gestured to my jacket, draped on my office chair. Decisions made when wearing a complete suit were evidently preferred.

Day to day management fell to former Radio 210 boss and erstwhile IBA executive Tony Stoller, who routinely strode the shop floor, like the department store manager he once was.

Whilst we executives dealt with minor matters, more significant ones, from licence awards to potential sanctions, were duly referred to the committee of Members at their monthly meetings.

The Members of the Authority by my time were a fascinating crew, headed by chairman Sir Peter Gibbings, formerly of *The Guardian*. Sir Peter was a frighteningly capable, quick-thinking chairman in his sixties with a fund of fascinating stories from a rich life, related with good humour.

Other Members of various shapes and sizes came and went as their terms dictated, many intent on making an honourable contribution, reading all the relevant Papers, listening to the debate, and probing wisely with huge intelligence and life experience. Sadly, it wasn't true of all, and I had to contain my anger on one occasion when it seemed to me that one Member hadn't given his Papers about a licence award the level of scrutiny that those writing them would have wished. Given the numbers around the table, however, I am confident his lack of meaningful contribution did not affect any decision. He just annoyed me.

In my very early days, Authority Members and staff were summoned to an 'away weekend' to dedicate some quality time to the major themes of the moment. In times of financial hardship, we were told the entire board and staff would travel standard class. This school outing was evidently the first time that some of the titled Members had seen red seats, and they appeared puzzled when there did not appear to be one to sit on.

Partners were invited to a social part of the occasion: an evening formal dinner. Chief executive Tony Stoller had a discreet word beforehand and suggested that maybe it was a little soon in my tenure to bring my male partner; not least, I suspect, because even hiring an ex-disc jockey must have already caused a few raised eyebrows in the establishment. I agreed with Tony and, in the climate of the time, he handled it utterly appropriately. In any case, I suspect my Paul would have preferred to spend the weekend anywhere but there. A mischievous thought ran through my mind concerning the possible reactions of the chairman and other elderly members. What would their pulse rates have been if I'd wandered into the large chandeliered room with the campest lad I could for the occasion, on my arm?

The culture was odd for me in many ways. I recall another social occasion when Authority Members met with other movers and shakers. Conversation round the oval dinner table moved to honours; and each chipped in fondly with the account of their trip to Buckingham Palace. It was not a conversation to which I could readily contribute, save to proffer an account of winning my purple Boys' Brigade badge for collecting silver paper for a guide dog.

Culture aside, much of the job was fascinating. Given a latent interest in politics and law, the ongoing dialogue with civil servants and top lawyers proved of huge interest. As the 1996 Broadcasting Bill was being considered, which was to herald the licensing of DAB, we'd inspect each clause line by line to tease out the implications. A couple of sections in the Broadcasting Act 1996 were inspired by points I had made, and I confess that those paragraphs did deliver some job satisfaction.

I recall the small talk before one of those meetings, when one of the top advisors from the Authority's lawyers, the renowned Allen & Overy, remarked that something had occurred to him as he 'sat in the drawing room' that morning. On that occasion and many others, I feared I'd repaired to a fascinating parallel *Upstairs Downstairs* world.

Another interesting legal battle which illustrated the complexity of regulatory decision-making was the case of Amnesty International. Amnesty had challenged the Authority for being ruled a political body, and therefore banned from advertising on radio, whatever the contents of their script. The fact that many people sympathise with the objectives of Amnesty is undoubted, but that was not the point. The matter was about whether the law permitted such a body to advertise. The eventual ruling, which permitted the body to advertise, was educative, appearing to me to be a cunning fudge hinging on the definition of the word 'mainly'.

One area of concern to many listeners was that of radio contests. Frequent complaints were received about alleged unfairness or non-arrival of prizes. No rules had been broken because there weren't any. I introduced one, the wording of which remains to this day in the Ofcom Code. That short paragraph was later to be responsible for fines exceeding £1 million as the premium rate phone scandals were exposed, eroding trust in our medium. TV was affected too, with a penalty imposed for the famous faked competition on *Blue Peter*, following a technical problem that meant viewers calling for a 'Whose Shoes?' contest did not get through. Instead, a visiting child was asked to pose as a caller, and won the prize. 'We'd like to say sorry to you because when this mistake happened, we let you down.'[18]

To me, amidst all the 'pop and prattle', radio is still a strangely magical and influential medium. Never did that become clearer than when I was despatched to Kenya. The Commonwealth Broadcasting Association had asked the Authority for some assistance in establishing a fair licensing process for privately owned stations.

My holidays are usually confined to the greenery of an overcast UK or any blob on the European map which you can get to directly from East Midlands Airport. This brief period in such a rich and different culture was, therefore, eye opening. The quarter of Nairobi where I lodged was typical of cities around the globe, but only a few yards away, up dusty tracks, lay a quite different world. Purely seeing a white face, young bright-eyed teenagers would see hope and tug at my jacket imploring me, in perfect English, to help them seek a future.

Seeing the challenges, I wondered why they would want our jolly commercial radio. The reason was quickly apparent. Although Kenya had democratic elections, a representative democracy requires that voters make an informed choice, which demands the consideration of relevant facts and opinions. In a country with only state-run media, and where literacy levels are low and television consumption outside the big cities rare, radio was a key platform, indeed the only platform, for readily conveying information. Now, mobile phones are widely available, bringing more access to citizens across the world, but in the '90s, radio stood alone.

There was some privately owned radio in Kenya, although the licensing process appeared to be shrouded in mystery, generating questions, at least, about the identity of the ultimate influences behind such stations. Having met station owners, government officials and community leaders, I started to devise a suitable approach.

I was invited also to conduct a radio workshop. On a routinely beautiful day, we assembled in a large hut on the edge of town where I passed on what I felt might be useful information. One of the delegates shook my hand firmly on arrival and assured me he had come to listen and to learn. I was humbled by the respect I was afforded and the hunger to achieve.

My lasting memory of my spell in Kenya is the warm evening we spent sitting on the edge of Nairobi National Park, the wide eyes of animals glinting in the darkness. Conversation flowed as we were treated to a meal of roasted meat, hacked as we watched, from hefty beasts which were dangling over the flames.

Whether my lofty suggestions were considered, I shall never fully know, but I enjoyed the Kenyan experience hugely and the power of my beloved medium was patently clear once more.

I reflected on my Kenya days recently, when visiting Quentin Howard, the technical supremo of forces broadcaster BFBS, best known for having engineered the safe launch of Classic FM and using recordings from the birds in his garden as a test transmission. He told the story of how a BFBS representative in blue body armour parachuted into Afghanistan, with a satellite dish and receiver under his arms, much to the surprise of a marine on the ground who later reflected: 'Our morale was rock bottom. That one action changed the morale of my troop and enabled us to finish our mission. I don't think we would have got through alive.'[19]

27

CHALLENGES

My Radio Authority office boasted a huge prototype DAB (digital audio broadcasting) receiver assembled on a large piece of plywood. Buzzing away and smelling of Scalextric, it was likely one of the first sets in the UK.

The BBC began an operational DAB service in London in September 1995. Listeners were soon able to invest in their own set, although the early domestic models carried a price tag of around £1,000.

The Authority was addressing the new challenge of just how to license operators of this innovative technology which was said to offer more stations, through spectrum efficiency, with more resilient signals. I became the internal expert on our remit, having read the new Broadcasting Act from cover to cover numerous times, admittedly whilst detained on a very delayed train back from an appointment with nothing else to read.

I appeared out of kilter with established wisdom in suggesting that listening choice, not audio quality, would drive DAB take but I think I have been proven correct. As the number of extra radio stations has grown, so has take-up, despite many such stations being broadcast in mono with relatively low quality.

The Authority did consider the matter of audio quality in terms of the minimum capacity, or 'bit-rate', which must be afforded to various formats on the DAB channels. It debated whether it should regulate minimum levels, but chose not to. The decision was illuminated at another stately home away day, where sounds were demonstrated to us. A control experiment was staged, akin to sitting in the optician's chair being asked whether you can tell the difference between the circles in the red – or the green. When it comes to audio quality matters, it occurred to me that a group of the over-sixties and a half-deaf disc jockey were likely not the best judges.

European summits are always fun, not least when you hear delegates in headphones laughing at a joke that was made five minutes ago. At a key Brussels assembly in 1997, I heard representatives from many countries insist that the following year would be make or break for the new technology. Without new stations, it would not catch on, but without the sale of receivers, it was hard to see who would be willing to create stations.

The senior team of Radio Authority staff were impressive. David Vick was possibly the best known, being the quizmaster with the job of breaking the news of licence awards to winners and losers. David's work ethic was impressive, as was the calibre of his thinking, his diligence, his conviction, his integrity and his enthusiasm. I respected him hugely, even though there was once a cross word round the management table when the licensing timetable was amended. I think we may have sworn at each other, but the chief executive wisely pretended not to notice.

Another challenging personal complexity was the Doncaster FM licence. Just prior to leaving Lincs FM, I had been deeply involved in assembling an application to steal Hallam's licence for the town, which was being re-advertised competitively by the Authority as it reached its end. Back then, Hallam broadcast to Sheffield and Rotherham under one licence, and to Doncaster under another, with all its programming shared across the two. The situation was a legacy of dark economic times when the former regulator had bolted on new neighbouring franchises to existing ones rather than risk failure. In more recent times, however, the Radio Authority, which was keen on what it called 'localness', issued guidelines which suggested that a licensee was generally expected to broadcast a minimum proportion of its hours from and for the licence area. It seemed to us, therefore, that Hallam was highly vulnerable. That is not to say its performance was poor, it wasn't – it was well run and enjoyed impressive audiences, but simply seemed not to be doing in Doncaster what the Authority suggested was now required.

A decent Lincs FM bid for the Doncaster licence, under the name 'Trax FM', was assembled. Then came my unexpected jump across the fence from poacher to gamekeeper. I had swapped sides at half-time.

In these circumstances, and all others, the Radio Authority did its utmost to be scrupulously fair. There would always be some challenges with staff moving from and to the industry – and the only alternative would be never to employ anyone who had any relevant insight from the other side. My interest in the matter was clear for all to see and I was rightly removed from all connected work.

The affair became more troublesome, however, when the Authority re-awarded the licence to Hallam and a determined Michael Betton engaged top lawyers to take the conflict to judicial review. No one had ever succeeded in successfully fighting a licence award, but typically that did not deter the principled Captain Michael. He lost that battle too, but in time won the war, when Lincs FM was awarded a new, additional Doncaster licence. Trax FM was belatedly born.

A footnote to the affair was only related to me with a smile as I left the Authority for the last time. All paperwork on any matters in which I should rightly not have been involved was secured wisely in a soundly locked cupboard above David Vick's desk. No one, including me, had realised that my keys to the cupboards in my office were the same as to those in David's.

I worried about the established process of 'beauty parade' licensing. It was conducted with utter thoroughness and impressive diligence and therein lay the problem, in my eyes. The Authority invested much time in analysing the voluminous applications and considering hefty volumes of research, before questioning applicants further about matters such as who would host the Thursday country programme, how long the lunchtime headlines would be and how long the chairman had really lived in Trumpton. Applications would then be rated by a host of criteria and the marks and analyses given to Members alongside a copy of the application itself so they could arrive at their judgment.

The difficulty for me was that the delighted winning applicant would then simply be given a 'Promise of Performance' by which it should abide, of about the size of an old paper driving licence. That document would detail the output essentials, but not the detail of the application. Staffing levels would not be stipulated, nor the identities of people involved in the company and many of the things on which it had been judged. If a listener complained about a station, it would only be held to account if the matter concerned had been included in the Promise of Performance. I also had reservations about the length and detail included in Promises of Performance, given stations merrily applied to change their minor elements, and we usually said yes.

I volunteered a plan to replace Promises of Performance with 'Formats' and presented my thinking to Members. These new Formats would be pithy documents which summarised the key defining characteristics of a station. I suggested that these should be drafted by the applicant and included within their submission. Accordingly, during the application stage itself, both the regulator and third parties could compare with ease how one station would genuinely sound on air, if licensed, compared to another.

Whilst I left the Authority before the plan was implemented, I was pleased my successor, Martin Campbell, followed it through and it remained in place for twenty years until it too became unfit for purpose.

There was also a huge frustration at the Authority that licences could simply be sold on after being won. The losers, therefore, could still become winners just months after the award – at a cost. In the words of former Capital CEO David Mansfield: 'Some people made a lot of money.' These complexities highlight the limitations of the well-intentioned licensing process; and with the arrival of many more stations via DAB, it is easy to see why the curtain should rightly fall on the beauty pageant.[20]

28

THE PEOPLE'S PRINCESS

We all remember where we were on that August day in 1997. I was half-asleep, hearing the story unfold in the early hours of the morning on BBC 5 live. As the description of Diana's condition in the Pont de l'Alma road tunnel changed, and the caution in the presenter's voice grew, I jolted into full consciousness.

British radio awoke that Sunday morning to the challenge of deciding how to respond. Those I knew at radio stations called me frantically asking for advice on establishing how other stations were responding, or seeking a regulator as an alibi for their actions.

By this stage, the Programming Codes I had helped to draft no longer led stations how to respond to a royal death, beyond a general instruction not to offend. They recognised that each station's audience would view such events in very different ways, just as the BBC TV news channel would handle them differently from the cartoon channel. Similarly, the BBC editorial guidelines simply stated: 'It is important that individual output areas are conversant with their own rules concerning the treatment of obituaries.'

A dusty folder had lain on the windowsill at Radio Trent in the '80s, containing a bundle of dog-eared typed sheets bearing instructions on what to do if some significant individual took their last breath. The manila file included a list of the royal family, bundled into neat categories, depending on their relative importance, beginning with Her Majesty The Queen. Just below the names of blue-blooded royal nieces I'd never heard of lay the names of less significant individuals like the Prime Minister.

When we young presenters of the '80s rehearsed our plans to take the needle off the Boney M song in favour of the national anthem and a touch of Mozart when the Queen Mother died, many of us wondered whether preparations seemed a touch generous. The UK mood had moved on from decades of royal deference into a contemporary cynicism. Would anyone now, apart from the loving relatives of those affected, really have an appetite for much more than a quick news flash and maybe a toning down of any adjacent trite content?

Such was the increasingly republican temperature through the '80s and '90s that, had any radio programmer been asked, the month before the accident in Paris, just how they might respond to the death of the ex-wife of a balding prince, I doubt they would have given a particularly sympathetic answer.

It was clear, however, that, on this occasion, the nation was stirred. As Robin Lustig, time-served BBC Radio 4 *The World Tonight* presenter, confirmed to me, it was 'one of the most bizarre inexplicable weeks in British modern history'. Robin had been charged with conducting vox-pop interviews at Kensington Palace capturing the mood 'and the vehemence that was expressed towards the royal family. A lot of people blamed [the royal family] for what had happened to Princess Diana … they had been unkind to her. They had ostracised her. And somehow they were to blame.'[21]

Robin worried that his angry sample of citizens were atypical, but the BBC quickly realised that these individuals reflected the sentiment of the nation in those strange summer weeks. The BBC 'couldn't ignore the steadily developing mass hysteria, nor could it feed it'.

For the news and talk stations, the response was predictable, although Radio 4 examined its tone and dropped the signature tune to its *PM* programme. Even on upbeat music stations, however, regular programming was suspended, in favour of newsflashes and segues of sensitively programmed music. Capital famously went near-classical and BBC Radio 1 broadcast ambient tunes. The mood of the inaugural day of Xfm in London lay in peril, and the new indie rock format station launched with an announcement that the first programmes would be dedicated to Diana 'as a mark of respect to someone who we saw going her own way and standing apart from the rest'. In the words of Absolute's Christian O'Connell, it's when you are handling the dark times that you realise how much better a broadcaster you've become.[22]

Mark Goodier, then host of the Radio 1 chart, which would normally have been aired on a Sunday evening, told me: 'I said there's no way we can do a chart today – it would be absolutely crazy.' Mindful, however, that to drop this institution was a big decision, Mark suggests that his controller Matthew Bannister had an unprecedented conversation with Capital's lead programmer Richard Park and it was agreed that neither station would broadcast the rundown that night. The decision that the nation should live without its weekly rundown was without precedent.[23]

In the days shortly after Diana's death, I was summoned to one of the Authority's regular large evening dinners, held just close to Harrods. The regulator often convened such gatherings with invited guests to chat through relevant matters under Chatham House rules. I remember distinctly the lively one attended by Pete Waterman to discuss the music industry.

As I had arrived a little early, and typically seeking to avoid a surfeit of small talk, I chose to spend a few moments visiting the grounds of Kensington Palace to see the scenes aired on TV so frequently in the days since the accident.

In this traditionally hard-faced capital city, I witnessed people on the upwards escalator at Knightsbridge brandishing large bunches of flowers and some on the downwards escalator visibly upset. No photograph or TV pictures did justice to the scenes outside the palace. A long queue of people silently making their way through the gardens surrounded by flowers piled feet high as far as you could see, pausing to read the generous tributes. The fragrant smell thick in the summer evening air.

This had been an extraordinary period for British history, and one which arguably changed for ever the way this 'stiff upper lip' country copes with emotion.

The incident was also evidence of the nature of radio's true close friendship with its listeners. There was no necessity for music stations to respond in the way they did. They adjusted their mood because they knew their friend, the listener, was shocked and upset – and they wanted to say the right thing.

On too many tragic occasions since, radio has pulsed with the nation's heart. The quiet quality of the medium is exemplified well by James O'Brien's beautifully chosen calm words on LBC following the Manchester Arena atrocity in 2017 in which twenty-two people lost their lives at an Ariana Grande concert. Rather than rant on terrorism, he spoke as a father, drawing powerfully on the contrast with the innocent happiness in the moments before: 'You know what it's like. You don't watch the show. You watch your own children enjoying the show. They will have been watching their little girls dancing in absolute undiluted glee.'[24]

29

ACROSS THE BORDER

Radio conferences are all very well; one bumps into old friends, as well as a few rivals whom one pretends to like and several former colleagues who've been overpromoted, all wearing dangly lanyards and carrying identical bags of festival tat. People in the industry, however, are busy and stations can often find something better to spend the money on.

The nature of a regulator's job means that one is often invited to conferences and has the time to attend. At one two-day event whilst I was employed by the Radio Authority, I bumped into John Myers, the amply framed no-nonsense northerner who ran the large network of regional Century Radio stations, then owned by Border Television. I liked the Century brand, an entertaining mix of music and personalities – and I liked John. With the industry becoming more cautious and corporate, he combined canny business sense with blunt intelligent honesty, expressed with endearing charm.

Over a polystyrene cup of lukewarm tea between two overlong conference panel sessions, he wandered over and we chatted. He suggested to me, as we parted, that if I ever got a little tired of life as a regulator I should get in touch. John was renowned for getting bored fairly easily; he related a story of a previous conference to which he took a company entourage, only to lead them straight back home again: 'We got back on the bus, mate. It was so dull.' His sly invitation to me was repeated the following day and I followed it up out of curiosity. His offer was to join his company, with a view to managing one of its stations. John tended to build his businesses around the talents of the people he identified, rather than shoe-horn recruits into an established structure.

The time was probably right for a move from the regulator before I became seen as a crusty suit out of touch with a Britpop world. Melody, London's eccentric light music station that was owned by Lord Hanson and later rebranded as Magic under its new owners EMAP, had already talked to me about a programming opportunity and I correctly shared news of both approaches with Authority management at the earliest stage. A decision was reached to join John at Century, and I prepared to jump the hurdles to exit my suited spell at the regulator.

On my farewell day from the Authority, I was on the receiving end of a prank call from Capital Gold's gifted presenter and impressionist Mike Osman. My colleagues had suggested the stunt and guffaws ensued when it dawned on me that I was not really on the phone to an awkward complainant.

Getting out of the Authority was even more difficult than getting in. Rather than transfer straight back to the mad radio world, I was obliged to be 'sanitised' by an unpaid gap of some months, permitted to take on specific radio projects, if rubber-stamped by the regulator, but I was not yet allowed to join John's empire. I suspect there were those who felt I should never be allowed to cross back, but they would possibly not understand the lengths to which the Authority went to ensure it was not compromised, nor the fact that my influence on any licensing decision had always been *de minimis* – and I certainly had no vote on the outcome.

I took full advantage of the break to return to on-air presenting and ended up back in Nottingham hosting a few programmes on what had become the oldies service, Classic Gold GEM, and occasionally on the Classic Gold network. How great it was to be back home briefly in the bowels of Castle Gate playing Mama Cass and JAM jingles.

The Leicestershire town of Hinckley also beckoned, where my partner was setting up the new Fosseway Radio, owned by Lincs FM, which was spreading its wings once more. I also spent a short spell consulting at one large station where the key issue seemed to be that the programme controller and the managing director didn't speak to each other. I appeared to be getting paid for running up and down the stairs as messenger.

30

THE TURN OF THE CENTURY

As Tony Blair smiled and waved in the sunshine at his landslide election victory in 1997, I prepared to return to Radioland. My role at the bright red and yellow branded Century Radio was becoming clearer. I was to assume the controls of the station back home in the East Midlands, Century 106, as programmer and managing director. The station boasted: 'Music, sport – and big personalities' and claimed to be 'the East Midlands' biggest radio station', if only by dint of it being the East Midlands' only regional station.

Century was sensibly based on the edge of Nottingham city centre. The general location had seen inner city demolition and had been cleared to make way for a large retail hub, with ambitious plans for all manner of attractions. The BBC building was erected at one end of the huge site and the one housing Century lay at the other. As the economy dipped and the city vision changed, however, few others ever joined us and the barren wasteland dividing us symbolised the division between the two sides of our industry.

The Century building was typical of most radio stations of its era: no longer converted stately homes, but bright, budget plasterboard premises, protected by a security guard with a very large dog. The premises were prone to flooding and, in later years, the drains refused to take the strain of heavy rain. Water flowed in, narrowly missing the studio areas, but laying an unappetising few inches of water and smelly contents unknown on the remainder of the ground floor. These were not quite the sorts of number ones and twos we had in mind.

This large regional station, serving Nottinghamshire, Derbyshire and Leicestershire, had emerged as the unexpected star of the fly-on-the-wall TV series *Trouble at the Top*, which followed the ups and downs of particular businesses addressing challenges, with cameras trained particularly on the lively individuals within.

This series became 'The John Myers Show' as the TV programme producers delighted at finding this rich, entertaining character – and in eventually uncovering some real trouble at the top as he'd taken control of the station in Nottingham. In one episode, John famously fired the religious programmes producer. The scene with her in his office was pure fringe theatre as John explained how he was going to install a new Sunday morning programme, so no longer needed a producer. 'The bottom line is what you're doing at that time of the day – nobody listens,' he told her, before explaining his general approach to programme management: 'If they don't deliver audiences they're gone.' John told me later he had some regrets about how he'd handled it and I'm sure the producer, who conducted herself immaculately in the exchange, may concur with his view.[25] Century 106 had endured a challenging childhood, launched originally in 1997 as a more sedate and mature Radio 106 in a joint venture between the ITV company Border TV and CLT (originally, Compagnie Luxembourgeoise de Télédiffusion). After a reasonable audience performance at launch as 'radio for grown-ups', the weekly audience figures had diminished to a worrying 7 per cent of adults in the area.

As Border assumed full ownership, the East Midlands brand name had changed to Century, in line with its other regional stations, although its audience was disappointing, certainly compared to its established sister in the north-east of England. Revenues, too, were in short supply from a slightly dysfunctional sales office.

This exciting opportunity brought me into contact again with Ron Coles. Here was the man who'd encouraged me at Trent in my early days; the man I had walked out on at Leicester Sound; the man who had then stolen, with annoying skill, the prospect of a Leicester licence when I was at Lincs FM. I was now to take his job.

Business is business and, at the top, we all know this. Alongside the decent rewards, the likelihood of falling in and out of favour as ownerships and company directions change is high. I suspect he knew that he was unlikely to be around no matter who took over. I respect Ron and we remain friends, but I can imagine at that moment, I was unlikely to be popular in the Coles household. I even inherited his statesmanlike dark blue Mercedes, a car with the sort of doors which thud reassuringly. It was my mother's favourite car and if I took her on an outing, she'd command me to slow down so the neighbours could see her pass.

Inheriting someone else's radio station is like wearing someone else's shoes. It takes just over a year to break them in – and despite one's determined efforts – the process will always take that long and painful blisters will persist for some time.

The station showed off a brand-new Century sign over the door, but inside, cultures collided as staff from the old regime cautiously mixed with the new. For me, a real indication of audience size came when I queried why the breakfast show presenter had only taken one call for a contest. 'Because there weren't any others,' he replied.

A host of new presenters were hired, who I hoped would make a difference, including the hugely entertaining and complex Bernie Keith, now firmly established with the BBC in Northampton. His act was pure theatre and prepared with diligence. There is only one Bernie, and I had to tempt him away from the south coast, prompting an understandably hissy call from that station's MD: 'Hands off Bernie.' I hired a few favourites too from past lives; presenters often follow programme directors around.

At school, the chubby guy and I were always the last to be picked for the football team. The game was never my forte and I have long since ceased to feign interest when dull men enter a room and can think of nothing better to talk about. I was a little troubled, therefore, to discover an hour-long football phone-in on the schedule each evening and even more alarmed to find that it genuinely seemed to be generating audiences in this, and indeed other Century markets. It was inspired scheduling.

In Nottingham, the gifted and confident Darren Fletcher, now – and then – a respected commentator, joined ex-pro Larry Lloyd, who had been part of the Nottingham Forest 1970s cup-winning sides, to chew the fat with callers each evening. The pair had become like an old married couple, with hugely entertaining banter on and off air, combined with the occasional fallout. Larry was a big burly lad and he was no longer as fit as he had used to be. On one occasion, his heavy steps slowly approach my embarrassingly spacious office and a wheezing Larry proclaimed that he was never going to work with 'that man' again, I dashed downstairs to hear Darren in high dudgeon shouting much the same. Like *Coronation Street*'s Jack and

Vera, the two always made up and all would be well. Thanks to Larry and Darren's contacts, they managed to deliver Brian Clough live on one memorable show, some time after he had last spoken publicly.

Another personality I relished dealing with was fiery lunchtime presenter Adrian Allen. Hired by John to help us meet the required demanding 40 per cent speech quota, Adrian hosted a daily phone-in. Again, this unusual programming tactic, delivered by this outspoken yet warm, stocky presenter from the north-east, delivered an increasingly impressive audience share. Whilst we swerved a few regulatory near-misses, Adrian, at his best, delivered moments of incomparable radio. A phone-in that features the wife one day and the mistress the next must be worth listening to. Like many presenters of his ilk, he sometimes chose to be as awkward with me as he was with the callers, but we understood each other.

A culture change was needed at the Century operation; it was a station that needed to believe in itself. As MD, I led it as best I could. After tolerating moans and groans patiently for, alas, too long, I held a 'shut up or get out' staff meeting. It seemed to do the trick and a reassuring steady flow of people later wandered into my office to empathise. When managing change, it's easy not to recognise the size of the quiet majority. The Monday after, everyone found a decent bottle of wine on their desk, accompanied by a note emphasising the positive finale to my rant.

The legendary Harry Dunne was brought in to boost the efforts of the commercial team. Harry had become well respected on northern radio stations and managed his staff in the good old-fashioned way. His sales meetings were pure performance. He'd tell stories; he'd pause; he'd walk around the room; he'd pause again. Then his voice would be raised – and raised again. At the crescendo, he would bang his hand on the wall so the plasterboard shook and shout out a key point about something that was not happening: 'and – it needs to start today'. If you were underperforming in that team, you needed to prepare yourself. This was as much like a presidential rally as a sales meeting and, in his own way, Harry produced results. He also felt he'd been shafted by a previous employer that had now become a rival – and this fired him up. He was not going to let a lacklustre sales executive get in the way of his victory – and his staff knew it.

Industrial revolution had hit the radio business during my regulatory sojourn. The Trent group had digitally dallied in the early '90s with an early playout system for its ads, known as DAMS. A semi-expletive was an appropriate name as I gather the system got so warm it would not function until it was re-installed in a new ventilated location – a process which took months. If you jumped on the studio floor, the ads stopped playing. Later in the decade, digital playout extended to all output. Studios, once a messy hive of CDs, vinyl discs and tape cartridges, were reduced to a couple of PCs, some powerful software and an infection of screens.

Whilst Virgin Radio was launching its first website and investigating streaming, and bbc.co.uk went live in 1997, Century was not leading the way with technology. Like so many sensible early adopters, I had invested in AOL email at home, even if it was driven down the phone line and at a very slow speed, but there was no connection in my office. I recall bringing to work a twelve-foot phone extension cable to plug my own email access into the Century phone system. The wobbly wire stretched across the office like a clothes line and allowed me to communicate with those who were a little ahead of us. In the building, typed memos still had to suffice, and the typical presenter taradiddle about not having received an email about some critical matter had yet to become a satisfactory alibi.

John Myers would visit our station to establish all was well, wearing his smart jacket, with tie and the compulsory Century lapel badge, delivering Biddy Baxter wrath to anyone not wearing theirs. Despite his showbiz approach to radio, however, John Myers was also a quiet thinker. In my early days in the role, he'd regularly chat over how things were going and wisely probe my thinking in depth. At the end of one memorable meeting, he shuffled his papers and suggested to me that I didn't need these detailed supervisory chats any more: 'You know what you're doing.' I'd clearly passed the test into John's trusted inner circle and he delegated absolutely.

Radio is such a passionate business with so many decisions being artistic and dependent on qualitative appraisal that it is hugely challenging to delegate effectively – but in expanding organisations it is crucial.

31

THE EMPIRE GROWS

The Millennium bug caused us no issues, nor did it cause many headaches for anyone else, apart from a reported problem with tickets at a couple of bus stations in Australia. I spent New Year's Eve in Nottingham's Old Market Square, letting off bright yellow balloons. When the name of your station is Century, a new one surely must be marked.

Century Radio's parent, Border Television, was one of the last in a dying breed of independent ITV companies, and was enjoying dipping its toe in the water of the radio world under the stewardship of John Myers – not least when it saw the value of its new wireless assets rise and rise. Owning huge Century FM licences in the north-west and north-east, alongside the promise of East Midlands success, constituted a decent radio group which was being eyed up by others with increasing enthusiasm.

The phone rang one afternoon and Peter Brownlow, the likeable chief of Border TV, summoned me to a summit later that day in a motorway service station. As we sipped our tea amidst the smell of the all-day breakfast, he broke the news that John, who had defined their radio business, was leaving. Years later, John told me about the frustration he'd experienced. He had created so much value for the company, yet he felt that his contribution to the company was not recognised appropriately.

I was offered the job of group programme director, alongside my East Midlands management role. For the first time in my career, my daily show was forfeited and I became a full-time executive, managing the pack of stations until their likely sale. I assumed, amongst other offices, John's impressive desk overlooking the waterfront at Salford Quays, where Century 105 was based, and became familiar with the A1 as I journeyed to the powerhouse of the Century regional station in Gateshead.

Board meetings were traditional affairs, convened in Carlisle. Harry Dunne was now capably in the top commercial hot seat and I covered everything else, as Border executives listened to our ramblings whilst munching cucumber sandwiches. I imagine they comforted themselves with the thought that a decent sale price for the radio business would be encouraged by improving ratings and profits. They also knew that the general acquisitive climate, some competitive tension amongst bidders and the strategic value of our regional assets would likely be dominant factors.

Delighted at being offered the top job, I'd not focused too much on the details of my contract. Like many people in our great business, money has never been the chief motivator for me. But when offers came in for Border, from Capital, then Scottish Radio Holdings, followed by Capital again, I looked up the mentions of share options on the signed A4 sheets in my bottom drawer and realised I was about to have a lucky day. Capital bought Border for £150 million, with a plan to release the TV business to ITV in due course at an agreed price.

When Capital first arrived to survey its new Century assets in the year 2000, I peered out of the first-floor windows of our offices. A succession of stretched black cars pulled up and the smooth Capital management team got out. The scene reminded me a little of black and white footage of wartime Europe.

Two hefty security guards burst into my office and escorted me off the premises, as my time in management there ended and the era of Capital Group ownership began. It was an uncomfortable moment – and I was not planning to leave without a fight.

At least that was the rumour I later heard from various sources. Tales like this fascinate me. Whoever decided to create the wholly fictitious story had clearly decided that one security guard was not enough: it had to be two.

The truth was altogether more prosaic. I'd resigned freely, and Capital Group's lovely representative was journeying from its Birmingham station to introduce the East Midlands staff to their new owners. When she phoned me en route, I reassured her I'd put the kettle on, which I duly did. With the staff assembled, I said my farewells and announced the acquisition, before handing over warmly to Capital's representative. The staff meeting passed without incident and we all gathered for a fond farewell and many glasses of Mâcon-Villages wine later that night.

I could have lingered, but felt it would be easier for them and for me if I moved on, and a decent contract thankfully anticipated this outcome. My decision was made easier on learning that Capital's on-air strategy for my East Midlands station was to be male-focused 'fun and football', rather than classic adult contemporary music with gradually declining amounts of speech as the regulatory reins loosened. It was reassuring recently, as I chewed over the good old days with Giles Squire, a hugely successful programmer for decades at Metro, to hear him echo my views. It was to be a short-lived Century strategy: the licences are all now operated as adult contemporary and performing impressively.

As I handed in my keys and wandered out the front door for the last time, I took some credit that we had inherited a problem station and doubled the audience, despite a relatively brief tenure.

My former boss Chris Hughes, who was still in a senior post down the road at the Radio Trent business in Nottingham, confided in me recently that, as competitors, they were all very pleased we'd packed our bags, as Century was beginning to power through in their own audience research measures.

Not for the last time in my career, I felt the end had arrived just that little bit too soon. That distinctive personality radio format could have enjoyed significant lasting success in the East Midlands.

32

ANOTHER GALAXY

When one chooses a career in media, a job which lasts for more than a couple of years is quite a welcome surprise. As the rival bidders for the Century empire had scrapped in the playground, I'd had the luxury of a little time to plan my next career move. The answer to the question 'what should I do next?' lay close at hand.

Radio stations had discovered that effective selling of airtime to national clients necessarily entailed selling large cohesive quantities of it persuasively and simply. Stations accordingly grouped together to ensure they were large enough to matter to the crazy ad buyers in London. At Century, we'd called upon the services of Chrysalis Radio to represent us in the national market – and to sell our audiences alongside their own. Chrysalis enjoyed a vital London foothold and owned the Heart and Galaxy brands, comprising two adult contemporary Heart stations, one of which served the capital with enormous success, and four Galaxy dance music stations.

In my Century spell, therefore, we met Chrysalis staff frequently. I found them to be like the Stepford wives of the famous 1972 film. All employees appeared puzzlingly perfect: utterly professional, utterly efficient, utterly objective and utterly pleasant. It seemed so perfect, frankly, it seemed odd. They were passionate about radio and a ready fund of anecdotes suggested they knew how to have a good time, but they also displayed a sense of calm focus which was absent elsewhere. Their stations leant on exhaustive research and benefited from a marketing sophistication which attached real importance to well-delivered cohesive brands. Such science was rarely evident in many of the UK's older stations which were more like emotionally driven family businesses desperately trying to grow up.

I spoke to Phil Riley, the chief executive of the radio division of Chrysalis, and he chirpily suggested he had an immediate opportunity for me. I'd like to say the process was more challenging than that, but it really wasn't. The gig was to head their Yorkshire operation as managing director at the mighty dance music station Galaxy 105 in Leeds. This was the first format with which I'd not had a close affinity. My days of sweaty clubgoing, strange hand gestures and a baseball hat facing backwards were long gone; in fact, they'd never really occurred.

Familiarity with Fragma and Daft Punk, however, was not of immense importance, given this was the first post I'd ever taken where I was not to be programme controller, nor would I be on air. I was just a humble managing director, whereas I'd grown accustomed to doing ten jobs at once and working at great speed. In the cases of my many rescues and launches, had I not run around, there would not have been a station at all.

Life was a challenge in those early Galaxy days. I'd left a cherished job; moved into temporary lodgings which smelt of wet dog; and, at the end of the very first week in the role, coped with the death of my mother, Betty, from cancer aged seventy-six.

Mum was Hyacinth Bucket. A woman who'd ruled a household of seven with a powerful influence, living on modest means in our stuccoed semi – but the second she left the house, she performed to impress. Life was a stage for her. She liked to dress well, and when appearing in local dramatic productions, as she frequently did, would only accept starring roles. She was all-knowing, recognising every ailment, given she'd seen it in so many of her children, and always able to dispense no-nonsense advice with the lack of subtlety for which a mother is licensed.

Her love affair with radio was typical of her generation, as illustrated in a 1952 diary I discovered when clearing the house:

'6th February. The King died today. George VI. Gave it out on the radio at 11.16 a.m. The Wireless closed down. It does seem miserable.'

'31st March. Had nice evening listening to radio with lights out.'

'22nd November.... cleaned car all day. Art's mended wireless, it's super now.'

She had her quirks, like any mother, but I recall a moment in my mid-teens when I was penniless and needed funds for something which she knew was important to me; she emptied her purse into my hands and said: 'I haven't got much, but you can have what I've got.'

Grief hits when you least expect it. You cope with all the complex administrative matters surrounding death and handle the funeral in a professional, coping manner. Indeed, in those early moments, you sometimes pause to ask yourself why you don't feel more upset than you appear to. It's when your guard falls, often at the most bizarre moments, that the sadness bites.

Just after my mum had died, Jan Tiffany, my wonderful shoe-loving PA at Galaxy, capable of anything in the world apart from booking trains, generously picked up an iced bun for me whilst she was on a lunch break. On her return, she rifled through her bag, stacked with shopping, and handed me this favourite sweet treat in its sticky paper bag, a little worse for the journey. The fact that it was delivered in the familiar, sorry squashed state, with the paper bag sticking to the icing, reduced me to sobs. The greasy bag symbolised every single caring gesture my mother had ever made in my life. Those tears were better out than in, as Mum would have said. Only when your parents have gone do you realise quite how much of them you inherit.

Jan, like Wendy at Leicester Sound, had assumed the unpaid essential role as mother to all at Galaxy. A cheap blue chair in her office became known as the crying chair, where young presenters and assorted staff would open up about relationship and family problems, as well as any career issues. She dispensed frank advice and, whilst never betraying a confidence, made sure that any bosses who needed to be abreast of something were delicately informed. In a station populated by young adults facing the dirty realities of life for the first time, pastoral care from the likes of Jan appeared to me to be crucial.

Chrysalis believed in investing in its staff and it was decided that employees should be despatched to a weekend team-building exercise. Nothing filled me with horror more than going on one of these futile charades; however, feedback on this one from Chrysalis staff had been alarmingly impressive. Some individuals had seemingly undergone life-changing experiences and teams that fought became unhealthily co-operative. To show my leadership credentials, I attempted to suspend my hatred of the absurd proposal for the sake of others who might benefit.

Off we went, clutching our required clothing and rations, ready for a weekend's play in a wonky farmhouse in Derbyshire. Crazy activities ensued, including being abducted by a Land

Rover in the middle of the night and dumped at some location. With compasses and clues, we were instructed to find our way back and there were jolly mental and physical challenges along the route. It was all about making sure you clarify the brief, identify skills, place the appropriate folk on the right jobs, appoint a leader, think about the goal and all that tosh.

The next day it was abseiling. Oh, joy! The completion of my journey down the cliff was greeted by a fake 'woop, woop' from the organisers. 'Don't you feel good now you've achieved that?' they questioned, as I unleashed myself. My mouth smiled politely, but my eyes likely betrayed, inwardly thinking I had derived neither pleasure nor benefit from the exercise. Had someone's life depended on it, I would have been the first to grab the rope and that would be the only reason to bother. The weekend dragged on. On the final night, tired and annoyed, and with a couple of drinks inside me, I sobbed and left. Just weeks after major crises in my life, my mind had been messed with and the timing wasn't great.

Back on the day job, I adjusted and began to savour the luxury of having time to think. Not to be lifting the paving slabs every day, but just polishing them and making sure they all fitted together well. That principally meant arbitrating between the commercial director and the programme director if we were to both build an audience and sell it successfully to clients; healthy conflict which exists at just about every commercial radio station in the world.

33

NUMBER ONE FOR DANCE AND RNB

One of the first expense claims I signed off from my new management chair at Galaxy was 'Hire of dwarves for event'. To this day, I cannot explain why we should have been even thinking of hiring people of short stature, and it was likely ill advised, but the moment serves to illustrate life at this eccentric outfit. Some radio stations are soulless, whereas others have an abundance of fire and energy which hit you as soon as you walk through the door, and Galaxy 105 was one such station.

It was based in a brick-built former clothing factory on the outskirts of Leeds. Routinely, we'd call for assistance to deal with an elderly lady who would sit on the doorstep claiming the premises belonged to her as she'd been left them by King John in his will.

Galaxy's car park was shared with those working in more sensible industries and guarded by men in braided uniform, whose only pleasure in life was to stop people entering. I heard the tale of Boy George, who hosted a network specialist music show for a time, arriving for his programme without the necessary green parking pass. It's alleged he tried the 'But I'm Boy George, and I'm coming in to…' trick, only to be greeted with 'I know perfectly well who you are, but you are still not coming in'.

Galaxy was a station targeted at twenty to twenty-nines

and knew its audience well; indeed, the presentation staff lived the same lives in this thriving, proud city with a throbbing yet well-behaved nightlife. 'Number one for dance and RnB' was the station's on-air claim, albeit it took some persuading and influencing skills from the group programmer to ensure the strapline was adopted by all four Galaxy stations. These were the times when local programme directors really did direct the programmes on their transmitters, but the friction amongst them over those half a dozen words illustrates the downsides of local government.

The station was unafraid to be 'edgy', when edgy was in, and puffed its chest with pride when the Advertising Standards watchdog banned an ad it had commissioned on the sides of buses.

The initial programme director was Jean Branch, a wonderful ex-record rep who managed her clan either in the way a mother manages her children or as an agent manages their talent, or maybe they are the same thing. Jean made way for the incredibly enthusiastic New Zealander Andrew Jeffries. His energies were well timed and I gather he brought with him some socialising habits with his presenters which were unexpected in this country, such as riding a go-kart with him or joining him in the hot tub.

It was Andrew who presciently paused to consider the future of the breakfast show. The programme was performing decently, but Andrew questioned whether it enjoyed sufficient growth potential. He alighted on a promising alternative presenter from Viking, a smaller commercial station in Hull. Although only twenty-seven, the presenter was an accomplished performer and already amassing a decent audience through a show which delivered real cut-through character. Simon Hirst, known to his

the appointment to Hit40UK, Hirsty tells of sitting on a favourite Yorkshire hill overlooking the familiar local panorama, reflecting on the enormity of the gig.

Although it sat on a tight, youth-formatted station, the award-winning breakfast show built sufficient listener trust to gain permission to go off piste when the moment was right. One such occasion was an impromptu link about bullying where each presenter opened up about their own painful experiences. Unlike many stations, they did not have to plead for reaction, their listeners just wanted to talk to their friend.

Whilst authenticity is key to the best radio, there was one secret which Hirsty kept painfully. She had gender dysphoria.

Presenting as a man for thirty successful years, her career built to such an extent that every year of success took her further away from being able to open up about who she was. She simply had ever more to lose. Whilst some of her closest friends knew the truth, she feared she would lose many others, were she to appear her true self.

In 2014, after too many dark days and having considered suicide on occasions, she decided to go public with her secret – at whatever cost. By this time, we were not working together, but she called me. Given she'd just left her job abruptly and the speculation was that she was about to move to another important gig, I thought she was about to share the news of her next role. Instead, in her typically friendly Yorkshire accent, she explained to me her dysphoria.

The next time we met, she was not presenting as the enviably good-looking, crop-haired lad I remembered, but as Stephanie. An attractive woman who attracted a glance only for that fact as we dined out in Birmingham.

The public denouement was destined to be dramatic. In

autumn 2014, Stephanie appeared on BBC 5 live to open up to its late-night presenter Stephen Nolan. Typically, she chose her beloved medium of radio as the platform for her story, speaking openly, at length and with good humour about her situation. It was an astonishing hour of honest radio; a well-judged interview that attracted much favourable and sympathetic coverage in the press and on radio and TV.

Such was the closeness of the relationship Hirsty enjoyed with her audience, she took them with her. The tone of the social media response was tear-jerking, and this neighbourly Yorkshire community simply stuck up for its own. I was reminded of this at a conference recently, when German writer Sebastian Fitzek said: 'If your main character is likeable, the audience will follow their journey until the moon.'

It was clear too that Stephanie's courage inspired others wrestling with life's challenges. Not for the first time, someone popular, using the medium of radio, had single-handedly helped to reshape the views of a nation.

Sadly, her former station, which by now had adopted the Capital brand, took the view she should not continue on air on the breakfast programme, and thus she was prevented from having an open and honest conversation with her own audience family she'd craved for over a decade. I can start to understand why they might have drawn breath, but, on balance, they missed out on one of the most compelling pieces of British radio that might ever have happened. And I'm not sure her station's stance was a fitting human response.

Days later, the annual glittery Radio Festival was convened in Manchester. All key industry figures routinely attend this celebratory event, both the BBC and commercial animals, from senior management to bright young things. Given Hirsty's news, the organisers shoehorned in an extra Q&A sofa session with her.

It was the first time her entire beloved radio industry had seen her since she'd opened her heart on 5 live. As she walked on stage under the spotlight, radiating happiness and relief – and looking a million dollars – her friends and colleagues rose to their feet as one and applauded. There is polite applause; there is enthusiastic applause and there is protracted, truly visceral emotional applause. Knowing that she'd feared the worst for so many years, this was Hirsty's beloved industry shouting: 'We still love you and we want you to know it.' As conference moments go, it was one of the most memorable and moving.

34

COUNTING LISTENERS

One million people is a lot: the equivalent of more than three times the population of Coventry or the O2 Arena filled fifty times. For Galaxy in Yorkshire, it was an ambitious listener target for an already successful station and required that a quarter of all adults in Yorkshire would be tuning in each week.

I rashly promised the staff a wild party or weekend away if we ever hit a million, quietly failing to trouble head office with the likely cost of the pledge, as I imagined it was likely that I would have moved on by that distant moment.

Galaxy had performed reasonably well with audiences over time. It launched in Yorkshire, licensed under the Kiss brand on Valentine's Day 1997 before abruptly becoming Galaxy a few months later. It moved from deep dance credentials to what became known unkindly as the 'Shania Twain years', before finding success again with a popular dance and RnB approach.

In my time, weekly audience figures, which stood at 800,000, crept up believably and sustainably, inch by inch. Then, one bright October day in 2002, the surprise news filtered through. Our spirited station had officially become the largest outside London, and the magic 1 million mark had been surpassed. Putting to one side the national stations or those broadcasting to the huge London area, we were the largest of all UK radio stations, BBC or commercial. Although Galaxy staff rarely needed to be given a reason for a drink, here were a million reasons for merry-making.

A large audience brings its problems. Presenters can start to strut around, legitimately asking for more money and making more demands – and programme management worry about losing the talent that appears to be paying dividends. In Yorkshire, revenues from local advertisers posed a counterintuitive challenge. Given the station broadcast its programming and advertising content across the whole large region, a local garage owner would be asked to pay more for his ad spots in view of their rising worth as the audience grew. As dizzy heights were scaled, the cost became simply out of reach for some local companies.

National advertisers provided little comfort. The agencies which controlled the purse strings of the major UK brands were London based. Their employees had grown up listening to Capital, and they now loved the music on Xfm, concluding that everyone else's listening repertoire was much the same. Galaxy was but a chocolate bar to them. Radio was not top of their media list and there was certainly little interest in a radio station based further north than they would ever reasonably think of venturing.

One of our best sales executives, rugby-playing Yorkshire lad Jason Willacy, told of the time he'd been asked about our weekly audience numbers by a grumpy agency head in London. 'A million,' he'd answered, only to be greeted by an impatient rebuttal from the head honcho, presumably anxious to go to talk to someone who sold a more exciting medium: 'I don't mean how many people live in your area, I mean how many listeners.' Jason replied with the impressive figure again, beginning even to doubt himself. This ad buyer could not believe that any station which had the temerity not to broadcast to London could command the attention of quite so many human beings. How could so many people choose to live up north anyway?

Whilst the station was delivering healthy profits, there was a frustration that the fruits of the enormous growing audience were not being fully realised. With further local revenue growth challenging, owing to the immense scale of the station and national revenues failing to yield the benefits warranted, the only answer floated in our endless strategy days seemed to be to create a Galaxy station in London so that our name would become as familiar as Capital Radio to the ad buyers in the City. The eventual solution, delivered nine years later, was even simpler. Once in the same ownership, the Yorkshire Galaxy station, along with others around the UK, simply assumed the Capital mantle.

Many companies, whatever their field of business, conduct staff surveys, despatching insistent emails inviting participation, to which most employees fail to respond. There are more interesting things to do in life than complete lengthy dull questionnaires comprising questions that don't always make sense in order to provide information for people who are unlikely to take any notice.

Periodically, Galaxy, and all the Chrysalis Radio stations, would commission such a survey. Richard Huntingford attached significant and genuine value to the projects. He was the parent company's chief executive: a small, clever, inspiring man with frizzy grey hair and, if my PA's estimate is to be believed, a 28-inch waist. His approach set company culture. Friendly and approachable, he was one of those bosses who know the names of – and something relevant about – everyone in the company.

Whilst always cordial, Richard was also a decisive, instinctive businessman. I admired him so much that I turned into a jabbering wreck whenever I attempted to chat to him.

Once the results were in, Richard would personally pay a visit to each station. Rather like unveiling the new no. 1, we managers had no inkling of whether we'd be deemed hero or zero as he presented the findings in front of us and our workforce.

The Leeds results from Galaxy 105 were spectacular. In the view of the independent analysts, the company had been judged 'world-class'. I recall one survey question which was along the lines of 'my manager gives the support I need to do my best work every day'. I welled up as the bar chart for the large programming department flashed up, suggesting every single person at this large eccentric radio station agreed strongly with the statement.

The result was a tribute, I believe, to Mike Cass, the programme director who'd inherited the station days after it hit the 1 million listeners mark. He called me from his pre-new-job holiday and joked that he likely wouldn't bother coming after all. There's no worse job than assuming the mantle of a radio station which has just reached record audiences.

Our relationship was an odd one. Mike and I first met at Leicester Sound when he'd arrived as the most annoying teenager ever, determined to 'help out'. I was equally sure this chubby, spotty, highly irritating lad would not be helping out any time soon. He disappeared obediently, only to return shortly afterwards, but as a changed character. Mike had become the sort of lad every radio station needs. He watched, listened, learned and helped out anyone in any way he could. As I left the station and handed over the reins, I shouted over my shoulder to the incoming managing director and suggested he fill an outstanding low-level vacancy with Mike, to afford him the start that he so richly deserved. Although new bosses traditionally ignore the wishes of their predecessor on principle, Mike was duly appointed. He went on from that minor post to become one of the top UK programmers.

Mike's trajectory illustrates two truths about our industry: most of us start at the bottom and many of us bump into each other more than once.

One thing every business gets used to in these changing times, is restructuring. At Chrysalis, a regional managing director post was to be created across both the Manchester and Yorkshire stations, with the Manchester MD and I both pitching for this stereo trans-Pennine gig. I was the lucky one and was handed an additional set of keys to our Manchester station, which had proved a challenge in audience and revenue terms.

Internal interviews are always fun, and I often wonder what the interviewers are likely to uncover in a stilted hour-long grilling that they didn't know from working with you for two years.

35

ANOTHER SAGA

The UK radio cake was being iced with a further tier of major regional radio stations. Real Radio, an adult contemporary music and conversation format, was spread across Yorkshire and Wales, and found a home in Scotland on the former Scot FM transmitters. Original and Wave 105 opened in the south of England.

In the West Midlands, older audiences were treated to a new station backed by Saga, the holiday and financial services company targeted at the fifty-plus market, and in 2003 that company was also awarded an East Midlands licence. Plans for both stations had been assembled by my former colleague Ron Coles, and my partner was appointed to programme the East Midlands station.

As Saga 106.6 FM was a fresh station on my home patch, programmed by my hard-working other half, Paul, there appeared little need to post an audition tape through our own letterbox. It was accordingly not too challenging to garner an invitation to host a weekly show. It was typically generous of Ron to allow me through the door of his station as we bounced into each other's lives yet again.

With the consent of my weekday employer Chrysalis, which seemed to accept with alacrity my scratching my broadcasting itch elsewhere, I agreed to a Sunday freelance contract which

I could easily honour whilst still holding the Galaxy regional MD role.

Some people play football by way of weekend recreation. I wanted to score with a few jingles and songs. As many broadcasters would agree, whatever else you do, nothing can quite rival the endorphin rush of 'having a good show' and that drug was the catalyst for my giving up my weekends rather than the show fee. As many presenters will confirm, show fees at most stations, unless you are the star, have not been blessed over the years with the luxury of a 'triple lock' guard against inflation.

Saga East Midlands was housed in smart premises, located on the edge of Nottingham close to the banks of the Trent, decorated with Warhol-inspired artwork of Bing, Dusty and Elton. It slid on the air with great professionalism, sounding as if it had been there for years. In a sense it had, with a clear lineage back to Trent days. Many of the presenters had grown up on the radio in Nottingham, their lives echoed by their listeners. John Peters, who'd been the first ever voice on Radio Trent and GEM AM, kicked off the station in the East Midlands and was back in his old dawn slot on the schedule.

For many Saga listeners, John's warm voice reminded them of happy days, busy lives and growing families. An interesting study written by Anne Karpf from London Metropolitan University adds weight to the theory that the regularity and daypart 'zoning' of radio listening means that voices are associated with times of the day and of life. As their own clans left their nests, John's listeners were pleased to have him back home.[26]

The Saga line-up was also blessed with the legendary ex-forces broadcaster and TV continuity announcer David Hamilton. He had been a key BBC Radio 2 broadcaster, having squatted on Radio 1 and 2 simultaneously in the '70s when the two stations linked up each afternoon. Accordingly, it was difficult to avoid David, as his cheery tones beamed out to the UK, and indeed some of Europe, on FM, medium and long wave. David's BBC afternoon audience share from those days will likely never be achieved again by any UK broadcaster.

David recounts the tale of the legendary Radio 1 Fun Day at Leicestershire's Mallory Park racing circuit in 1975, when an appearance by the Bay City Rollers, the teen idols of the '70s, attracted a crowd that was larger, younger and more hysterical than envisaged. As the Rollers flew in to land on an island in the middle of the lake and surrounding track, the screaming fans sought to cross the water that divided them from their tartan heroes. As David recalled, it was lucky no one was hurt, although his own programme on the day continued with typical proficiency.

'Diddy' David Hamilton, who tells me his epithet was bestowed by Ken Dodd, has never written a book called 'the true radio professional', but he should. In his later career at Saga, less in the limelight than he once was, he carried off the 'I used to be a star' mantle with sufficient skill to lend a special feeling to being with him, but he also did it with great charm and an absence of demands. David's hugely professional approach to his work suggested he wanted to be judged by what he did now rather than lean on past victories. With live shows in Nottingham, plus voice-tracked, pre-recorded shows on other stations in the stable, plus some network shows, his work ethic amazed me, not least because he was already in his mid-sixties. Like the music industry, radio keeps you young.

It was typically generous of David to turn up for a private gig in his sparkly gold jacket for our civil ceremony reception in 2006. In the evening sunshine on that beautiful August night in the rooftop grounds of London's Coq d'Argent, overlooking the Gherkin and St Paul's, David played the part to our mostly radio crowd with a retro 'Radio 1 roadshow' dedicated to me and Paul. As the night proceeded, the champagne flowed and the fireworks fizzed to the choreographed sound of a radio jingle soundtrack.

David Hamilton's new afternoon show on Saga in the East Midlands was well received and his 'music game' returned, which had been a staple of his BBC programmes. His old features, including 'Beauty Tips for Women' and 'David's Daily Dolly', wisely did not.

Meanwhile, at the weekends, I settled in on Sunday mornings, hosting a traditional request show which I tried to do in a relatively fresh style. Gone were the *Family Favourites* days of long lists of names 'and anybody else who knows me', mentioning the house number and street of each contributor. Most responses still came by mail, however, given the target demographic. In my day job, I don't think we'd ever have noticed had the Galaxy postman not turned up.

Waking on a Sunday morning felt as exciting as the dawn of Christmas Day as a child. Albeit on a hobby basis, I was back on air in the East Midlands doing something I loved, on a brilliant radio station. I often grit my teeth when presenters appear lukewarm about what they are paid to do. If you hate it as much as your demeanour suggests, move out of the way and let someone else have a go.

The way listeners confide in their chosen station is always astounding. Callers can sometimes be heard opening up to their non-judgemental friend, the radio presenter, in a way they've never spoken to anyone before, regardless of the thousands of people eavesdropping. This quiet unassuming medium enjoys tremendous intimacy and power.

One letter came from a mother whose daughter had gone off the rails and was later found dead in a derelict Nottingham city centre warehouse. She wanted a song to be played on what would have been her daughter's birthday. In radio presentation, just like in journalism, part of you sympathises with genuine honesty when reading tragic stories like this, and I concede that the other part relishes the chance to deliver such compelling material. In radio, the very best content comes from listeners.

Nothing disappoints a programmer or presenter at a commercial radio station more than grabbing a lift from someone in the commercial team who has their car radio locked to Radio 2. In charge of revenue generation at Saga was a friend, sales director Lisa Macdonald. Some occupants of similar posts in the industry treated the efforts of the programming team with disdain, failing to value the integrity of the on-air product; indeed, some didn't ever trouble to listen to the stations they represented. Lisa was not one of these people. She cared about what was broadcast, about how her commercial material fitted in and about her relationships with the programming team. With long blonde hair and friendly eyes, she made vibrant company and was an experienced operator.

My impression was, however, that this wonderful individual was troubled and lived a complex life, and her worries extended beyond the monthly revenue figures. Following some growing concern from friends, I remember taking a call and learning she had disappeared. When a conversation like that happens, it is as much what is not said as what is said. Hours later came the awful news that this capable, much-loved person had chosen a spot which meant a lot to her to take her own life.

Funerals are never joyous occasions, but usually you can manage a half-smile when you recall fond memories of the times you shared together and console yourself with the fact that they lived a rich and rewarding life. At the funeral of someone who has committed suicide at such a tragically young age, there are no such platitudes, no such comforts – just bleak sadness. There are no suitable words you can say to comfort family and friends; there is nothing you can offer beyond a handshake and a sympathetic murmur.

There was standing room only in the large building for the farewell service. Some songs are always associated with a moment in time and, for those present on that dark day, Abba's 'Thank You for the Music' will for ever symbolise the loss of a friend and colleague.

I'd prefer to remember Lisa, champagne glass in hand, throwing back her head laughing and relaxing outside our local pub. She was an inspiration.

The world of radio is full of complex characters and it is hugely upsetting just how many of us meet the ends of our careers or lives all too prematurely.

Lisa's beloved station continued, although her colleagues never forgot her. Saga carved out a decent audience across the East Midlands, quickly building to over a quarter of a million loyal listeners.

As a brand extension, I could see the value of the radio stations to their Saga parent in generating profile and a platform to market its own goods and services; I could also see the instant 'awareness' for the radio stations that the relationship with the Saga brand offered, not least through its established communication channels and valuable mailing lists.

The station names, however, were arguably a challenge both to advertising agencies and to those listeners who would have loved the music and personality format but felt their lives had not yet reached what they considered the gnarled-hand-on-walking-stick 'Saga stage'. Norman Quirk, who ran the Scottish Saga station, commented: 'At the moment you start to talk to people about Saga Radio and they think it's Zimmer frames and stair lifts. What we have to get across is that the Saga Radio is not a station for old people; we are a station for older people.'[27]

The Guardian Media Group, which had been appointed to sell the stations' airtime to national agencies, faced the challenge of selling the proposition to the young ponytailed lads buying media at London advertising agencies who seemed to view fifty-pluses as people who had already made their minds up about everything they would ever buy, and who would likely keel over and die by the weekend.

The station provided a home for many time-served broadcasters, even if only for an occasional shift. At one stage, my old colleague from hospital radio Steve Voce was briefed for a few programmes. You always remember the people who helped to put you on the path to your chosen career, and I held Steve in high esteem both for that, and for his general warm presentation style. Steve had also pursued radio professionally after hospital radio, popping in and out of several stations.

I gather that, when being briefed for his Saga shifts, Steve had appeared a little confused about some of the equipment and about locking up the premises after he'd finished his weekend stint. Paul and I, however, tuned in eagerly from home to his first programme, looking forward to hearing his familiar tones on air.

It was to prove a shock. Steve was clearly having difficulties, seeming to lose his way, forget what he was saying and what was to come next. It was both worrying and puzzling, given his calibre and experience. We concluded he was unwell and that he needed help. Paul prepared to call in and take the reins, as his boss, but we agreed it might be more helpful if I, as an old friend, appeared to drop in 'whilst passing'.

Behind the heavy studio door was not the Steve I remembered. This familiar figure was struggling to deliver what he had done for years. His state was one of agitation, knowing that something was wrong. I helped him limp to the end of the programme, exactly as one would a new presenter, establishing step by step what he was going to say the second he opened his mic, and then what he would do next. I was teaching him what he had taught me thirty years before.

We learned later that Steve had developed early-onset Alzheimer's disease; he was only in his fifties.

He was to appear on radio again, but this time talking about his Alzheimer's. I met him at the BBC after one interview and we joked about the old times which he remembered well.

Once diagnosed and treated, Steve lived a decent life for some time, supported by the devoted, loving care of his wife Nikki. The path for this cruel disease is, however, a certain one, leading to an inevitable downward spiral, at present at least. I last saw him in a wheelchair at a hospital radio reunion that Nikki was keen for him to attend. By this stage, he was no longer himself but was aware he was attending a special occasion of some sort and I rushed to find a five-inch spool of tape as a prop to remind him how we'd both edited so many miles of it in our lives. He smiled.

There are times in life when you pause to be thankful for what you have, and wonder why something so awful chooses someone so decent to be its victim. Steve helped me enormously in my radio life, and I shall be for ever grateful. On our second ever meeting in 1977, he'd promised me he would train me how to use a portable tape recorder, but never got around to it. We joked about that for years. He never did train me. Now he can't.

Within four years of the East Midlands launch, both Midlands Saga stations, alongside the Scottish station and a licence for a new outlet in the north-east, were sold for an impressive price to Guardian Media, who rolled out their Smooth brand across the powerful regional frequencies in 2007. The saga was over.

36

ANOTHER TOY TO PLAY WITH

As I jumped in the cab in the rain from Manchester's Galaxy 102 to visit the hospital to which an employee had been admitted, having tried to take his own life, I wondered what I was going to say to him.

I hope I said the right thing; to my knowledge, his life continues happily, likely no thanks to me. Whatever leadership and management training you have, and I've suffered a few bouts, nothing can prepare you for the sort of things a career in radio throws at you. With its incredible highs and lows, even over the course of a single day, it's pure Shakespeare.

My Manchester office was a glass erection in the station's spacious premises, located on the second floor of a shopping centre in the cool part of town, noteworthy for a distinct absence of shoppers.

After a couple of weeks, I asked the identity of a cheery lad with spiky blond hair who had delivered a welcome cup of tea to me at my desk each morning as I arrived after a painful drive over the Pennines. It transpired that this agreeable, conscientious guy, who wasn't on the payroll, simply wanted to understand the radio business better and funded his own bus fare to get to the station to help out on a voluntary basis. I didn't need to know much more; it was clear he'd engineer his success in radio. Now, Simon Morykin enjoys a peak show at Sheffield's Radio Hallam.

It is refreshing to see such people still exist. I have a theory they are rarer, with those of the X Factor generation seemingly demanding a highly paid breakfast gig two weeks after joining the industry. I recall the young lady on work experience at Galaxy who turned up at ten thirty. I reminded her that we normally start at nine, to which she retorted: 'Yeah, but I was out last night.' As in the case of Simon, I could probably have predicted what life would bring her.

I also recall the challenge in rostering a technical operator to oversee the New Year's Eve output which was being transmitted on all Galaxy FM services, plus the national DAB service. I shook my head in disbelief that no one seemed willing to forsake a few pints in favour of the large black studio chair. In my teens, I would have crawled up the motorway on my hands and knees for the privilege of pushing up faders on a Starship Enterprise pumping out music to the nation. What could possibly be more exciting?

I recognise it's a change in the ethos of society. We have, probably rightly, all come to expect more from our jobs, better conditions, more fulfilment, better rewards, faster progression – but staff and presenters who make undue demands too early in their career do not lay themselves the best foundations. The lad who told me that his parents had encouraged him to demand more money as he had a degree certainly got short shrift.

Programme director Vaughan Hobbs ran the programming department at Galaxy in Manchester. A gifted music programmer from Australia and a man of few words, he was a little frustrated sometimes by the UK's less direct approach to life. I liked and respected this good-looking man, although with his mop of black hair and piercing eyes, he could look pretty frightening. I recall his being thoroughly disappointed and surprised by one set of audience figures, back when they were published at the crack of dawn, when tolerance levels are low for us all. His anger was evident, his hair ruffled, his eyes wide open and staring. I edged closer to the first-floor window to put myself in front of the gaping hole leading to the Manchester streets below, for fear he might jump out. He didn't, but he certainly made clear his frustrations about audience measurement.

Vaughan relished the radio stunts which were commonplace back home, and devised a 'Three in a Bed' promotion, staged in a sponsor's store window, under the glare of passers-by. The lucky contestants, challenged to stay *in situ* through the day and night, were a chap with his wife and mistress. The affair became even more dramatic when a local scally ram-raided one of the adjacent shops.

Decent breakfast presenters can sail too close to the wind. At Galaxy 102 in 2003, we were fined when a twelve-year-old child taking part in a contest was asked what she thought about a previous caller who'd suggested giving his wife a slap was a good idea. The child rightly suggested the caller was 'a fucking wanker'. Following a single complaint, the tapes were called for, just as our regulator changed from the Radio Authority to Ofcom at the end of 2003. There was a concern about language, as well as asking children about the topic.

Following Ofcom's tardy investigation, and numerous procedural exchanges written in chilling language I remembered well from my regulatory days, we were summoned to what appeared like a gruelling high court hearing. Lawyers and stenographers lined one side of the room, Ofcom officials the other, with us staring straight ahead. Ofcom's new wonderful

Thames riverside home was impressive, compared to the former Radio Authority's lodgings. The luxury lavatory appeared to me to be sufficiently large to accommodate a modest radio station.

We were fined £2,500 and acquired the dubious honour of being the first radio station ever to be fined by the new regulator.

Our annual staff appraisal forms were typical of many companies, with one box labelled: 'Things that Went Badly' and another headed: 'Things that Went Well'. I naturally scribbled down the expensive regulatory breach in the negative box. In true Chrysalis style, my boss Don Thomson moved it to the positive one, commenting on how well he felt I'd handled it. Goodness knows how much he had feared we'd be fined.

There was an occasion when one of the two Manchester breakfast presenters found their co-host had become emotionally 'close' to a presenter of a rival breakfast programme. Whilst the two Galaxy presenters were clearly not an item, it was still felt to be a betrayal. Such is the close bond of a breakfast duo: two people who likely spend more time in each other's lives than with their real-life partners.

The following morning, the double act turned up for the programme, but refused to speak to each other on air. As a boss, waking up to a show which is just destined to fall over is a horrible experience. One of them hosted the show, ignoring the other, who just popped up unannounced every half-hour to deliver the travel news. Later, I brought them in my office for a chat and proved why I am not a marriage guidance councillor. One stormed out, slamming my glass office door so hard that the walls shook. It all ended happily.

It was just another day at Galaxy 102, a station which used to display proudly a huge line graph of how the numbers of listeners was growing closer and closer to that of our rivals, admittedly mostly through their falls rather than our progress, at that stage. In true 'edgy' Galaxy style, our competitors were not labelled on the chart by their name, but by an expletive.

37

MOVES ON LONDON

In a giant game of expensive Monopoly, the commercial radio industry was trying to make sense of the commercial network which had grown from the original nineteen stations to a matter of hundreds. Life is difficult when you own the Strand, but your rival owns Trafalgar Square and Fleet Street. You can't do very much and the game becomes very dull.

At strategy days in random hotels, I cannot imagine that our Chrysalis Radio management team was the only one playing out exercises with coloured pieces of paper and imagining that life would be better if we all gathered in the playground and swapped stations to make cohesive sets. We owned the youth brand Galaxy, but EMAP, later bought by Bauer, owned Kiss. Capital owned Century, but we owned Heart. GWR owned some stations in decent cities, but then again so did EMAP. If the network had launched in a confused mess, it was now just a bigger one.

Chrysalis took a deep breath and decided if it were to win the game, it needed to boost its London presence, and maybe it could afford to relinquish its challenging Galaxy station in Bristol. The deal agreed was complex, not least because of who was permitted to own what on competition grounds. But, after some very long nights, Chrysalis claimed the once-great news and talk station LBC in the belief that it could restore it to its former glory.

That first commercial radio station in the UK had suffered

a troubled life since its birth. As one of its first employees, Ian Rufus told me that few staff at LBC's launch in 1973 even knew anything about radio. He'd been given a far higher position than he'd expected, simply because so many other staff did not appear to know which end of the microphone to speak into. The money ran out quickly and Ian recalled staff taking typewriters home in lieu of salary, given that they had not been paid. The station was off air frequently as arguments with the unions raged.

The station, identified for many years by its iconic jingles by *War of the Worlds* composer Jeff Wayne, did eventually acquire a fond reputation in London, although it continued to lose money. Some suggested wryly that LBC stood for 'Losing Bundles of Cash'. In 1993, LBC failed to have its licence to broadcast renewed and went into receivership. Its own news bulletin in September that year announced: 'LBC's chairman, Dame Shirley Porter, who took over earlier this year, is shocked and saddened. She said London will be the loser.'[28] The LBC name died and the new licensee, London News Radio, took over in 1994, broadcasting as London News 97.3 and London Newstalk 1152. Ownerships changed and changed again, and two years later, when operated by GWR, the company concluded that the former licensee's name, LBC, appeared to have more recognition than the new one, so the old familiar brand returned. Even this change was not without incident: whilst I was at the Radio Authority, I'd learned of plans by Egyptian business magnate Mohamed Al-Fayed, father of Dodi, to register LBC as a trademark to be used on his Liberty AM station in London. The ingenious cheeky plan never came to pass.

Chrysalis took the view that it could revive LBC's fortunes, and Phil Riley, the chief executive of the Chrysalis radio division, was a firm believer, not least because, as a fan of American radio, he knew of the success great news stations in the United

States enjoyed. Briefing visits to New York were arranged, so the secrets of 1010 WINS – all news, all the time – could be shared: 'You give us twenty-two minutes – and we'll give you the world.' To this day, that station, broadcasting on AM, still appears in the top five stations in this busy radio market.[29]

Phil was an inspiring, towering individual with the biggest feet you've ever seen. Like many in his position, he held firm beliefs about most things and expressed them with conviction. Unlike many others with his degree of conviction, however, he did listen to and take account of rational argument backed by evidence – and he was one of the most honest, generous, loyal, intelligent people I know. An early riser, bored easily and with an enviably quick brain, any disaster today would be addressed by a creative and confident remedial plan by dawn tomorrow.

Studios for LBC were quickly installed over Christmas, built adjacent to those of Heart in the company's characterful west London premises, formerly the Phoenix brewery. Investment in the on-air product was significant and some huge names wandered through the door to host programmes or contribute.

Notably, the wise decision to switch frequencies was taken. The rolling news service moved to AM, with the news talk station LBC moving to FM. The format with which it could win the audience battle was switched to the best platform.

After a year or so, however, the venture had not shown quite the immediate promise expected and the cost of the operation was becoming painful. Having rejected overtures about being a group programmer for Chrysalis, I was offered the LBC managing director and programme director post.

The little lad in the shed was about to run what had been the first ever commercial radio station, delivering news and news talk to one of the world's most exciting cities.

38

LONDON'S BIGGEST CONVERSATION

Day one in a new role is an odd one for any manager. You're supposed to be running something, and know you'll be called upon to make decisions within hours, but you have no idea what you are doing. What's more you don't even know where you're supposed to sit.

I was fortunate, as I arrived at LBC that Monday morning at around eight o' clock. Early show presenter Steve Allen had finished his infamous dawn programme and was looking for someone to talk to. An endearing gent with an expressive face worthy of the finest *Carry On* actor, he was in his fifties and wore baggy shirts; he'd once revealed on air how he wore new underwear every day of his life.

He looked me up and down with a nod that said: 'Another one. I've seen them come and I've seen them go.' He had. Steve had been there almost from the outset, off and on, from presenting news shifts in his early days to settling on overnights or the early breakfast show. Whilst he was ever concerned about not fitting in and various managements not liking what he did, he outlived them all, and will likely continue to do so with his truly unique talent.

The programme controller suggested to me that Steve really excelled away from the glare of the peak shows, where he could feast a loyal large band of attentive listeners with an unbridled biting chat. Despite experimenting now and again, he seemed allergic to taking listener phone calls, preferring to talk to himself, clutching the tabloids, despatching dismissive entertaining remarks about many of the minor celebrities pictured within.

Steve showed me to my new office, located at the end of LBC-land, a little hidden away from where the presenters had their desks. Some months later, a helpful engineer installed a light I could flick on from my desk altering staff when I was free. It was a nice idea, from the company's truly excellent 'can do' technical department, but I did not want to feel like a doctor and could imagine, with some ease, the likely remarks from presenters about my deploying such a device.

Steve lay on the large black leather couch in my new home and led me through the schedule, programme by programme, with fitting remarks about every presenter. I suspect it was not the sort of induction HR would have liked, but it was truly illuminating and highly entertaining. Had it been on air, it would have been the best programme rundown ever. Steve is a peculiarly gifted and irreplaceable presenter.

Comedian Sandi Toksvig hosted a daily lunchtime show. I first met this highly intelligent presenter as she was climbing the stairs, followed closely by her loyal producer, who carried her lovely dog on a cushion. I could tell LBC was going to be quite unlike any other station.

An unkind, oversimplistic view of radio stations is that they tend to have sometimes challenging breakfast presenters, with the remainder of the day filled with characters in declining order of awkwardness. The LBC talk format meant that every show was as demanding as a breakfast show – this extended to their respective hosts. The presenters' office was a veritable soap opera, with some presenters getting on, some who clearly didn't, and when they were not having words with each other, they were falling out with their producers.

The company's busy HR division was run by my kind of woman. Faced with the latest challenges from my motley crew, she'd offer me the sort of speedy practical solutions on which fast-moving media businesses rely. Memorably, one day as I poured out an intemperate interminable account to her of one set of staff demands, her considered professional advice in broad Cockney tones was offered: 'Tell 'em to fuck off.' I am a huge fan of dealing with staff fairly, but worry that extant HR laws mean that it is altogether too difficult to move on from someone who is clearly doing themselves and their colleagues few favours.

On air, the LBC format was also deliciously unpredictable, and therein lay its value. Radio which relies on listeners calling in is addictive listening in the hands of the right presenter. Whilst regular callers can often make a decent contribution, it is often the phrase 'first-time caller' when the drama really begins. After decades of listening, something is said that motivates one individual to call and a first-hand account of something significant surely follows.

Presenters can be moved to tears from some calls. Whilst their response is genuine, their broadcasting instinct will cut in as the caller's voice quakes. 'Are you OK to carry on…' says the presenter sympathetically, quietly crossing fingers for further emotion. 'Yes,' says the caller, without exception. Of all forms of radio, talk radio is the purest.

On this format, by its very nature, the presenters are everything. When a regular host is on holiday, listeners will notice. It's like going to your friend's house and finding they're not in: it's likely that you wouldn't choose to have tea with a random neighbour instead. Listeners always have a close affinity with their radio station; but with a talk format, the presenter–listener relationship is a true, lasting bond.

LBC generated an emotional listener response. Some listeners, however, were less than enthusiastic about what they heard presenters say, and the police were summoned on more than one occasion to deal with suspicious packages, letters signed off in blood or threats to presenters' children. Talk radio is radio magnified.

Nick Ferrari had been installed on the breakfast show in 2004. I was aware, however, that the Chrysalis parent company chairman, founder and entrepreneur, Chris Wright, was not the biggest fan of Nick's programme. When I was having my final polite 'meet the chairman' chat before my appointment was signed off, he made his views clear. I nodded, cocked my head to one side and furrowed my brow sympathetically to indicate I was listening. I suspect he thought I was agreeing and that I was poised to make the change he'd preferred. I gather the only reservation he expressed about my appointment concerned my patent blue shoes.

I'd spent some time listening to Nick, however, and was resolute not to make a change. Sometimes, with key strategic decisions in radio programming, or indeed any other business, doing nothing is a good day's work. I'd formed the firm view that if you were going to broadcast talk in the morning, in a world where the BBC existed, Nick Ferrari was an impeccable solution. That was despite Mr Ferrari's insistence on calling me 'Mrs Lloyd'. A counterintuitive, mischievous camp undertone sometimes twinkled in the rich character of this very straight man in a showbiz world.

Nick combined the communications skill of a gifted radio presenter with the persistence of a press journalist and the wit of a comedian. A serious journalist with a tabloid instinct who could sharpen any subject to a killer question and reduce any interviewee to a wreck, if he chose to do so. Yet all that tough meat was seasoned beautifully with a dash of humour as large as he is. He was the consummate storyteller, dramatizing every anecdote.

Amidst the most serious of topics, Nick could still volley a humorous aside with the listener. Like most great talk broadcasters, his performance entertained and the content informed. A journalist of the old sort: persistence and truth. Great broadcasters like Nick identify instinctively the headline, the drama, the story and often the humour in each moment. Then they squeeze out that value.

You'd pay to dine out with Nick. He was great company and a genuinely decent and generous guy, albeit thoroughly intolerant of those who did not do their jobs capably. He expected commitment; and his appreciation of those around him when they scored for him was something to which they attached real value.

Most people had to try very hard to do what Nick appeared to do effortlessly.

It is to be expected that this clever man, who could choose to be awkward even with the Prime Minister, was always unlikely to roll over and comply with the latest LBC management diktat. When we once dared to change the contracted LBC taxi firm, I was treated to a lengthy phone rant from Nick. He was in performance mode and enjoying the scrap. I explained why we'd changed, but he argued back as if I were a truculent politician. Eager to resolve the matter, I reassured him that he could open the Yellow Pages and pick any firm in London he wanted. He did just that. Shortly afterwards, his company of choice let him down one morning – and our official firm dashed to him, at short notice, to save the day. The matter was never mentioned again. Until now.

Journalist and pundit James O'Brien is now an accomplished performer on LBC's mid-morning programme, with a genuinely unique approach. Not only is his liberal political home a place where few other broadcasters on the format around the world live, his exposition of topics is utterly illuminating. He carries his audience and himself on a well-informed voyage of discovery and is even heard changing his mind mid-programme on the strength of a caller's personal testimony – and listeners confess they have done the same. Like the best in his field, he is both opinionated and likeable.

James was appointed to his daily show in the Chrysalis years and, unusually for media careers, he has been allowed the benefit of time to perfect his own eloquent act and build a deep understanding with his audience. He speaks to his listener intimately, asserting, challenging and on occasions asking forgiveness. He takes the same approach as his broadcasting heroes: 'They connect on an individual level, rather than seducing a crowd like a demagogue can.'[30]

Thanks to UK-wide DAB exposure and canny social media, audio and viral video content, James's stock has rightly soared and it is fitting to see him hosting BBC 2's *Newsnight* from time to time. Were I casting that programme, I'd hire him.

Many LBC presenters are showmen, and some sought to earn a few quid and have some fun by creating stage shows where they addressed the audience in person. In essence, it was just another radio programme, but on stage; and one in which loyal listeners felt they were getting privileged insight into the character of the person they chose to spend so much of their life with. A good test of a great talk broadcaster is whether people would pay to hear them speak.

One such event that I attended in a large Croydon theatre, hosted by Steve Allen, was a phenomenon. His presence alone was sufficient to impress some people, once they realised that the voice they spent their days with had a body too. I turned around in my seat at the front and gazed at hundreds of smiling faces. This was a sell-out gig, with the people there united simply by their love of Allen.

Some radio industry engineering chiefs seemed to view broadcasting as a thorough inconvenience, indeed in one station the department was quietly labelled 'the programme prevention team'. The 'techies' had no grasp of immediacy, moaned when legitimately called out of hours and treated anyone from the programming team as an utter idiot until proven otherwise. I have probably shouted at only four people in my career and two of them have been engineers.

The team at Chrysalis, under calm, intelligent Bruce Davidson and inventive Dave Walters, could not have been more different. Dave would park himself in my office, lean back on the chair with his hands clasped behind his head and volunteer his latest bright idea: 'How useful would it be if…'

One such idea in 2006, capitalising on presenter loyalty, was subscription podcasting. Such is the irreplaceability of talk radio content, we suspected listeners might be prepared to pay for access were we to create the right interface. Our 'premium podcasting' became the darling of the media press, reaping appreciable revenues.

Beyond the many bright ideas and clever solutions, this impressive team understood the emotional impact on a presenter of a well-maintained studio; when explaining new technology to people like me, they could translate the impenetrable into words I understood. I have much respect for the clever, often unrecognised, technical clan who drive our industry. As delivery, as well as content, now brings competitive advantage, they are key to our future.

The LBC format's proven close listener relationship did not translate to revenue. Despite drawing huge, thinking audiences who would listen attentively to every word, and were at a stage in their life where they have a few pounds in their pocket, London advertisers did not attach sufficient value to the station. In the United States, the format can carry a premium, but over here we sometimes felt we couldn't give it away.

That problem owes a little to the BBC's existence, although LBC carves out a decent London market share, but owes more to the attitude towards older audiences by media-buying agencies. They fail to understand the persuasive potency of talk radio and are said to hold the view that attitudes about brands are formed earlier in life than the age of the format's audience. Such attitudes also drive down the price of older audiences for all media, which means agencies have the choice of many alternatives at a knock-down price, not least cheap and cheerful daytime TV. For years, too, not only was LBC the only commercial station of its kind, its footprint was London only and it could not promulgate a message nationwide.

LBC was still suffering losses, not least due to the huge taxi bill for guests and contributors. Each interviewee would demand a cab to get them to our building in a part of west London where they would not usually be seen. Such busy people also requested the car wait for them so they could exit promptly after their performance. Our alternative approach of relying more on content from presenters and callers than guests was driven by programme strategy, but brought welcome collateral cost savings.

When running a youth music station, one can count on a company board keeping a safe distance from day-to-day matters, given they readily concede that they have neither product understanding nor interest. They judge by figures. With a news and talk station, however, everyone appears to have a view on the content. Having expressed some opinions on presenters at the outset, parent company chairman Chris Wright appeared keen to keep abreast of LBC matters and I was summoned to a meeting, a couple of months on, to discuss progress.

Chris, the clever co-founder of Chrysalis Records in 1968, based himself in a large office, replete with artefacts of a fascinating life. Thankfully, the cricket on the television proved a stronger attraction than my LBC tales, so as I began my account he turned his chair sideways to watch that instead. Enjoying such overwhelming success and wealth so early in life gives one the confidence to be enviably eccentric, as illustrated by his affectionate portrayal in Ruby Wax's fly-on-the-wall TV profile of Chris. I recall him arriving extremely late to operational board meetings pushing a shopping trolley, whilst he was served his lunch between agenda items.

One sunny day, Chris kindly invited us to bring some clients to share his box at York races. As our guests took their seats, he gestured that we'd be positioned next to George and Judy, who sounded like a couple of his random neighbours. It transpired that the George concerned was Beatles producer George Martin, the chairman of our Heart station. Our gleeful, middle-aged car dealer customer rarely turned around to watch any horses, preferring instead to gaze lovingly into his idol's eyes.

I was told of one board meeting where, seeking to divert

attention from a controversial marketing agenda item, one Chrysalis executive suggested the board listen to the new Heart jingle package. The couple of identifications were duly played to an unimpressed George Martin. No one rose to the challenge of arguing with one of the greatest record producers of all time.

Our radio company, with its 'bring a dog to work' policy, had rock 'n' roll in its soul, and that suited me.

39

A NEW DAWN

LBC was dubbed the black cab drivers' station, a station you could turn on to hear old folk moan. The programme controller of the FM service, the patient Scott Solder, and I sought to bring it up to date.

Clever Scott, later editor of 5 live Breakfast and deputy editor of BBC TV current affairs, was a master of language; he could analyse not only what presenters said, but how they said it. He'd instruct presenters not to judge their programmes by the number of calls, and would illustrate the point by using the topic 'Are you feeling ill?', which would surely light up the switchboard, but not prove terribly interesting. It's a topic I've never tried, but all of us in radio know the proven caller power of old confectionery reminiscences, the colour of crisp packets and 'what's your favourite biscuit?'

Brand research was commissioned from a capable agency, Sparkler. When they suggested that the LBC corporate yellow was 'cheap', I had not the heart to mention Selfridges carrier bags. Sparkler did, however, help us to a conclusion that brand comprehension of the current LBC was low, and was confused by the fact that no one knew what LBC stood for. We alighted on the word 'conversation' as our defining word, and came up with 'London's Biggest Conversation' as our positioning statement.

We sought to ensure the topic balance more closely represented the subjects people chose to chat about in their everyday lives. Alongside the news agenda, we sought a little lighter talk entertainment too, mindful that human beings don't just discuss news all day. We'd even carried out some ad hoc research by sitting in a coffee bar eavesdropping on conversations and making notes to ascertain which subject areas were most popular. Holidays and work gossip ranked highly, with 'the price of spectacles' bizarrely entering the chart. Some accomplished personalities were hired, with Anna Raeburn reprising her famous Capital agony phone-ins and Jenny Eclair, Jon Holmes and Iain Lee adding entertainment and modernity to a braver schedule.

Iain had made his name as a stand-up comedian and presenter of *The 11 O'Clock Show* on Channel 4 and *RI:SE*. I rated him as a unique talent. Whatever else Iain did in his varied career, his radio work stood out, allowing him the freedom to be himself and, dependent on the show, the time to try things out. His stand-up experience and incredible creativity paid off in his delivery and build. Iain's asset was that he had little filter, which allowed truly great, spontaneous radio moments to occur. The worry for his managers was the very same matter. Thankfully, his considerable intelligence usually kicked in and issues were rare, but the very nature of his act, combined with the nature of LBC's vocal regular audience, meant that we were poised for a busy time with compliance management.

Iain attracted a phenomenally loyal following, but when I picked up the phone in my office and heard the shaky voice of an annoyed listener saying 'I'm [seventy]. And I've been listening to LBC since it started in 1973…', I didn't need to be Russell Grant to know who they'd be calling about. 'What have you done to my radio station?' they'd cry. The calls were tantamount to a landlord ringing his tenant in disbelief on learning that the tenant has just knocked down the living room's supporting wall. Any radio executive understands that, just like football clubs, a station belongs to its fans, not to you.

One caller suggested she had been annoyed by Iain 'seven times so far today'. I imagined this angry woman sat in her Chelsea flat, fuming as she ticked off her frustrations on a five-bar gate scribbled on a pink Post-it note.

One of Radio 1's aphorisms through the years has been 'ratings by day – reputation by night', with the more daring programming after dark, but its very presence contributing usefully to the station's brand reputation. In that vein, concluding that maybe drivetime was a little too risky a place on the schedule for Iain at the time, we moved him to late nights where he could be more himself and listeners could enjoy him at his unbridled best. The decision was not too popular with him, as presenters understandably have a very clear idea of the pecking order of shows. In time, we both chose to work together again and I am confident, from what he's said more recently, that he now believes my intentions were honourable.

If we are to have a future generation of radio listeners who care passionately about the medium there's got to be a home somewhere for the renegades.

Even in innocence, there's a funny sinking feeling you get when you see people in police uniforms asking for you; that same feeling you get in your stomach when you pass a mobile speed camera and you're never quite sure whether you were going too quickly or not. Two police officers were shown up to our floor and I led them calmly into my office. It appeared one of our team of presenters had used an inappropriate word and the police were investigating as a matter of race relations. The complainant who'd heard the broadcast had not troubled Ofcom, he'd gone straight for criminal law. I handed over the recordings and the presenter sweated. The bobbies never returned.

It was not the only legal encounter; in another incident, it was alleged that a presenter had suggested a listener had taken drugs. Whilst that may or may not have been the case, we ended up writing a modest cheque for the matter to go away. All radio carries risks, but talk radio carries more than most.

I am cheered when complex presenters, who proved a handful when we worked together, get in touch much later to reflect with humility on their younger selves. It's probably happened more than a dozen times now, and I often wonder what prompts the late night email out of the blue, decades after we've worked together. Broadcasting talent is only truly annoying when it is both difficult and not very good.

40

RADIO GOES GLOBAL

Whilst I was fending off the complaints at LBC, Chrysalis head office was on the prowl, as it sought to grow its excellent music radio brands further. Luckily, a well-timed radio marriage had produced an unwanted child ripe for adoption.

In 2005, the southern-based Capital group merged with GWR, which owned many local stations elsewhere in the country alongside Classic FM, to form the mighty new GCap, with over 16 million listeners. The regional Century stations became part of the new mega-radio group, although competition concerns dictated that the new group could not retain ownership of my old home, the Century station in the East Midlands.

Chrysalis entered with its cheque book, given this was a prize strategic asset for us. The station could be rebranded as Heart 106, pairing up neatly with the existing West Midlands successful Heart station. Being able to sell Heart audiences to advertisers across both ventricles of the Midlands created real incremental value.

We proudly took the keys of Century 106, the station I'd left with a lump in my throat when it was sold to Capital five years earlier. In August 2005, the Century signs I'd originally helped to put up came down and Heart's familiar red logo was hoisted. Although I never ran the new Heart East Midlands station for

Chrysalis personally, there was a feeling of satisfaction in being free to walk through the door once more as it joined our clan. Buying back a station you've held close to your heart is like buying back the house you grew up in.

Meanwhile, Guardian Media, under the stewardship of my former boss John Myers, had quietly built a network of stations echoing John's old Century empire, under the Real Radio brand. Under the nose of Chrysalis, John then bought the remaining Century stations from GCap. He too walked back through the door of the stations he'd created.

This sudden purchase by Guardian Media came as a shock to Chrysalis bosses. Indeed, the two chief executives, normally good buddies, fell out briefly. The ball had been stolen by the boy next door. What's more, Chrysalis had wanted to buy Guardian's radio assets itself, given the two regional radio businesses fitted like a beautiful jigsaw, but it was to miss out on that too.

The rules of the consolidation game are simple: if you fail to acquire, you are acquired and Chrysalis thus began a 'strategic review'. That's often a polite way of saying your house is on the market, yet pretending you're not desperate to sell.

Such times are uncertain for all. When a radio business is on the market, it still needs to maximise audiences and revenues. If the staff know the future is uncertain, they tend to speculate needlessly or leave, but if they are unaware, they worry why their formerly decisive management have become wishy-washy about any plan for anything beyond next Tuesday.

Particularly in the last few days before any deal is completed, one is impotent, forbidden from making any decisions. The answer is making oneself scarce. I recall wandering off to Notting Hill for many leisurely mint teas and an amble round its lovely old bookshops a couple of times a day. Colleagues saw me dashing in and out the building and concluded I must be inordinately busy. I really wasn't.

The successful bidder for the radio leg of Chrysalis in 2007 was an unknown new Irish-backed company, flatteringly created for the purpose of acquiring us, via a wholly owned subsidiary called Global Radio UK Limited. Global Radio had two directors at the outset, one of whom was Ashley Tabor, chief executive of Global Talent Group, a music publishing, artist management and rights ownership business. Ashley was a dashing blond, thirty-year-old man-about-town who, as a bright young thing who loved the medium, had once been a helper at Capital. The company stamped its pedigree early with the announcement that former ITV heavyweight Charles Allen would be chairman.

I confess I sniggered as I saw the name 'Global Radio' for the first time with its hasty debut logo, complete with the sort of transmission wiggles that graphic designers always seem instinctively to add to radio company logos. The name looked a little rich for our modest company that had been evidently so small, it couldn't quite punch its weight to growth. The aspiration was clear, however, and it now seems a thoroughly fitting label for what has become the largest radio group in in the UK. The company we had built formed a well-run, clean, successful foundation for a dominant UK player, complete with the brand-led approach which Global was to progress obsessively with considerable energies and investment.

When you're the prey in an acquisition swoop, you generally divine whether the new owners want the old top team to hang around; but in this case, that was not clear to us at the outset. Gradually, more details emerged, as we learned a familiar figure was to play a key role. A late afternoon email pinged into my inbox from our chief executive, Phil Riley, informing me that Richard Park, the industry's best-known programme director, was to be part of the new Global company. Phil's notes were always brief, but this one was particularly so. That information suggested to me, to him and to others, that the new owners would probably want to do things their way, as indeed they had every right to.

Richard Park was a Scot, then aged almost sixty, who'd once ridden the pirate waves on air before a spell at a young Radio 1. He'd moved to the new Radio Clyde in Glasgow, and then down to London to steer Capital to great heights, before leaving to do just the same thing at Magic. With a formidable track record, and TV stardom from his 'headmaster' role in the talent show *Fame Academy*, most people in our industry have a 'Parky' story. No one can doubt his achievements.

As the new management seized control, the existing de facto heads of LBC, Heart and Galaxy were asked to present their brands to Richard Park and Ashley Tabor, who sat across the table like father and son. This was *Fame Academy* once again, this time with the chance to win our own jobs. The programme controller and I performed what I recall was a compelling presentation on our beloved LBC. It ended up being cut tellingly short, and there were few questions. Richard scribbled a discreet note halfway through and pushed it under Ashley's nose. Who knows what it said.

I like certainty and asked to see Richard. A royal visit was duly arranged and on the stroke of the hour, this sharp-suited man strode purposefully into my office, looking much younger than his years. Like a politician, all his thoughts were well marshalled and simply expressed. His assumptions were presumed to be your assumptions too. He described to me the LBC he envisioned, which was more news driven and where topics rotated frequently like A-list songs on a music radio station. If Madeleine McCann were the top story of the day, that's what people would hear when they tuned in. He also suggested people generally were becoming more interested in the news. Whether by pure serendipity or evidence of his proven programming instinct, I fear he was correct. The last few years have been fascinating ones for the UK and world news agenda, with stories which have truly hit a public nerve.

I suggested to Richard that we might fall out were I to stay. He said we wouldn't. I believe a great radio station can only have one captain. There are many ways of reaching a port, but one person must choose the direction otherwise the ship will get nowhere or sink. As Global now owned the company, it was only right they should determine the path to be navigated.

On my last day, I popped up to see Ashley on the busy management floor and his eyes suggested he feared a scene might ensue in front of his new colleagues. I merely shook his hand and wished him sincerely every success. Whilst not everyone will agree with the strategy the company was to adopt, I believe that without Global's passion, confidence, professionalism and investment, our industry would be worryingly poorer.

In the general election campaign of 2017, the Nick Ferrari interview with shadow Home Secretary Diane Abbott was a standout moment. Ill-prepared for the interview about investment in policing, Nick's few well-chosen questions floored her. Nick's interview was transcribed in every national newspaper, featured on *The Graham Norton Show*, and was played in its entirety on Radio 4's *PM* programme. Across that whole campaign, one then witnessed other broadcasters draw on the techniques Nick had demonstrated so well.

It was by no means the first time that Radio 4 has picked up on political stories created by LBC. It is now a confident station with a real ability to make and break stories with panache, as well as provide addictive, rich coverage of rolling news. It boasts an enviable PR machine – and has perfected the use of video and social media. It has mastered the art of hiring the right political figures to host exactly the right programmes, and its newer daily recruits, such as political pundit and publisher Iain Dale, are perfectly cast. To say LBC is back at its peak would be to ignore the fact that its former so-called peaks were also enormously troubled by financial, audience or corporate challenges. In truth, this truly great radio station has never been in better shape.

Whether my approach, operated at necessarily lower budgets, might also have worked, we shall never know. I believe there is more than one way of doing talk. I used to refer to 'music radio without the music'; and I mused whether a station where the likes of Wogan and Tarrant just chatted would have brought an audience, and I feel it would. But Global have had a chance to prove their excellence would shine through – and it clearly has.

I gather current management prefers to look forward rather than back, and is a little reluctant to remind anyone of the earlier days of this landmark station in British radio history, but I like to think that we were part of its rehabilitation and that the current LBC is much more like the one we left in 2007 than any earlier incarnation. As Chrysalis inherited the station in 2002, *Campaign* magazine noted: 'LBC attracts 480,000 listeners and aims to double its audience to one million by 2005.' Admittedly, its growth took longer than we'd envisaged, and the life span of a fresh owner, but ten years after our acquisition, LBC 97.3 hit the million.

After one moves on, one naturally drives by one's old home to see if the new occupiers have changed the colour of the paintwork or knocked any walls down. I take pride from the fact that: the formats remain on the frequencies we put them; LBC is still podcasting and earning from it; peak times of the day are still occupied by the personalities we installed and valued; and I'm pleased that they retained 'London's Biggest Conversation' until it necessarily became its derivative 'Leading Britain's Conversation'.

I'm most pleased that the station overall has shown the promise which was identified by the Chrysalis team as they chose to buy it. It wasn't such a crazy idea after all.

41

LIKE A VIRGIN

The original Virgin Radio was based in a wonderful old building at One Golden Square in Soho, a much sought-after address in one of central London's historic squares, just yards from Piccadilly Circus. It is more fitting to recall that a musical instrument manufacturer once stood on the site, rather than the fact that the area was a plague pit some three centuries ago.

The historic drama imbued in the foundations may have helped to lend this radio station its rich character as it launched on AM across the UK in 1993, with London FM coverage added two years later. Virgin was a rock 'n' roll brand and tales abounded of the Chris Evans days. That atmosphere was still evident on my arrival. Bands rocked up to perform live, customs persisted and drinks were delivered to the office on a trolley on all manner of pretexts. The culture was summed up by the album covers on the walls of the stairwell, which had been embroidered by prisoners in their cells.

The remarkable Richard Huntingford, having managed the Chrysalis group and presided over a successful exit for its significant radio arm, had been left without a sizeable empire. He was thus a logical choice to head Virgin, broadcasting on AM across the UK and on FM in London, as TV group SMG (Scottish Media Group) plotted the station's disposal in 2007.

Given that I was about to be free and the lovely Richard was just about to collect a fresh swipe card to admit him to a new radio empire, it seemed foolish for me not to have a chat about opportunities, not least as he was poised to be both Virgin Radio's chairman and chief executive, following the departures of its management team to Capital.

I was invited to an odd meeting with Richard about Virgin whilst he was still *in situ* in his office on the second floor of the Chrysalis group building, although his mind was already elsewhere. Here was a man who'd sold his old radio business based on the floors below, and who now had an eagle-eyed view of its new owners strutting around.

It brought to mind the fond rumours I'd heard about the head of London's Melody Radio, as they handed over the radio offices in the building owned by the station's former owner, Lord Hanson, to new owners EMAP, who were poised to convert it to Magic. I'm sure the reports are thoroughly apocryphal, but I have a picture in my mind of Melody's boss gurning through the glass in the adjoining wall. Handing over any business must always be odd, but in radio there's that odd lacing of emotion between the parties, not least when they remain operating as neighbours.

Looking back, Richard was clearly auditioning for senior staff as he took up his new role and I should have prepared a little more for our get-together than a few scribbled notes on a screwed-up piece of paper. I now know that other ex-Chrysalis staff had also been 'chatted to' and I imagine they had assembled impressive funky strategic presentations and presidential speeches.

I was, nevertheless, appointed programme director, adding the responsibility for marketing to the title a few months later.

It strikes me that radio stations should not trouble to order business cards, given that posts in our industry rarely last long enough to finish a single box.

I don't think I was necessarily the slickest or the best candidate to reposition the Virgin output to maximise audiences. I fear I was appointed because I had a commercially sympathetic attitude to maximise short-term profits, on which company value would eventually be based, and would keep staff motivated during the change. I managed the latter principally through bringing in large bags of chocolates and copious supplies of sweet chewy rubbish from the grateful tobacconist next door. Virgin was as wonderful a place as I'd been told, and, amidst earnest discussion on new music and festivals, Friday afternoons routinely brought the sounds of laughter as old Morecambe and Wise videos were routinely played on YouTube.

In my early days, I arrived to find colleagues in a state of annoyance one morning. The station's former chief executive Paul Jackson had paid an unannounced late-night visit to the premises. He'd been out celebrating with friends into the small hours and decided to bring his clan back to his old stomping ground, persuading the security guard that he really should be admitted, even though his days in charge were over. Messages had been daubed on flip charts and there was evidence that champagne had been discovered and merrily consumed. Juicy industry rumour suggested we called the police, but that would have been over the top in our rock 'n' roll world and was neither entertained nor warranted. The offender was simply informed that he had been a naughty boy and that his ex-colleagues were disappointed in his behaviour. Replacement champagne and a generous contrite note followed and the matter was closed.

'Studio J' I was told, when I enquired where I might find

Virgin's imaging producer. I paused, aghast that any station could have quite so many studios. 'Do our studios go up to "J" then?' I asked. 'No,' came the reply, 'there's also a K.' The rationale for the surprising surfeit of studios was that when the station had begun to consider spin-off digital stations, it was envisaged that each would require studio space. By the time digital radio consumer take-up had generated sufficient appetite for such stations, however, they could be operated on a single PC. The underground studios, therefore, smelt like a new car and lay largely unused.

I'd always envied the station's PR machine from afar. Whilst it had not been London's biggest station, it always appeared to amass its unfair share of coverage the way that Virgin-branded businesses do. Under the eyes of talented Cat Macdonald (now Martin) in the Virgin Radio press office, the arrival of a pizza in reception would manage to make the *Telegraph*'s front page.

42

ON BOARD

Virgin Radio employees all had an air of mature capability. The presenters were accomplished performers earning decent money. Top of the stack was long-standing breakfast presenter Christian O'Connell. When he'd begun on the show in 2006, 86 per cent of households didn't have digital radio, the best-selling phone was a Nokia and Mike Baldwin died on TV's *Coronation Street*.

As the programme launched, Lynn Barber at *The Guardian*, who I imagine was awoken early by Cat from the PR team banging on her bedroom window with a long stick, observed: 'I don't think he is the new Chris Evans – he is less frantic, less bullying, more likeable, with a much drier sense of humour. And he is much less laddishly offensive than most of the other pop DJs.'

Christian's time in the London limelight was preceded by an apprenticeship at 2CR in Bournemouth and an early spell at hospital radio in Hampshire. I found the man to be a true pro, habitually clad in his black leather jacket; a single-minded, clever operator. Witnessing his flair, when he hosted the commercial radio annual industry awards bash, was always an education. One's peers are always the toughest audiences. He measured the mood, with the fun poked at the big boys not the little guys.

On air and off air, he was a sharp performer with the skill to prep well and deliver as if he hadn't. Christian was serious about being funny, was willing to draw authentically on his own life's experiences and watched others with skill to harvest observational riches. He studied his influences with diligence and, unlike some other great performers, knew just how he did what he did.

Christian was good to deal with, with the rare knack of being able to detach the person from the performance to enable honest programme analysis. He was hungry for anything at all which might help tomorrow's show become better; and he got impatient if disappointed. What is infuriatingly common in radio is when a programme deserves better audiences than it receives, or when second-rate programmes generate results they don't deserve. In my time, Christian's programme was a case of the former.

The team were more accustomed to their company being up for sale than it not being on the market. Forecasting the future became a sport. On our arrival, one presenter had tried to read the tea leaves to determine the programme schedule I would introduce. He had even committed his prediction to paper and would whip it out of his pocket to share with others, as fact, in hushed tones. I was half-tempted to adopt his plan.

Our objective was to sell the radio business. STV's TV operation was clearly of decent value, but the radio business would be worth more if it wasn't sold as part of a job lot. Several UK radio groups were still seeking to extend their empires and there was always the outside chance of a newcomer.

Selling a business, if the process is conducted formally and competitively, usually begins in earnest with the assembly of a colourful 'Information Memorandum', which is much like a mega end-of-term school project. This document, which details the assets in the most persuasive way with tables of figures, glossy pictures and rigorously checked claims, takes an age to assemble as final drafts are repeatedly redrafted. By the time it is ready for printing and binding, you have convinced yourself that your business simply cannot be ignored.

The IM is then circulated to those who have expressed an interest, ranging from the potentially serious to the definitely nosey. Such candidates will likely flick to the crucial bits of the document and ignore much of the remainder, barely noticing all the hours of effort spent in drafting enthusiastic prose. Genuinely interested parties are then invited to a formal presentation where buyers and sellers meet. This early ritual is very much a polite speed date. The sellers puff out their chests and blow their trumpets showing graphs which point upwards, and the buyers suck through their lips and suggest the graph should really be pointing the other way.

The presentations to potential buyers for the Virgin business were convened in a large presentation room at the lavish Doric-columned premises of a merchant bank. I instantly stumbled across the control which made the fancy switchable privacy glass walls go cloudy, so that confidential presentations could be made without the cleaners seeing your gaudy pie charts from the adjacent corridor. I could have played with that for hours.

In and out came the potential suitors, with a discreet pause between, so that one group could leave without bumping into the ex-wife. Some of them were known to us, and others utterly unknown. With the familiar parties, I stared across the table at those who would replace me; whereas, in the case of the unfamiliar buyers without their own UK management teams, there was just a chance they might be my future employers. The goal, however, is simply to get the best price.

Our presentation kicked off with an impressive short brand video which aimed to set the mood and illustrate the scale and influence of the assets. At a time when the radio industry generally was still not awfully good at video, Virgin excelled, and this well-produced mix of on-air studio shots, festival footage and artist involvement afforded a great impression of the energy and music equity that underpinned the station. That quality of presentation is now commonplace in an industry that looked too shoddy for too long.

One group of overseas buyers stared over-attentively at the Virgin video. As we then paused for questions, the wide-eyed head of the team quickly asked for the name of the video's attractive female presenter.

Outcomes from the sale process for any radio business are always uncertain, and the only certainty is that things will not turn out as you'd imagined. Just like buying a house, typical negotiating tactics ensue and just when you think it's all over, you realise that it really isn't.

Energetic Clive Dickens was part of the winning consortium, with his colleagues from Absolute Radio International, which operated two FM licences in Oxford. Clive was a likeable guy, bursting with childlike enthusiasm, and exhibiting sufficient cerebral energy to power the whole of Sussex. His eventual investment partner for the deal came as a surprise: TIML, part of the Times of India Group, which owns the *Times of India* newspaper, said to enjoy the largest circulation of any English-language newspaper in the world. TIML were new to UK media and were looking for Clive and his team to manage their new acquisition.

The company was sold without the Virgin brand, and our staff, accordingly, knew that their beloved red V would disappear. For some stations, the name is just that; but for the staff of Virgin, it was a true brand in which they'd wrapped themselves. The prospect of losing it seemed not only a complex affair but one which they feared would put at risk the rock 'n' roll culture they treasured.

43

ANOTHER NEW DAWN

Diaries, which had been kept empty, were suddenly replete with meetings as the new owners of a station which was soon not to be Virgin Radio got to grips with their new assets. As we gathered on the dot of the hour, awaiting Times of India representatives, they'd happily burst in, slightly late and a little flustered, laden down with Selfridges yellow carrier bags. Owning a radio station in the heart of this great city had its benefits.

As I was to discover later for myself, settling on a new name for a radio station is never an easy task. After due consideration, the new owners agreed to use the one which happened to be the name of the Absolute Radio operating company itself. Once signed off, preparatory work for the divorce began in earnest. After a fifteen-year marriage, this station had to clear its house of anything connected with its bright-red branding husband and to an incredibly tight timetable.

If you've ever picked up an Innocent drink and quietly marvelled at the language and tone of the product communications, then you've likely just bumped into some work inspired by brand agency Albion. It was asked to advise on the Absolute brand changes, and it was a pleasure to work with their focused, stylishly dressed staff.

Although I was likely not going to be around for the long term, I was charged with managing the detail of the brand change project. In my earlier life, changing a radio station name just amounted to some new jingles, a new sign for outside the door and a few new packs of A4 letterheads. Now, with a multi-platform presence, life is more complex, not least when you are about to relinquish your former brand licence and are no longer allowed to use it in any form after the transition. In this case, we also feared that our old brand name might appear the following week on another radio station. That did eventually come to pass, but not for another nine years.

Rebranding plans were so detailed that A3 multi-coloured printouts were needed to keep track. There were meetings, meetings and more meetings. Cancelled meetings; rearranged meetings; meetings that were destined to be about one thing but were suddenly about another; meetings at 7.30 in the morning; meetings where one disembodied attendee boomed from the spider phone; meetings with venue confusion, where half the attendees gathered in one room and the rest in another, both groups wondering what had happened to the other. But there were also productive meetings with lots of custard creams.

My former PA and general programmes assistant, Joan, slid further down in her chair, until she was almost lying horizontally. A guttural grunt came involuntarily from her pretty lips as she ran her fingers through her long, curly hair. It was just another typical day for this hard-working professional, now supporting a coven of bosses, old and new. 'What time is it in Brazil?' she croaked. It transpired that, in a three-word email softened only by a puzzling emoticon, busy Clive had decreed that a meeting with some bizarre company be postponed. From a cold Google start, Joan discovered that the said company had head offices listed in the US and Brazil and decided to try

Brazil first to see if they knew of a man called Clive, and to find out if they were expecting him to make a conference call.

The task overall was clear. The old brand must not appear on air, nor on the digital displays on listener radio sets or on any other platform such as TV; it must not be on the website or any other digital manifestations either. Supplementing remorseless on-air coverage of the name change, texts were despatched to regular participants and pretty emails pinged to those who'd engaged online. The changeover date and time were choreographed to the minute.

Virgin had been a station with an impressive digital presence, probably further along the digital journey than any other company thanks to the inspired early efforts of radio 'futurologist' James Cridland, and the new operators were to take that ambition forward. Those achievements, however, created a hefty digital footprint which needed to be erased, including many of the star interviews and concert footage online which showed naughty glimpses of our former name. A canny idea was implemented, where the dull task of 'brand spotting' was crowdsourced, by creating a webpage showing successive clips of content, with listeners invited to tick whether the old red brand was in the shot. With each piece being vetted by numerous listeners, it was a clever efficient way of getting the job done and, seizing the zeitgeist, involving the listeners in the change.

I expected to hand over this teenage foster child quickly to its new adopted parents and bid a tearful farewell at the garden gate. After all, in our great industry, once a manager – or presenter – is displaced, they are usually despatched within hours with a macho curl of the lip. Swaggering new managements then invade, making a swathe of very sensible decisions, accompanied by a whole host of ill-judged ones, just because they do not trouble to seek the views of those who have lived in the house for a few years and know where the dry rot is and which walls not to knock down without an RSJ.

As Absolute Radio marched in, it was genuinely different. When they'd invited me to 'hang around' to help with the launch, I smiled, thinking they were being typically polite. They were, but I tossed my black bin bag to one side once I realised they also meant it. The new boss of operations, Clive, squeezed in a small desk for himself in a dark corner next to the coat stand; I remained in my office overlooking the sunshine of Golden Square with seeming diplomatic immunity from the regime change.

Like me, Clive was a fan of early starts, and as the dawn smell from Greggs wafted across the road, he'd wander into my office and share his plans fully in a way he need not have done. I was thus equipped to catch a few balls which might have been dropped and helped to advise which of their newly inherited staff were suited to which tasks. They trusted me and I trusted them. Knowing I would witness the first breaths of this Absolute infant, I cared.

When paying a first flying visit from Mumbai, the very senior Times of India representatives suggested they wanted to address the team en masse, so a full staff meeting was duly convened. Such was the number of staff and the level of interest in our new owners, that the meeting was necessarily held in the open plan area on the first floor, given that no single room was sufficiently large.

At the appointed time, the nod came that our guests were on their way and our irreverent rowdy rabble fell silent. All eyes then focused on the lift as it juddered to a halt in full view. The doors slid open gracefully and Mr Times of India emerged smiling – to amused rapturous applause. The entrance, which was wholly unplanned, was akin to Young Mister Grace arriving at the top of the stairs in the *Are You Being Served?* TV sitcom.

Maybe he had been well briefed, but his tone was judged brilliantly for this discerning audience. All I remember of the content, and I suspect I am not alone in this, was that he said their company culture was give and take: 'If you work too hard and too long one day, take it easy the next day – go and watch a film.' Predictably, the remark became a long-standing joke at fraught moments: 'I've had enough. I'm just off to the Odeon.'

I rarely stay at social events for more than an hour, not even the rare ones held in my honour, but my eventual Absolute Radio farewell a month or so into the life of the new station was hugely enjoyable and I stayed all night. I returned in the small hours to my overpriced matchbox-sized studio flat in west London with fond memories of some of the nicest and most talented people in radio. I felt the new owners had brought energy, vision and intelligence, and they allowed me to leave with dignity, even facilitating a valedictory blog on their own website.

For the good of commercial radio, I hoped the new Absolute Radio would succeed in its clear ambition.

The station was sold again five years later, in 2013, to Bauer, who appear to have derived fair value from its momentum.

44

BIG ISN'T ALWAYS BEAUTIFUL

Journeying to the Scilly Isles amounted to a jolly Anneka Rice jaunt. Having spent a relaxing night at the famous Headland Hotel overlooking Newquay's beautiful Fistral Bay, we jumped on board the plane to the islands. It was a baby plane: a sixteen-seater Twin Otter, apparently. The amiable chap in the front seat, whom we presumed to be the pilot, turned around, and parted the curtain to impart the necessary safety advice.

A juddery half-hour later, the dear Otter touched down at St. Mary's airport, and we made our way to witness a new community radio station in action at one of the outlying posts of the British Isles. The Scillies are home to a traditional community depicted fondly by the first, defining, BBC 2 TV series of *An Island Parish*, although I'm told it's a bad idea to mention that when visiting.

Community radio had been a less than popular concept during my time at the Radio Authority. The regulator's stance was that small-scale radio already existed in the commercial sector and, in a sense, it did. In 2002, however, this third layer of radio, supplementing local/regional and national stations, was patiently trialled with a feasibility study of fifteen 'Access Radio' stations.

The experiment was judged a success and Ofcom pledged to facilitate 'the development of a distinctive new tier of radio'.

It was envisaged that such stations could cater for whole communities or for different areas of interest, such as a particular ethnic, age or interest group.

Community radio stations typically cover a pint-sized geographical area with a coverage radius of up to five kilometres. They are deliberately run on a not-for-profit basis, unlike many stations I had worked at which achieved losses quite by accident. Frequencies are identified which could not support commercially sustainable services, but which could be used for non- or partly-commercially funded stations.

I nursed a healthy scepticism of the overall project, quite willing to be proven wrong. At worst, these stations would exist purely for the sake of those assembling programmes, have appalling compliance standards, and tread on the toes of other small traditional commercial stations which were already struggling. At best, they could be stunning.

My worries about compliance appeared to have some foundation. In 2014, a quarter of all community radio stations were investigated by Ofcom about not observing their 'Key Commitments'. There were numerous examples of bad language and failure to supply recordings to the regulator – and one station stopped broadcasting when the bailiffs turned up to remove studio equipment.[31]

In contrast, some community stations provided an incomparable public service. The example with which I became most familiar was on the Scilly Isles, run by one of my best friends, Keri Jones. I was once told that you have friendships for a reason, a season or a lifetime – and Keri fell in the latter category. One of those friends you catch up with once a year and yet pick up as if you saw them last week.

Keri had hands-on experience at several stations; indeed I'd first met him when he was a quiffed student, helping out at Leicester Sound, discharging duties far below his abilities with intelligent charm.

Besides some experience in large radio markets, it was to be small stations where he was to carve his reputation and which were to equip him well for the Scilly venture. He helped to run such stations as Mix 96 in Aylesbury, Valleys Radio in south Wales and some small trial stations under the Authority's restricted service licence model. At Pembrokeshire and Carmarthenshire, some of the lessons were painful, not least when a group of radicals broke into the premises, purporting to represent the interests of a Welsh nationalist group. The arm of one of his staff was fractured in the resulting fracas. The culprits were arrested and imprisoned.

On dark days such as that, Keri was inspired by the tranquil photograph on his wall of the five Scilly Isles. Once he sold the Radio Pembrokeshire business, with a timing of which I remain jealous and at a price he deserved, Keri was free to follow his dream of setting up a community station based in that beautiful part of the world.

As we witnessed on our visit, the views across the road from the Radio Scilly premises were enviable, but Keri's work was hard in initiating, and then personally delivering, a solid local radio service, day after day, week after week. Intelligent automation facilitated by proprietary software kept the station alive whilst Keri darted around his islands, and content was always fresh and topical. Few much larger stations would manage the ten-minute news bulletins which Radio Scilly provided and Keri would shake his head in disbelief at the output-to-staffing ratio at his station versus that of the BBC local station across the water.

Radio Scilly defined utterly local radio. The times of boats between the islands were read out by Radio Scilly boatman Fraser, before being daubed in chalk on a board in the town centre. When some clothes needed to be retrieved from a dry cleaner's in Penzance, an appeal would be broadcast by Radio Scilly to find someone else who happened to be making the journey to the mainland. The school dinner menu, at St. Mary's only school, was aired daily, and cue scripts introducing news items necessitated simply reading out the first names of those featured, given that listeners would likely know the contributor.

Every street we walked down with Keri during our time on the main island, a cap was doffed, and Keri would tell us in which programme item the Scillonian was involved. One memorable helper, for a period which was wisely brief, was a taxi driver who hosted the rock show. He had decided that the length of its raucous tracks afforded him sufficient opportunity during the programme to carry out brief taxi journeys.

Small communities hold secrets, and radio stations can serve as a powerful independent catalyst for action. Anonymous letters were often deposited on the stairs of the station, containing allegations of poor local conduct. Keri's partner Andy recalls a key news story where he sourced information from the Environment Agency regarding an incinerator which was bellowing out far more fumes than the rules allowed. The matter was exposed and the incinerator demolished.

Council meetings were attended, with stories covered extensively, much to the chagrin of the local council which had previously enjoyed the luxury of less scrutiny. Similarly, a lack of openness on civic salaries was exposed and systems changed.

It came as little surprise that the efforts of Keri's Radio Scilly were challenged, on occasions. Angry complaints were lodged with the regulator: 'The council complained that it was treated unjustly or unfairly in the programmes as broadcast because it was not given an appropriate and timely opportunity to respond to the allegation made.' After due consideration of Keri's thorough response, Ofcom found his station not guilty.[32] Following an enjoyable couple of days savouring the Scilly sights and traditions, a cool glass of wine in a friendly Hugh Town bar and some calm moments on warm, neighbouring Tresco, we left – taking with us clear proof, if ever it were needed, of how influential a small, well-run local station can still be. In Keri's view, all it really takes is one committed individual.

45

INFORM, EDUCATE AND ENTERTAIN

I'd driven past the BBC building in Nottingham thousands of times. As I navigated the roundabout, adjacent to the filling station, now just a random car wash, I would gaze across wistfully: even the BBC logo outside makes one shiver. Almost a century of history is vested in just three black letters, denoting Wogan, Humphrys and the Empire. A BBC lanyard dangling round your neck is enough to impress most parents.

Fate can dictate one's career to an alarming extent. Although one seeks to take control, it is inevitably linked to the mood of an organisation at the time; the views of people in whose gift your potential roles are; and the decisions of others to vacate their posts to make way for you. My career happens to have been spent largely in commercial radio, but it might easily have been otherwise. I have always felt a genuine passion for the BBC and had a heartfelt desire to make a real contribution to the greatest broadcasting organisation in the world.

The BBC and I had never had a great deal of professional contact, but as Smooth Radio acquired the regional Saga Radio stations in 2007, I felt my Sunday morning programme would likely sit more at ease on BBC local radio. After discussions with the friendly managing editor at BBC Radio Nottingham, the effervescent Sophie Shardlow, I prepared to broadcast for Auntie in my home town.

The day when my name would appear in the *Radio Times* had come. Few people would honestly suggest that a mention in the *Radio Times* meant nothing. Like many others, I have collected copies over the years of this venerable organ, from back when the magazine was printed on what appeared to be school toilet paper and was not sullied by mention of dirty ITV.

As I anticipated, life is different at the BBC. Those from the commercial sector are viewed with a little suspicion and you quickly discover that everyone around you is a journalist. Some even prefaced sentences with: 'Being a journalist…' Rather than bowing deferentially, I was almost stirred to respond: 'Being someone who's worked in radio for thirty years…' I hold the view that being a good journalist is a real skill worthy of admiration. Some journalists may also be good newsreaders, programmers, programme presenters, managers or leaders. Some may not.

There are processes to be followed at the BBC: forms to be filled in, online training courses to be completed, each one enviably thorough. Passwords must be generated for systems which then ask for another password. One such system asked me for the name of my first pet. It then suggested that the word was not permissible as it had insufficient letters. I concluded that having a dog with a long name was a prerequisite for BBC employment and the process was somehow a microcosm of the organisation. You had to fit in with the BBC; it was never the other way around.

Jeremy Vine wryly observed much the same thing when he told me: 'At the BBC, you don't matter. Until you've actually broadcast in the BBC, you don't really exist at all. Even if you went missing, they wouldn't notice unless there was an enormous blood stain.'[33]

Preparing for this part-time weekend role, I was pleased to see a few familiar faces, not least fellow commercial radio escapees, and the managing editor offered genuine support in helping me across the threshold to this new world.

On air, opening the fader for the first time and saying the letters B, B and C was a moment I truly relished. Like the logo, the sound of the three letters carries so much weight, just remembering that they were uttered immediately before major announcements in our country's rich history, from the famous abdication announcement in 1936 to the declaration of war in 1939. The former is a fascinating piece of audio to listen back to. Following the continuity announcement by the DG himself, John Reith, there is a noticeable bang. After suggestions that traditionalist Reith had slammed the studio door in disgust at the King announcing he didn't fancy being King any more, it was explained that Reith had simply kicked the table leg as he made a hasty exit, the sound of which boomed in through the AXBT mic. It is interesting to note that, following the announcement, the BBC simply closed down for the night in reflection. Now, there'd likely be endless dialogue into the early hours from shivering correspondents outside Buckingham Palace.

Like all BBC local stations, the dusty BBC studios in Nottingham were being prepared for a 21st-century upgrade to an innovative 'virtual' system based in the cloud. This beast was to replace all the under-the-bonnet complexity of every remote local site with two large cost-efficient throbbing data centres.

Only radio folk could get nostalgic over bits of old equipment, but many of us do and it's reassuring that some are rightly being preserved as museum pieces. The earliest BBC local stations had comprised a Mark I desk, with its rotary 'pots' (faders), a couple of Thorens turntables, or grams, as the BBC dubbed them, and two Ferrograph tape machines, with the exciting aerobics of pressing cartridge machines still to come.

Radio Nottingham's original mixing desk was replaced in 1979 'enabling more sophisticated broadcasting techniques to be used', even though the new one had the faders going the wrong way, as far as I'm concerned.[34]

The desk at which I sat in 2006 was a subsequent traditional analogue installation, fed by a digital playout system, but still surrounded by generations of much-loved playout systems, including CD, DAT, minidisk and even cassette.

Feedback to my early BBC programmes seemed favourable. One receptionist was even stirred to remark: 'I thought you sounded a bit commercial at first, but I like you now.' Whatever station you're on, those who are not on air, whether from inside or outside the business, never quite appreciate how devastating their well-intentioned casual words can be. Absolute Radio's Christian O' Connell relates a text that he received saying: 'We're coming to see your live gig, but my husband's not coming, as he can't stand you. LOL.'

My BBC work back on the shop floor grew naturally, following the disposal of Virgin to Absolute. I even grew to comprehend at least some Delphic BBC utterances. Programme promotions were 'trails'; journalists were 'beejays' (broadcast journalists); shows were always 'programmes'; and 'workplace' was a mysterious team that would mend things in the office.

As fellow presenters took a break, I filled in, notably on the breakfast programme. This was the first time I had ever hosted an all-speech programme. In due course, like many BBC local radio breakfast programmes, it was to become a double-header, but at that stage it was a solo affair and probably one of the most demanding jobs in British radio. The many people who have hosted such programmes will recognise the challenges. Without songs, ad breaks or a co-presenter to lean on, this guest- and feature-driven format is the equivalent of being pushed out on a tightrope on your own at seven o'clock in the morning, hoping you can get to the other side by nine o'clock without falling off.

As I interviewed one person, another unfamiliar face would be shuffled quietly into the adjacent chair. I crossed my fingers and hoped it was the person next on the running order. It was easy to see how the famous 2006 incident on BBC TV news could happen, when Guy Goma, an unemployed computer technician awaiting a BBC job interview, was mistaken for an internet expert expected on a programme and interviewed live.

Some reports and interviews came in via ISDN line or phone and, if they were not there when expected, one had to do something else.

Travel news was aired every quarter of an hour, fed from a remote travel centre which was feeding other stations too. One would accordingly only be allowed to cross to them within certain time windows. Split-second timing to the junctions was, therefore, critical. A crucial, hard-hitting live interview would hence be curtailed in favour of a travel bulletin, often limply telling listeners there were actually no travel problems.

At all times, you are hugely reliant on excellent programme production, which I generally received. The most worrying times were ending one piece, recognising the symptoms that the next was in doubt for some reason. You look through the glass to see frantic moves to sort matters, but no one has quite got the time to tell you what you should say when you next open your mouth. Other programmes unexpectedly benefited from suddenly being previewed at inordinate length.

Half of your brain is worrying about timing and thinking of the next item, whilst the other half is concentrating on what you are supposed to be doing now. With such demands, missing a key pick-up in an interview is easily done, and it was frustrating to hear a suggestion of a key question buzzed into your headphones.

When presenting the early afternoon programme, on a regular basis for a spell, I recall one moment where I was taking a few enjoyable listener calls and playing a favourite song, gazing out of the window to my city bathed in sunshine and recognising how much I enjoyed being on the radio. It's a puzzle why those of us who just love being on air trouble to engineer our way into management.

After a few months of jobbing BBC on-air work, however, whilst still exploring other options, I thought I should seek a proper job. Concluding that the consolidated commercial radio world was unlikely to have a suitable home, I turned my attention to identifying a permanent position at the BBC via its busy online portal.

Hidden amongst such vacancies as 'Tutti 2nd Violin, BBC Philharmonic' and 'online journalist for the Persian Service', I alighted on one for a post in 'English Regions', overseeing all local radio and TV in the relevant area. It seemed a suitable opportunity and I duly began work on the lengthy BBC application form, trying desperately to recall what I did when and what grade I got for O-Level Geography.

By way of preparation, investigative conversations were convened with senior colleagues and I observed how refreshingly willing BBC people are to share details of what they do and how they do it. They also happily divulged the frustrations of their own roles and with the Corporation as a whole. Every staff member spoke of the organisation as if speaking of an annoying errant brother they still loved unconditionally.

Each employee in the BBC appeared to be desperately trying to make some sense of a very odd organisation, which, were it left to them, would be a whole lot better. Large organisations are all the same, and I often muse on who is actually messing them up, if every single person you speak to wouldn't be doing it the way it's being done.

I perused some BBC staff attitude surveys around the local radio network. This anonymous data contained the results of many of the familiar themes included in similar surveys from my past lives, although the BBC graphs astounded me. How could morale and faith in management be so low among staff who worked for the finest broadcasting organisation in the world, which enjoyed a guaranteed income?

An interview was convened, which I appeared to pass, despite not really offering a convincing answer to the question of how we might make the next direct elections to the European Parliament interesting to listeners. In time, the referendum result would suggest that it is likely impossible.

A second interview was arranged at the old, fondly remembered Television Centre, where a selected bunch of the good and the great gathered around a large oak table to quiz me on how I might operate were I offered this senior regional post. As local radio, for reasons that are beyond me, sits in the BBC News division, one attendee was the then BBC head of news, the admirable Helen Boaden.

A hypothetical challenge was outlined and I was invited

to suggest how I might address my management team were I coping with it. Rather than explain my modus operandi, I geared up into full performance mode to demonstrate how I would take charge of the make-believe crisis. Such was the energy of my rabble-rousing speech, complete with desk-banging and generous gesticulations, that I knocked over the water jug on the table, the contents of which then proceeded to drip slowly onto the laps of the BBC's senior executives. Now there really was a crisis. Helen and her colleagues rallied round, making reassuring noises and offering paper handkerchiefs from their pockets and handbags. Little mounds of soggy tissue appeared across the desk, arising from the shallow lake. I tried to carry on regardless, doubting I'd be confused with any other candidate.

Taking a break for a few days, and about to ascend the Salève mountain in Geneva, my phone rang and the voice of David Holdsworth offered me the regional post for Lincolnshire and Humberside. David was controller of BBC English Regions and had been with the Corporation a long time, but had spent his early days in commercial radio, memorably being the newsreader on the first day on air for the former Wyvern FM station (now Free Radio) in Worcester.

I was delighted to accept the post, hoping that it might allow me a springboard from which I might play a role in the future development of BBC local radio. A new BBC office beckoned, located in the impressive and colourful Hull premises where BBC TV and Radio Humberside were housed.

Shortly after I arrived, I seized an early opportunity to sit down and chat privately to every member of staff, a ritual I had performed in all the places where I had been MD. These informal, off-the-record chit-chats always turned up some consistent themes that needed addressing, and one or two easy fixes. I recall, in my commercial radio days, finding out from one such exercise that one explanation for our commercial and programming teams never mixing was that the office keys were not compatible. Staff couldn't mix without breaking in.

At the BBC, the conversations were a little more complex and I sometimes struggled to translate the answers into English. When trying to establish who did what, it emerged that some individuals had been shunted from one city to another and 'attached' here and there, regardless of the collateral damage created by the uncertainty of 'back-filling' for their own job: 'I'm here filling for Sally for six months, as she has gone to Derby, and we are not sure if Sarah is coming back from *You and Yours*.'

One individual struggled valiantly to explain what his job was. After asking him three times, and being greeted with all manner of random job titles, I had to start from basics: 'When you come in and sit at your desk in the morning, what do you do?'

Those in jolly commercial radio often point inappropriately at BBC staffing levels, without taking the difference in format duly into account. The more news and talk you carry, the more people you need. However, even when mindful of the necessary demands, I regret that I still found the BBC inefficient. Not only could it manage with fewer staff in some areas, particularly management, I believe that the remaining staff would have been happier and the programmes better, had some positions been removed. But, it is reassuring that such a restructuring has begun.

The BBC has the dilemma of having to prove itself as being of sufficient universal appeal to justify the licence fee, and yet also remaining distinctive. If success is not defined absolutely by audience figures, what does it look like? Despite all the operational oddities, there were many hugely gifted individuals who tried their best to create great radio and TV, sometimes without the appreciation they deserved. I adore the BBC and everything it stands for.

In February 1966, a delicious aquamarine pamphlet called 'Local Radio in the Public Interest' was published proudly by the BBC as it laid claim to local radio. In just fifteen musty pages, Auntie set out her stall for the next phase of broadcasting in the white heat of the Harold Wilson era.

There was an insistence on truly local stations, not made-up regions: 'Long experience of regional and area broadcasting has convinced the Corporation that a station addressing a plurality of local groupings is continually at a disadvantage – as its listeners can never be sure that what it is saying is really meant for them, rather than for the people in another town.'

Far from the 'monolithic' BBC image, the pamphlet argued that responsibility for local radio would be delegated: 'The aim would be that listeners would come to regard their local station as our station not as the BBC station in our town. The BBC would not try to impose a central pattern or any form of detailed overall control on its local stations.' They would 'do much to make listeners proud of their community and willing to take part in its affairs'.

Station managers would be 'of the best possible quality … expected to participate in local affairs'. They would be 'close to their listeners' and decent means of keeping in touch with their views would be established.

I describe the pamphlet in detail as I feel, if anything, in recent years BBC local radio has moved to observe the opposite of those 1966 assertions. What's more, the fact that the entire local radio philosophy could be outlined at a length equivalent to a modern-day compliance memo speaks volumes.

Like many large organisations, I found the BBC dysfunctional, despite its best intentions. It appeared to spend as much time running itself as it did producing output. If local radio suffers from the organisation's complexity, then the national networks must surely do so by an even more expensive margin. I recognise, nevertheless, that it would be as politically and practically challenging to deconstruct the Corporation and rebuild it in a better mould, as it would be to do the same to the NHS. Both are treasured public institutions where useful change in one area, even if only to benefit another, is hugely difficult to engineer without it being emotionally dubbed 'cuts'. It demands confident, strong leadership.

Before my appointment to the senior post in 2008, I'd been moved to write a paper giving the benefits of my perspective and offering to help identify more satisfactory ways of operating local radio. I suggested that if the network were 'cut off' from the BBC machine, afforded an income stream instead and left to get on with the job, yet still allowed to buy in BBC material and functions as it wished, it would produce better programming at a much-reduced cost, provided that this was overseen by a skilled manager. I observed that, in my time in London, LBC was producing twice the number of radio stations, at half the cost, achieving double the audiences of BBC Radio London.

46

RADIO 4

'Forties, Cromarty, Forth.' 'Tyne, Dogger, Fisher.' We all nurture an unlikely broadcasting ambition. Mine is to sit in a dimly lit studio delivering the shipping forecast on BBC Radio 4 on a windy, wintry night whilst the rain is pattering on Home Counties' window panes.

Whilst the remainder of radio – and British life – has changed beyond recognition in the last fifty years, the distinctive characteristic of Radio 4 is how it has remained defiantly the same, whilst still managing to stay fresh and relevant through subtle changes in pitch and tone. Any controller rushing in to make changes, without due thought, is rightly given short shrift by the station's discerning audience.

As former Radio 4 controller Helen Boaden observed, 'You have to know it beyond your intellectual knowing. You have to have an instinct about what its most conservative audiences will tolerate.'[35]

In 2006, the BBC faced a revolt over the decision by Helen's successor, Mark Damazer, to axe the 'UK Theme', the jaunty five-minute medley of British folk songs, arranged by Fritz Spiegl, which had started the Radio 4 day for almost thirty years. 'This seems typical of the BBC's constant desire to disassociate itself from anything that could be construed as nationalism,' wrote one complainant with their temple throbbing.[36]

As a glance at a current *Radio Times* confirms, a surprising number of Radio 4 programmes remain as they were in the channel's Home Service incarnation. In my early teens, the red transistor radio in my little back bedroom would routinely be tuned to the *Book at Bedtime*, which had become a formal part of the regular Home Service schedule in 1962. Like some other Radio 4 rituals, its beauty arises as much from its calming sound as its content.

Desert Island Discs moved to the Home Service in 1951 and remains hugely popular, despite the herring gulls heard as part of its familiar signature tune being native to no remote island. William Hardcastle's booming voice heralded the first edition of *The World at One* in 1965 and *Any Questions?* was aired on the Light Programme and Home Service.

Today dawned in 1957 on the BBC Home Service. By the following year, Jack de Manio became its defining voice, renowned for being unable to translate the reading of a clock face to a radio time-check. Another former presenter, Brian Redhead, was quoted as saying: 'If you want to drop a word in the ear of the nation, then this is the programme in which to do it.'

One of the *Today* programme's most challenging chapters opened in 2003, following a two-way interview with correspondent Andrew Gilligan. He had referenced the claim in a dossier that Iraq's military planning would facilitate weapons of mass destruction being ready within forty-five minutes of an order to use them, and he had suggested that Downing Street had ordered the document to be 'sexed up' in that way to render it more compelling. The BBC's source for its reporter's assertion was identified as Dr David Kelly, who was subsequently questioned by a Foreign Affairs subcommittee, and then found dead two days later. An inquiry was commissioned and the ensuing

Hutton Report criticised the reporting and BBC management. The fallout from this early morning broadcast resulted in the resignation of Gavyn Davies, the chairman of the BBC's board of governors, and director general Greg Dyke.

The *Today* programme remains on air to this day, although the formerly deferential tone politicians grew to expect has faded. It is said that the first querulous sign of the change in tone from broadcasters came in 1957, on TV when Reginald Bosanquet tackled Prime Minister Harold Macmillan over a by-election: 'Sir, as time is short, could we question you on a domestic matter which I think is uppermost in our minds at the moment?' 'If you must,' Macmillan replied.

Although programmes like *Just a Minute*, *You and Yours*, *The World Tonight* and the evening news programme *PM* are saplings by comparison, they have still been around longer than any commercial radio station. *PM* is usually hosted by Eddie Mair and I shake my head in wonder as this clever Scot allows radio to be the best it can: the pauses; the short, barbed questions, those daggers covered in cotton wool; the deadpan retorts; the potent questions masquerading as statements; the deadly acid coated in politeness; the tasty menu at the outset.

PM began in 1970, following the 'Broadcasting in the '70s' report which paved the way for the BBC radio services to carve out more definite identities. The programme boasted a 'twiddly-pom' signature tune, thanks to the Radiophonic Workshop, whose work adorned many BBC stations in the '60s and early '70s. This later gave way to a portentous orchestral piece and I often dreamed of co-hosting with the legendary Valerie Singleton, who presented the programme for over ten years from 1981, delivering the programme menu perfectly into the brassy 'Da-da, da-da-dah-dah-dah'. Roger Mosey, one-time editor of the programme, told me Valerie had said to him as he arrived in post: 'I bet as you were watching *Blue Peter*, you never thought you'd be my boss.'[37]

There is no theme tune now, but Eddie's powerfully chosen words are better than the best orchestra in the world.

My childhood friend Harry, whose garden backed onto ours, came from an interesting family. His father was a renowned violin maker and hand-crafted these wonderful instruments in a garden shed; his mother was saving the earth long before it was trendy, collecting all her old Sainsbury's cardboard carrier bags with their string handles and taking them somewhere useful in her rusty dark green Renault 4. As I was beckoned into their kitchen, I'd see a huge Hacker radio set on a swivel base dominating the kitchen table, and we would be shushed as *The Archers* signature tune rang out.

The Archers began in 1951, and this 'everyday story of country folk' is still an important fixture on the schedule. The BBC's Godfrey Baseley was the early producer who was instructed to include a maximum of eight characters: 'A father or mother, or both; young lovers; adult lovers; a comedy character and somebody to hate.'

The series notably touched a nerve in 2016 with its storyline about marital coercion and domestic abuse, attracting major media coverage. That level of interest echoed the coverage in September 1955 when a dramatic Ambridge fire claimed the life of a popular character, in a plot designed to suck attention away from the launch night of ITV.

Aside from the obvious, there are quiet corners of true brilliance on this astounding station. Despite hating the name 'The Listening Project', which sounds to me like a working title someone forgot to replace, these interstitial 'potters-wheel' pieces of intimate conversation are an example of radio at its emotional best. These treasures have moved me to tears when driving home from another vigorous week in the world of commercial radio.

This station, which rules London listening by some margin to this day, is my guilty pleasure. If the BBC stands for anything, it is Radio 4, and whilst I have had little to do with the station, save from a fleeting appearance on a couple of programmes, there is a special place in my heart for this world leader. Although I am sure it too could be operated at lower costs without any impact on quality, I would protest naked down Pall Mall if any future government, BBC or regulatory madness dared to place the output of this precious station in peril.

47

BAD TIMING

It's always good to have a short tenure for one of the roles on your CV. Lazy interviewers will then gleefully alight on the easy question, wasting time asking you why it was so short a spell. Providing you have a decent answer, such filibustering ensures that they have less time to interrogate you about other areas where you may be weaker.

Rumour has it that I stayed in my regional BBC management role for just a week. In truth, it was closer to a month.

In 2008, another high-value transaction occurred in the commercial radio sector, as the new Global Radio, comprising our old Chrysalis stations, successfully acquired the much larger GCap group. Whilst Global had not become literally global overnight, it was certainly one step closer.

Following the completion of the deal, Global owned an impressive number of local stations, dominating the south and the Midlands with the Galaxy, Heart and LBC brands, as well as the national Classic FM. Global's weekly audiences rose overnight from over 6 million to more than 20 million. UK radio now was concentrated principally in the hands of Bauer and Global, with UTV and the smaller operators some way down the stack.

The Office of Fair Trading, however, had furrowed brows about Global's concentration of ownership in certain geographic areas following the acquisition, asserting that the choice of commercial radio offerings to advertisers in those areas had been materially diminished. In other words, if you were a local garage owner and Global increased your advertising rates unreasonably, there would be a reduced number of alternatives for your campaign and your negotiating position would thus be weakened.

The foundation of the concern is the apprehension that radio is a distinct advertising market. The contention does not accept that, if radio raises its rates unduly, then the advertiser just won't bother or will choose an alternative like ITV; or Sky AdSmart; or buses; or mailshots; or YouTube; or newspapers; or roadside posters; or petrol pump ads; or Facebook.

Whilst the existence of rival operators in a market may offer welcome job prospects for those of us working in the medium, and whilst some listeners might argue they value the perceived listening variety it may bring, I am not persuaded that the concern about advertising markets is well founded in a digital world where alternatives are proliferating and self-evidently stealing radio's cash.

To avoid referral to the Competition Commission, at which stage the deal would have fallen through, Global volunteered to the OFT that it would sell some stations in the Midlands, namely BRMB, Beacon, Mercia and Wyvern in the West Midlands; and Heart 106 in the East Midlands. A buyer needed to be found quickly for these five key FM stations and their AM offspring. This was to be a fire sale.

Several parties expressed an interest in these important stations, not least Global's major adversary, Bauer. Another interested party was my former colleague Phil Riley, who was now free following his exit from the chief executive post at

Chrysalis Radio and who was seeking backing from investors. I'd previously indicated a willingness to be involved in the possible venture although, as the weeks went by, I conceded that pulling off the deal seemed highly unlikely. When I was offered my job at the BBC, the plan had completely died, so I took up the post in Hull, never dreaming that circumstances would change.

Just a few weeks later, sitting in my bright BBC office, feet on the desk, quite enjoying a calm day and getting used to playing with television as well as radio, I took a call from Phil. His familiar, determined tones boomed: 'We're back on.' I smiled, with little intention of leaving the job I'd just started.

Phil, however, is a difficult man to say no to, and I found myself on the train to Birmingham one evening preparing to present 'Project Gershwin' to the potential investors. The habit of giving names to secret company plans is well established, and makes one feel like a Secret Service agent. I recall once spending more time deliberating on a project's name than its contents.

The investors were persuaded of the merits of the plan and funding was duly agreed by LDC, the private equity leg of Lloyds Bank. It seemed fitting to me that it was the bank I'd worked for aged eighteen, the sort code for which I still knew off by heart. Whilst Bauer were still very interested in acquiring the stations, we manoeuvred ourselves into pole position and LDC, and all of us in the management team, prepared to get out our cheque books. Quite unexpectedly, we were about to bet on a radio horse we'd called Orion Media.

The night the deal was expected to be signed became a long one. I left Hull after a day's BBC work, thinking matters would be agreed that night, but knowing that this might not be the case, and that I could be back at work the following day trying to disguise my exhaustion. Early evening came and went, as did mid-evening. As late evening approached, I was summoned from LDC's Nottingham office to the Birmingham offices of the lawyers. I grabbed a cab to join the remainder of our team in the old wood-panelled offices. Tables were piled high with multiple copies of carefully drafted documents and debate on contentious points ensued. In another office, miles away, much the same thing was happening with the vendors.

At a dull moment, and there were many of those in the small hours, I stretched my legs and wandered down the long, tiled corridors of the lawyers' offices. There is something surreal about being in an office you don't know at four in the morning. It's always puzzled me why these things happen in the dead of night and don't get completed in time for *Coronation Street*. For the investment team at LDC, however, this was business as usual, almost part of the ritual. For them, to be tired was not acceptable; this was the time when their clever brains needed to be on the money. Their long-suffering partners had presumably got used to them walking out the door on Monday, returning on Wednesday and sleeping until Friday.

The birds twittered loudly in Birmingham's Cathedral Square and dawn broke on what had become a memorable morning in May 2009. After a furious document-signing session, we linked up live with the Global Radio team by a large speakerphone on the desk, feeling a little like linking to Stockholm for the Eurovision voting. We'd claimed the prize and Ashley Tabor and a cheering, tired mob from the other side wished us every success. Champagne flowed. We were the proud owners of some significant Midlands radio stations. Surely running them would be the easy bit.

There was no price reduction from the Hilton Garden Inn in

Birmingham, even though I'd only slept in their bed for ninety minutes after I'd fallen into it at six o' clock. The alarm rang and I prepared to take a deep breath and call David Holdsworth at the BBC promptly, to let him know his new recruit was about to bugger off again.

To say the call surprised him would be an understatement. Understandably, he wasn't happy, having just press-released my appointment. I'd have been the same. He spluttered that we commercial folk were different by our very natures. I don't agree, but the art of coping with resignations from posts like mine seemed a little alien to the lucky Corporation.

Wanting to appear helpful, I volunteered to David that I'd return to work that morning to tell my senior team the news and clear up any loose ends. Having splashed cold water on my face and driven from Birmingham to Hull to have the necessary conversations, I discovered, on arrival, that my BBC pass had been deactivated. As I banged on the door in a puzzled way, and gesticulated to the receptionist to buzz me in, I realised that as far as the BBC was concerned, I no longer existed.

The role was wisely not replaced – and I am comforted to know that my inconvenient departure at least helped the BBC bank some savings.

48

THE MIDLANDS

BRMB was the key West Midlands station in our new portfolio; few listeners knew what the four letters denoted, but it didn't really matter. To Birmingham folk, it was their local station and regarded with huge fondness.

BRMB had been the UK's first commercial radio station outside of London, launching in 1974, and enjoyed a purple period in the '80s and '90s, owing in no small part to the performance of presenter Les Ross. On the breakfast show, this impish entertainer had ruled his city. His quick mind, his gift for turning the routine into entertainment, and his knack with, and understanding of, his callers were powerful gifts. He is one of few broadcasters who are still remembered with a smile long after the end of his astonishing twenty-seven years of daily early morning appearances.

The station was also famous for its stunts, including examples of 'reality radio' before the genre hit television. *Housemates from Hell* led the way, followed by a programme which attracted worldwide attention and considerable controversy: *Two Strangers and a Wedding*.

Like so many of the early stations, however, the mighty BRMB had lost its way. It had become a Woolworths, with everyone loving it being around, but few people bothering to shop there. Its glossy red rival, the original Heart West Midlands, had become well established and, in some ways, started to become the local station of choice, not least through huge investment in sexy marketing. Meanwhile, amongst younger listeners, the credible Galaxy had become a 'must-listen'.

Despite being decently run by some impressive operators over the years, BRMB, like several of the original stations in the big cities, had become famous for nothing, allowing the new radio supermarkets down the road to steal their customers. The fall from grace was even more galling as we walked through the door, considering that several of our management team had been involved in creating the competition we were about to face.

In charge of our new venture was our 'Gang of Four', headed by Phil Riley as chief executive. From the same stock, I was to be programme and marketing director and the calm and capable Mark Evans was appointed finance director. Good-looking Adrian Serle joined us from Bauer as commercial director.

The station had moved from its launch premises in former ATV offices at Aston Cross, and was now based in a modern building in what was to become a media quarter of Birmingham at Brindleyplace. Not only would Global Radio, in time, choose to base itself here, but it was also one of those locations where TV shows routinely choose to film any cheap drama which needs a hotel, bank, piazza or coffee shop. Watching all the people hanging around clutching clipboards, wearing lanyards and trying to look important, it struck me that surely it cannot possibly take quite so many people to make everyday television.

One of my jobs, however, on arriving at BRMB was to establish quite how many people it would take to make commercial radio.

Our Orion Media operation was dubbed a 'management buy-in', in that we, the management team, were parachuted into an established business. It is less common than a management buy-out, where the management are already part of the business and know where all the bodies are buried. We had the benefit of a huge amount of knowledge of the business, and indeed we knew many of the people within from past lives in our small industry but, in technical terms, there was still theoretically the risk of a corpse or two in a cupboard.

A little like buying a house, there is an anxious period when the deal has been agreed yet not completed. You know you are about to do the deed, as do the management and staff on site, yet you cannot put up pictures of your loved one in your office as the old tenant is still living there. Temporary office accommodation was arranged for a brief period in a building just feet away, whilst we watched through the venetian blinds, only calling into the station by appointment.

The strategy at the outset was to return the West Midlands stations to their former glories and become 'kings of our own backyard' once again. The plan also chimed emotionally with Phil Riley, as this was the station where he'd begun his impressive career, as a humble trainee in the early '80s. He was now back home – as the big boss. Whilst Phil was annoyingly evidence driven in all matters, and his personal investment in Orion was considerable, one could feel that success at this particular station meant a lot to him emotionally too.

The West Midlands business also included stations elsewhere. In Wolverhampton, we inherited Beacon Radio, housed in a former orphanage on the edge of town, said to bear the ghost of a poor baby who passed into the spirit world back in the nineteenth century. This Victorian building had been bought, back then, for £18,000 by one of its directors, and stroppy presenters replaced stroppy children. In true rebellious Beacon style, the building was purchased originally on a whim, without the knowledge of the board, necessitating a hastily arranged meeting to sanction the transaction.[38]

Beacon had launched in the sunny days of 1976, with a jingle package and sound more fitting for San Francisco than Bilston. It had been the last in the first tranche of stations around the UK. Beacon was of Radio Trent vintage and I felt an affinity with its battered, ill-fitting home. Its relationship with the regulator had been tense in its early days and a former Trent MD confessed to me that he had believed as long as Beacon managed to escape dramatic regulatory intervention, his own station would be safe with its lesser transgressions. Dale Winton had worked at Beacon in the '80s, after leaving Trent, and famously rebelled against an edict to mention the station name twice in each link by starting each link with 'Beacon Beacon...'

On our arrival, the Beacon operation comprised two stations under the same name, one for Wolverhampton and the Black Country, and one for Shropshire. These two unlikely bedfellows had been wedded by the regulator at a time when it presumed no right-thinking person would conclude that a service for Shropshire alone would be able to sustain itself. The IBA applied the same thinking to the Derbyshire and Doncaster licences in tough economic times.

In Coventry, we acquired Mercia. Formerly Mercia Sound, this was the first station in England in the second tranche, after the government began to grow the commercial radio network once again. The station was inspired by community radio thinking and sought a large spread of local shareholders. Unlike in many cities, its arrival in 1980 had preceded BBC local radio, and it attracted a weekly audience reach in its first year of an astounding 60 per cent.

Mercia's programme director in the early days, Ian Rufus,

recalled that even by the 1980s the regulator was still gleefully interventionist, insisting on a daily lunchtime classical music programme and objecting to the proposal to call the station WKCV, owing to the name sounding 'too American'. It is reported that the hasty replacement label Mercia was inspired by the name of a buffet at Coventry railway station.

Mercia was based in a less than salubrious area; it was housed in an old snooker club, with breakfast presenters climbing over sleeping bodies and syringes to get in the building. It was an early '70s concrete mess which had seen better days and, one frightening morning, I recall a piece of concrete collapsing over the entrance to one of the studios. Despite its location, or maybe because of it, Mercia was a station still very much loved by its people. It certainly played its part in its community with impressive fundraising for the Snowball Appeal and the smiling face of long-standing MD Stuart Linnell MBE was seen more often than anyone else in the local press, pointing to impressive figures on bumper-sized cheques.

The city lay so close to its dominant neighbour, Birmingham, that to have its own media which placed Coventry at its heart was a privilege people valued.

In Worcestershire, Wyvern FM lay in what passes for an industrial area in the heart of this beautiful county, with an enviable view of the Malvern Hills through the mist out of the studio window. Wyvern, its call-sign juxtaposing the names of the River Wye and River Severn, was the newest of our West Midlands stations. It launched in 1982 with an inaugural breakfast show which appeared to trouble to mention the names of most listeners. Wyvern served as an early home for accomplished Hit 40 and Magic London presenter Neil Fox, who observed that an early MD, Norman Bilton, had 'inherited a frigging turkey' as he took over his responsibilities at the then struggling station.[39]

Over in the East Midlands, we acquired Heart 106. It was odd to find myself again in this Nottingham building, in which I had worked in two earlier stints. As one of very few stations in the East Midlands, the competition authorities had firm views on who could own what, and this station was always in a tug of love in times of industry consolidation, emerging as an unwanted child whose name changed with each foster parent. Now we owned the station, though we continued to rent its Heart name and carried some of its off-peak programmes under a brand licensing agreement.

Plans for our Orion venture had been well thought through in advance. LDC seemed to relish huge colourful Gantt charts, illustrating what would happen on each day. I imagine they are quite useful in some circumstances, but my experience of such charts is that no one ever refers to them. I have certainly never woken up thinking 'what should I do today?'

We'd had the benefit of staff lists and details of the infrastructure, but the reality is always a different story. We knew we'd have to grow the staff and build our own head office team, given this business had been carved out of a larger parent, but we knew similarly we'd have to lose some posts. The early days, therefore, were painful for us, and more so for those involved, as we began the restructure. I hope we behaved fairly and honourably and I recall that those who subsequently left us were professional too. It helps when making such changes if one has been on the other side of the 'we don't really need you' conversations.

Restructuring also allows a station to gear up correctly to the demands of the age. Although some roles have shrivelled since commercial radio's birth a raft of new ones have been created: from IT to design, and video production to commercial programming.

During any regime change, staff will tend to drift into one of three categories. There are the suspicious ones with folded arms who really don't want any of your new ideas, thank you very much. There are the ones you can win round in time. And there are those who ask what you want to achieve, advise you objectively, and help you get there without falling over along the way. David 'Salty' Salt fell into the latter category. This intelligent, utterly dependable young man with piercing blue eyes had been helping out since he was a kid and had soaked up all there was to know. His quiet Black Country demeanour belied the calibre of his thinking; he was a rare character who was both hugely creative and organised, and who managed up and down with annoying skill when he chose. He was not on the staff when we arrived, but that was quickly arranged and he graduated quickly to deputy content controller. It is fulfilling to identify someone who will one day hold one of the great offices of state in this wonderful industry. As I said in his well-deserved Radio Academy award nomination, every station needs a Salty.

Global's Ashley Tabor famously said: 'I'm afraid to say there are not thirty-three good mid-morning presenters in this country and there are not another thirty-three good afternoon presenters. I wish there were, but there aren't.'[40] He probably had a point. We inherited many presenters of high calibre, including the likes of daytime presenter Dan Morrissey. Slim Dan, with cropped hair and earnest glasses, was a quiet sort of guy who, through solid preparation and innate talent, delivered real value on air. Tight daytime radio, which still delivers personality and laugh-out-loud moments, is an undervalued skill. In the words of a gifted programmer, the deadpan Francis

Currie, 'great music radio presenters are like a poet, saying a lot in a few words'. Unlike many, Dan also managed both to echo the tone of his presentation contemporaneously on social media and to spell perfectly.

Most decent businesses begin with detailed customer insight. Solid evidence viewed in context aids decision-making and helps you argue confidently against what the boss says his wife thinks. In our case, it helped to fuel some pretty graphs we could show to our investors who were unaccustomed to our bizarre intangible world.

We duly commissioned endless studies in the West Midlands, including several focus groups in gloomy hotel rooms. I moderated the sessions myself, assuming the necessary detached air of someone who doesn't know what a radio is – and thoroughly enjoyed the act. The sorts of people whose voices we wanted to hear were wisely recruited with care, via a capable research company. Not loyal listeners, but casual listeners and the sorts of listeners we aspired to own. Having said that, no matter how often we told ourselves that we had paid to hire people who didn't love us very much, it was utterly demoralising to sit through endless hours of chatter from those who didn't love us very much. Focus groups are seriously bad for the health.

There were the quiet ones in the room. There were the noisy ones who dominated, including at least one anorak who knew a little too much. And there was the gentleman who said he was going to the loo after being paid, and was never seen again. My favourite focus group participant was a woman in a brown parka who returned to the room just after the group had concluded and asked if she could take home an unopened packet of Pringles we'd laid on.

What emerged was a sobering insight into how people really felt about our station and our competitors. I grew to know exactly which words they would use when I asked about all the radio brands and discovered that listeners remember all the things you thought they would not, and forget those things you spent years planning. I had to restrain myself as listeners spouted utter rubbish, and suppress the inward cheer when a perception we had worked hard to change had indeed started to do just that. Some listeners I wanted to kiss with joy, others I longed to slap.

Listeners express surprising recall of the performances of some presenters and know scant little about others. Pretending not to be familiar with the names 'Chris Moyles' or 'Simon Mayo', I would wade innocently through a list of presenter names, from our stations and others, seeking to establish levels of familiarity. I fear that some nationally established figures would be shocked to know that 70 per cent of people may not actually know who on earth they are. Then again, when rich stories flowed from a listener's mouth about something one of our presenters had done on air a year before, it was gratifying.

In every group, there was always at least one gem of a remark which would change the way we did something fundamentally – for ever. Often the views of real listeners serve to overturn predictable, conventional radio wisdom in a refreshing way. Just refrain from asking listeners to predict their future behaviour. Just like you and me, they really cannot.

Our conclusions were stark. Everybody loved the fact that BRMB was there. It was local. And local is a very good thing. When we quizzed them on their listening habits, however, it transpired they'd not troubled to listen to their dear BRMB for some time and if they had, they remembered nothing about it. Group after group, the findings were the same. BRMB was famous. Famous for nothing. There was work to be done.

One thing was clear: they adored the reputation the station had for mentioning school closures on snowy mornings. Eyes lit up as focus group respondents nostalgically recalled sitting by their radios in their school uniforms praying that the name of their comprehensive would be mentioned on BRMB. I could relate to that, having lived through the '70s, when we'd sit by candlelight in scarves and mittens waiting for the next dramatic power cut update on local radio.

We judged, however, that being famous for school closures was not the strongest of foundations for our West Midlands radio brand.

49

A ROSE BY ANY OTHER NAME

Brand franchising is commonplace in business and works well for many branches of Subway, Pizza Hut and McDonald's. The formula is proven, risk is lowered, ingredients are purchased cost-efficiently and, even on the first day the outlets push open the doors, the brand names ensure they already seem familiar destinations to customers.

It worked well for us too. We had licensed the 'Heart' name from Global Radio for our East Midlands station, so to listeners clutching their radios in Leicester, Derby or Nottingham, the change in ownership to us was undetectable. Here was a brand we thoroughly understood from our past lives and it served us well to bask in their ongoing well-judged investment in the bright red 'feel-good' marketing. With that ongoing quality of brand support, underpinned by our own efforts running the business in the building locally, and hiring and managing on- and off-air staff, the station continued to thrive. Indeed, in September 2010, the station published its highest audience figures ever and revenues were hitting record levels.

In that same month, Global Radio announced they were to convert several of their radio stations across the country to the Capital brand name which was so famous in London. It was a proven strategy: they had changed the names of many of their other local services to Heart just months before, to expand that brand's footprint beyond London and the Midlands.

The dividend of the strategy was that they could aggregate all listening to a brand across the UK and sell that audience simply to the clients of London agencies, without having to explain that chunks of that listening belonged to stations that clients had never heard of, based in cities they cared little about. Brand marketing campaigns could also be rolled out with ease on any media, regardless of geographic boundaries, something from which we had benefited with our own Heart station. On-air programmes could more easily be networked, given they shared the same identity; on-air personalities became bigger and major promotions could easily be integrated on all stations.

For many in our industry, however, brought up during the era in which these colourful original local stations ruled proudly, the move was utterly unthinkable. How could this brash newcomer even countenance such vandalism – murdering much-loved heritage radio stations such as Hereward, GWR and 2-Ten in favour of Heart? Did 'independent local radio' still exist?

With clear foresight and focus, however, Global had carried off the Heart transitions in 2009 with typical conviction and operational perfection, alongside serious marketing investment. They had, at last, erased the uncomfortable legacy anomalies of a radio network designed by politicians and regulators of a monochrome age. They had engineered, not without pain, a cohesive and powerful radio network which could, at last, rival the BBC in scale, reputation and audiences. In general, listener volume overall did not suffer from the change and audiences were much more readily monetised. Global asserted, too, that local output at the critical drivetime periods remained local, as did the news content.

After the Heart transplants, Global still owned several stations which, for assorted reasons, had retained their former names. They also owned the large Galaxy brand, which, whilst hugely famous in its northern backyard, was unknown in London. That Galaxy issue was a problem that had kept us awake a generation before at Chrysalis. In a second strategic move, therefore, the company chose to lay its Capital brand across the remainder of its services across the country.

In the East Midlands, where we operated Heart, this announcement meant that Nottingham's Trent, Derby's Ram FM and Leicester Sound would become a single new regional Capital station, with comparatively little locally originated output.

We were conscious of the digital trend. Whilst listening through a TV set accounted for a comparatively small proportion of consumption, Heart listeners via TV in the East Midlands heard Heart London, not us. In due course, there would be nothing to stop Heart also operating its own programme stream on DAB too without troubling to license it to us any longer. In short, there was a risk that the long-term value for our FM radio licence could be eroded.

All these developments proved the catalyst for us to make some changes of our own. We chose to relinquish the Heart name and create a fresh East Midlands brand. We identified an opportunity to be the only station originating programming locally.

Our decision came as a surprise to the owners of the Heart brand and, as they took pains to point out, carried risks. Unlike the brand changes by our competitors, we were not inheriting any brand benefit or scale from the change; we were simply changing a well-loved familiar name for an unknown one we hadn't quite decided on yet.

Choosing a new radio station name seems an easy job – it's far from that. Endless brainstorms in airless offices ended up with colourful Post-it notes stuck all over the wall with hot contenders being ruled out, one by one, for valid reasons. Just about every word you dream up is already owned by someone. Typically, lawyers never do anything useful, like give a name a clean bill of health, they just charge a fortune to suggest some are riskier than others. The ones which are possible contenders then just don't seem to sound, look or feel right. Little wonder that so many start-ups now have silly made-up names.

It is also challenging to research how your favoured name will chime with audiences. I was comforted by the fact that I suspect any 1967 research, had it ever been conducted, would likely have concluded that 'Radio 1' would be a pretty lousy name for the BBC's supposedly exciting new pop service.

My theory is perhaps borne out by one letter to *The Times* in 1967:

> Sir, it really is an astonishing mistake that the BBC's Radio 1 is to be the pop programme and the Home Service is to be BBC (Radio) 4. The ordinary person and the ordinary foreigner will naturally imagine Radio 1 to be the most important and 'official' programme of the BBC … Whatever misplaced subtlety may be used to explain this apparent demotion of the Home Service, it is bound to be regarded as a surrender of cultural values and is deplorable.[41]

Our efforts suggested a few names of interest for our East Midlands stations, and 'Gem' was one of them. The jewel fitted the sparkly brand ethos and the station's female target audience andour research findings satisfied us that the target audience did not associate it with the area's successful former oldies station GEM AM, a brand name which had been suffocated by new owners by the late 1990s as the station had moved to more network programming.

Only people as old as me remembered that GEM (Government Employees Mart) had also been the name of a pioneering, American-backed Nottingham superstore in the 1960s, famous for being the very first huge out-of-town store in the UK. Typically, long after it became Asda, locals still called it GEM; a familiar experience for those of us involved in changing radio station names.

Our radio brand transition was necessarily abrupt. Never one to miss out on a moment of radio history, I volunteered to be the live on-air presenter as Heart 106 morphed into Gem 106 as the year 2010 ebbed away.

Having excused myself from a New Year's frolic at our local pub, I walked across a rowdy Nottingham city centre, rolling up at the station premises, to find dedicated head of music Paul Iliffe in a party hat, scheduling the music for the early days of the new station. From being a part-time operation, supported by big sister Heart, we were about to take off our stabilisers and stand on our own, twenty-four hours a day.

Dashing down the stairs into the studio, I took control of the networked output which was being fed from London. As Michael Jackson faded, I delivered the station's call-sign 'Heart 106' for the last time. After a brief pause, and the chimes of Big Ben, I uttered the words 'Gem 106' for the first time, with no reference to what had gone before, and fired in one of our hasty, yet excellent, new jingles from production house Wisebuddah. The frequency was now operating under its fourth name. Five years on, the very team who had put the Heart name on the frequency had just taken it off again.

I returned to the party, leaving an obliging young lad to sit through the night watching the automated programming through the small hours, to ensure our newborn would still be alive in the morning. The burghers of Leicester, Nottingham and Derby must have felt a little puzzled when they woke up with sore heads wondering why their favourite station had changed identity overnight without warning.

Whilst we were confident in the long-term wisdom of a name change, we were cautious about the short-term effects. Listeners often get a little confused between stations as they flick through the buttons, so we anticipated a short-term blip in registered audience levels. Our chief executive even wheeled out a lengthy 'managing expectations' PowerPoint presentation to confuse the staff further.

Those sensible efforts were luckily unnecessary and the eventual first audience results were a delicious surprise. We had delivered the best ever audiences for any station which had ever been on the frequency. It was a relief.

Listener confusion had felt likely as other commercial East Midlands stations, run by our rival Global Radio, had also changed their names almost simultaneously. My beloved local Trent, Ram and Leicester Sound had been united as a regional Capital station. Indeed, we'd floated the idea of securing the 'Trent' name for our own service. That may or may not have been a wise or feasible plan, but it would likely have been the final straw for listeners, who would have just reached for the wine bottle again and gone back to bed.

Gem emerged as one of the UK's most successful radio stations, delivering record audiences and profits, along with real programme quality, not least from the exceptional Sam & Amy on the breakfast programme, who later even enjoyed the privilege of appearing on Radio 2 from time to time. Under the gifted management of the launch PD, Mike Newman, supported by no-nonsense Paul Iliffe, the breakfast programme carried off the biggest awards in radio, even in the face of national radio names.

For me, the boy from Nottingham, to be able to lay some claim to what had become the East Midlands' most listened-to radio station was a privilege.

50

THE WEST

The East Midlands business was a simple one. One mighty FM transmitter beamed out a single programme service from a single building to everyone. The West Midlands, however, was a more complex affair entailing four sets of premises and, including DAB, over forty transmitters. Rationalising the operation was crucial.

The old premises for some of the stations had become unsuitable, not least the buildings which had been commissioned when Harold Wilson was in power, dads drove Avenger cars and radio station staff numbers were likely more than double. At Beacon's stately home, a presenter needed to go for a long walk and push a heavy oak door if he wished to chat to his programme director in his cavernous office. The lonely staff at Wyvern rattled around on their large floor, and the concrete Mercia building was past its best for a funky media business.

We prepared to move the Coventry operation into our Birmingham base and to sell off the Beacon premises in Wolverhampton, in favour of what I was told off for calling a 'lean-to' in the Black Country, given it was a decent, compact new complex. In packing the chests to move out of Beacon's old stately home, we acknowledged we were leaving behind forty years of memories. A fitting party was thrown on site to say farewell to the many people who'd passed through the building's doors over the years and who had left a piece of their heart. The Orion team did its best to honour the past.

On air, in trying to establish a new reputation for the stations, we sought 'talkability'. We wanted them to be famous again by creating content listeners cared for, talked about and were loyal to, and to raise the length of time people spent with the stations each week, which had fallen to worrying levels.

One measure was the return of a late-night phone-in, in the hands of the wonderful Caroline Martin. Although Caroline chose to move on in due course, and I reluctantly concluded that the investment should be differently placed, I loved this show of real-life stories. *The Sanctuary* delivered some compelling moments of late-night radio. When Caroline opened up about her own complex life, the listeners did too. To listen felt like being back in the 1960s days of shared phone lines; you would pick up the receiver only to hear the neighbour pouring out her heart on the 'party line'. There were tears and laughter. All human life existed.

'My mum spoilt my wedding day by having sex with my husband under the stairs ... havnt [*sic*] spoke to her since. As for husband we lasted 18 yrs ... manipulating t***. I get married again in three weeks she aint [*sic*] coming to this one!'[42]

The programme was another example of the late-night phone-in offerings across the UK that created something special over the years, from James Whale at Metro to Pete Price at City.

On our stations, listeners felt they could confide in Caroline – and that brought its own drama. The police were in touch on a couple of occasions when it seemed as if something that an unwitting caller had said was relevant to an ongoing investigation.

Troubled listeners also appeared to gravitate to Caroline,

and she would pass on any alarming communications for me to handle. I know we were not the only station to take a call from someone threatening suicide. One of the puzzling things about radio is that people feel their relationship with their station is so intimate, that they can confide in it confidently. I recall one call vividly, from a young lady who feared for her safety and said she was being kept in the house against her will. There was something about this conversation that made me suspect that she was in imminent danger. I contacted the police, who responded with impressive speed and focus, and I stayed on the line until I was confident that matters were in hand.

Years later, a bright cheery caller was put through from the reception desk. It was the woman I'd tried to help many months before, wanting to thank me for my role that night. Life had turned out fine.

One listener inexplicably left us a mobility scooter in her will. The gifted programming team tried to put it to good use by using it for a stunt in a celebrity interview. In a *Top Gear*-type affair dubbed 'Star Scooter', a female pop star, who shall remain nameless, was invited outside to drive around the perimeter of our building on the scooter, negotiating an obstacle course we had painstakingly arranged. As her manager made clear her objections to participating, an elderly lady on another scooter duly turned up and had the time of her life zig-zagging through the traffic cones.

Another celebrity mishap occurred when *X Factor*'s inimitable Wagner was set to appear on our Wolverhampton breakfast show. We'd arranged for a car to pick him up from Scotland, where he was staying, and to bring him to the station. Already cutting things fine with regards to timing, the star insisted on being taken on a detour to his house to feed his cat prior to his appearance on air.

The more competitive the market, the more important is a carefully defined music formula. In Birmingham, Heart was a perfectly programmed music variety and Galaxy's dance and RnB was a well-targeted winner. Radio 1 had found a distinct place in the repertoire and Radio 2 was becoming more mainstream; both BBC stations were aided also by a lack of ad spots. Kerrang! was available on FM across the region, and a growing band of DAB stations were starting to amass appreciable audiences, which had to be stolen from other services.

The West Midlands was a frantic place for radio. At the time, it was the only UK market outside London that enjoyed both a youth commercial brand and an adult contemporary brand surrounding, attacking the audience to the established 'heritage' station from both sides. And, like many of the stalwarts around the country, our station had demonstrably lost its way, oscillating from music policy to music policy as competitors arrived. To depress ourselves further, we assembled a pretty flow chart of all music format changes over the years, which I recall was too large to fit on a single PowerPoint slide.

Our West Midlands stations needed to identify a music position which was both distinctive and popular. A good deal of music research followed, resulting in our moving to 'today's best music mix', a contemporary-flavoured sound with some credible oldies and production values and styles that fitted the overall sound, with a slight guitar lean.

Heart, Birmingham listeners told us affectionately, was about cheesy songs, singalongs, and love songs; Galaxy was all about thump-thump. In time, after our concerted efforts, our station began to be described accurately as 'a mix', albeit a different mix from Heart, often demonstrated by listeners using outstretched open palms: 'A bit of this and a bit of that.' It was refreshing to see research suggest the understanding of our music proposition was growing although perceptions remained a battle, with our brand, confused by age, fighting against beautifully orchestrated sexy, newer competition.

More focus groups were convened, including the evening spent with male Heart listeners in their thirties who seemed blissfully ignorant of Heart's female targeting. Despite the pink promotions, the power ballads and the shoe giveaways, one muscular construction site worker with a bulging stomach claimed it was aimed at people just like him. Therein lay the success of that brand.

Our investors craved 'measurables', with the key statistic being the audience numbers published by Radio Joint Audience Research (RAJAR). Four times a year, our management team would gather in my office for the ritual of downloading the latest spreadsheets of figures as they filtered through. Imagine getting your GCSE results every three months. Faux cheeriness would belie the tension as we waited for the clock to tick round to the arrival of digits which would determine just how painful the next couple of days would be.

In sizeable markets such as ours, an unlucky set of audience figures could easily make a six-figure difference to revenues and blow the budgets apart. The specific implication of our operating solely in a single region was that any negative variances were not offset by positive ones elsewhere. Our observation was that results in big cities like Birmingham and Manchester were becoming increasingly volatile and that frustration, I know, was shared by our rivals.

Whilst the hard-working, intelligent teams at RAJAR and their contractors quietly conceded the research methodology was under serious stress, the industry was in no rush to replace it with a system that would likely produce very different results at a higher cost.

Great listening figures were celebrated; there were smiling faces across our office and everyone had a spring in their step. Graphs were drawn in cheery colours, effortless press releases were drafted and drink flowed the following evening in a neighbouring pub.

When the news was bad, however, I would fail to sleep as I prepared to deliver the disappointing audience figures to agitated staff the following morning – a gig akin to Theresa May speaking at her 2017 general election count. Anxious eyes would stare as I tried to deliver a positive, yet honest, message to a team that had worked its hardest to deliver success. The sales team would leave the room, fearful of their next appointment and missing the monthly revenue target; the marketing team would wonder why on earth they annoyed their friends and family by working every weekend at station events that seemingly made scant difference; the presenters would prepare for four hours in a studio feeling that no one loved them any more.

In the ensuing days, as I mined the data for a handful of positive titbits, barrack room programmers with alternative strategies for running the radio station would strut about, crowing that they had been right all along.

51

SEASON'S GREETINGS

As Christmas approaches, hard-working programmers in desolate tinselled offices wear silly hats and don't-disturb-me faces. Not only do they have to look after the programming for the following day, they need to plan the entire festive fortnight with military precision.

Atypical presenters are set to host atypical programmes between atypical news bulletins emanating from atypical places. What could possibly go wrong? And will there be anyone around to help when it does?

Is the three o'clock news on Boxing Day a network bulletin or a local one? Does Lisa know how to put herself on air and take the service out of the network feed? Has she got a zapper to get her in the car park? Will the breakfast show need more songs scheduled in each hour, given that the double act has been sliced in two and there's no one to talk to?

Newsrooms are busy inventing the news in advance for the lonely reporters on duty between Christmas and New Year. The bulletins will return, but the news won't.

Programmers identify who's remaining in the neighbourhood, in preparation for the inevitable Boxing Day call from a hoarse presenter who claims to be ill. You try to sound sympathetic and tolerant, as you face the prospect of ringing everyone on your emergency list, but you don't quite pull it off.

Meanwhile, life gets a little quieter for the sales executives. After a frantic flurry seeing off December's targets and making a good start on the January takings, their self-made clients have disappeared to their overseas holiday homes. In the sales office, it's time for banter, decanter and Secret Santa.

Boxing Day 2009 will remain with me forever. One of my programme directors called to say there'd been a 'bit of a problem'. When the phone rings on Boxing Day, you know that the phrase 'a bit of a problem' will likely be a delicious British understatement.

It transpired that presenter Tom Binns had not been entirely respectful to the Queen, or to several listeners who had pointed this out to him.

Tom is now known for his TV exploits and stand-up comedy. He'd also had some early history with commercial radio in Birmingham, so he'd seemed a decent appointment for a weekend show. We were looking for a few programmes to spice up the output and we thought he'd get talked about. He certainly did.

He was on the rota for a Christmas Day afternoon show. That's a lonely time, even on the biggest stations, with the presenter often alone trying to conjure up on-air Christmas spirit. With national news bulletins fed from the national news agency IRN, there is not even a fellow journalist around with whom to pull a cracker.

As three o'clock struck, Tom put up the fader and crossed to the latest news bulletin. However, instead of the anticipated pithy update, the audio feed was that of the Queen's Speech. In the midst of Tom's irreverent show, and much to his surprise, Her Majesty then launched into her traditional Christmas message to the Commonwealth. It had been a particularly worrying year, and the Queen began in an earnest tone by paying tribute to our forces in Afghanistan.

In common with many other stations of our format, it had not been intended that we carry the speech. Rather than make the best of a bad job and stick with it, as I would have preferred, Tom chose to fade the Queen out, with his own commentary: 'That's the Queen there. Two words: boring and boring. That squeaky voice, what's with that? I mean surely by now – you know it's 2009, nearly 2010 now – why doesn't she speak with a normal voice?'

Unsurprisingly, some listeners got in touch to question the wisdom of his remarks. 'The texts have gone mental,' said Tom. Warming to his theme, he then suggested that the only reason we still had a royal family was because of tourism, adding that France had beheaded their royal family and yet tourists still appeared to visit. He concluded the ensuing link by suggesting that maybe our royal family should suffer the same fate.

Whilst some listeners, maybe high on Christmas spirit, found the whole thing very amusing, others did not. One such listener, Joyce, was duly dubbed 'a stupid cow'. Another suggested Tom was a disgrace and that he would 'do us all a favour if he were hit by a roadside bomb', a remark to which Tom, understandably, took exception.

I rated and liked Tom, but felt that we had to act quickly. In the light of the remarks on and off air to listeners, alongside the questionable comments in the middle of a speech paying tribute to those who'd lost their lives, I concluded we'd have to let him go and called him to let him know we would no longer need his services in the future. He didn't agree with my verdict, but it was a professional conversation.

This episode came fifteen months after the famous Russell Brand 'Sachsgate' prank call that was broadcast on the BBC and that had attracted front page coverage. Tom suggested to me that the exposure from his outburst would likely do his profile good. I preferred to keep the episode quiet, for both our sakes. Inwardly, however, I knew that a news story involving the Queen at Christmas would likely excite journalists.

Over my reheated turkey, I began a damage limitation exercise. A carefully drafted letter of apology was despatched to Buckingham Palace and a pre-emptive note sent to Ofcom, who would doubtless have upheld a complaint on grounds of offence. I prepared my alibis and crossed my fingers.

We had just about got through the next day when the calls from journalists began. First the calls were local, then national, then from around the Commonwealth and finally from all around the world. On Google, I could see BRMB coming up in searches in all manner of languages.

It is commonplace in radio that more people complain about something they are told about than those who heard it originally. The story which appeared to gain momentum, however, was one implying that we had taken Tom off air simply for criticising the monarchy. In fact, as I had made clear to him, there are many places where a debate about the monarchy can be aired with passion, but Christmas Day, in the middle of the Queen's Speech on deaths in Afghanistan, was not one of them. In trying to save Tom's blushes, given that I always try to protect creative talent, regardless of where the blame lies, I had also not mentioned publicly my worries about how listeners had been treated. The public conclusion was, therefore, that I was simply a lily-livered royalist who revelled in censorship.

Emails arrived, by the hundred, hurling abuse at my decision. I replied patiently from my kitchen table to every missive. When the world is telling you how stupid you are, it does get to you after a while; being in the firing line is a lonely place.

I was also instructed by the chief executive to draft a briefing note to our new investors. Whilst we know these things happen in our crazy radio world, I suspect it was a fascinating crash course over the bread sauce for the top brass at the Lloyds Bank investment arm.

Crises like these, however, are good for the soul, and life in radio is full of challenging episodes. My advice to my teams has always been: deal with things decisively, wait – and matters will blow over. Today's crisis is usually forgotten three months on.

I gather Tom now relates this tale from his perspective at his stand-up gigs, and I imagine it's a very entertaining performance. On reflection, I did what bosses must do sometimes. Tom did what creative talent does sometimes. He's now enjoying success and I wish him well. It is radio's job to take measured risks. I'd rather do that than risk never hearing brilliance.

No one complained to Ofcom and Buckingham Palace wrote to thank me for my letter.

52

PENNIES FROM HEAVEN

The early morning outside broadcast from a Midlands university seemed a very good idea. The institution was keen to boast what an exciting place it was and the sales executive who sealed the deal considered the venture an excellent creative solution. After all, the client would witness the station's cheery breakfast show personalities live on their premises – and the sales person would hit their target.

Breakfast shows, however, have an annoying habit of being broadcast early in the morning. Students have a habit of sleeping. Not a lot happens early in the morning in a university building. As dawn broke, our presenters and producers duly rolled up with trunks of broadcast equipment and colourful branding, only to discover the university's open day did not begin until ten o'clock – an hour after the end of the programme.

Not for the first time, the team prepared to make a silk purse out of a sow's ear and do a proficient job on air to convey all the excitement that was not yet happening. The task was rendered more difficult by the locked door to the room with the necessary broadcast lines installed. It could be opened, but only by the chap who was expected to roll up at about nine o'clock.

The post-show debrief was a simple affair, with the resolve never to do anything like that ever again and to ignore, in future, any assurances from an intermediary that guests would be supplied, action would happen and all would be well on the day.

A year later, the same smiling sales executive rushed to the programming office on the last Friday of the month, desperate to hit their target, with an order form to sign off for an alarmingly similar outside broadcast. The client, it seems, wanted an outside broadcast and nothing else would suffice. Oddly, clients tend to find such isolated tangible activity more appealing than ongoing on-air messaging, but are often disappointed when roaring crowds akin to a Radio 1 roadshow do not turn up for the OB at the special offer weekend at their car dealership. The best radio is not particularly wonderful to watch.

Expecting the programming team and the sales team on any commercial radio station to live in harmony is rather like expecting leading figures on the Brexit debate to sit in a room and emerge with a sensible consensus. From my experience around the UK and Europe, no matter how many drunken team-building sessions are arranged, the two sets of staff return to their habitats next day, wholly convinced that the other side is lazy, mad or both.

There are, of course, exceptional stations where dialogue is refreshingly cordial and specific individuals appear to share a deep understanding of both areas, but this is rare. Sleeping together is usually the explanation for the latter.

Let's concede that presenters are a strange breed. They live in an air-conditioned cell, isolated from the rest of society and talking about themselves to people they don't know; giving all of themselves for hours each day and emerging spent. Their future is only certain for a matter of months. They work silly hours, with rarely a full weekend or bank holiday off, and are surrounded by people who want their job. They are constantly being judged on every word that comes out of their mouths and that judgement, when delivered, feels hugely personal. All this can result in insecurity and paranoia, which is often self-medicated with a dose of swaggering braggadocio.

What programme staff often fail to understand, however, is the wholly different pressures sales executives must endure – not least having to dress smartly every day. Their work is utterly measurable: they bring in revenue or they don't. Their lifestyles are built on an expectation of hitting targets, so when they don't, bills cannot be paid.

Sales staff spend every day of their lives being pleasant to people who they wouldn't necessarily mix with were they given a choice; they are required to take an unhealthy interest in their clients' lives, laugh at their jokes and tolerate the intolerable. When they tell people about their job, they are not greeted with the same sort of impressed expression that citing an on-air post attracts. Being an excellent sales person is a rare gift, yet, in our odd country, it fails to generate the respect it deserves.

For every story of an overenthusiastic listener a presenter can relate, a radio sales executive can cite equally odd behaviour from a client. I remember a client who was desperate to forsake his family in favour of a close relationship with one of our sales team – the attraction most certainly was not reciprocated. Then there was the poor sales executive being summoned in the evening to present a proposition to a client, who merrily sat in his dressing gown eating his dinner and watching the TV as she wheeled out her presentation. In local sales, clients are often determined, self-made individuals who like to do things their way. Business is gut driven and the deal you thought you could count on last week suddenly falls away, for no apparent reason. Sales people need to get very accustomed to the word 'no'.

In my earliest days in commercial radio, these two very different programming and commercial worlds rarely needed to collide. Presenters only visited the sales office for leftover sandwiches from client entertaining.

During my time at Orion, Ofcom consulted upon further generous changes to its advertising rules. As 2010 closed, the suits at Southwark Bridge cracked open another bottle of branded sparkling water to celebrate the sweeping away of decades of wordy compliance rules, being persuaded to the sensible view that, provided listeners were made aware of the fact that someone had paid for something to be included, we could largely do as we liked.

We embraced the potential this relaxation allowed, as our scale and agility permitted. My dream as a programmer was that we might replace some overlong ad breaks with something more interesting and, as a shareholder, I anticipated we could charge more for it.

The creation of dull contests as vehicles for sponsorship became no longer necessary; brands could instead be included at will, and embedded into an entertaining programme storyline. The new Ofcom rules, however, demanded that we signal the imminent commercial mention to ensure listeners could distinguish it from a personal presenter endorsement. Their suggested method was to use the daft phrase 'our friends at…' Commercial radio stations accordingly announced an enviable amount of new friendships. In truth, I believe this phrasing is as meaningless to the average listener as the letter 'P' denoting product placement on TV, but the device satisfied the regulator and afforded much welcome scope.

Ideas for this new 'brand integration' flowed from the endless 'brainstorms', which became a regular feature in all our diaries.

Experience suggests that alliterative or rhyming names for activity were particularly welcome. Radio wisdom suggests that, for most content ideas, the name comes first, with the detail determined later. I suspect Real Radio's 'Risk it for a Biscuit' was one such example.

The doggie wedding was one example of our teams rising to the challenge. When a vet sought a creative idea to spread its name, we suggested that we find a mate for a dog and then marry the two dogs. A suitably patient dog that seemed to need a partner was identified, together with a co-operative owner who would put up with our rigmarole. Various suitors were proposed and date nights for the canine couples arranged. I recall putting in a call to my favourite restaurant asking whether we might use her venue for photographs and the dog was also the subject of an arty photo shoot at a local cinema. The idea culminated in a formal wedding ceremony in the precinct adjacent to our premises.

Whilst the client will hopefully recall the positive impact of the promotion on her business, we remember the wedding cake made of dog food which was carelessly left in the staff kitchen without being duly marked.

In answer to another brief from an amusement park, a record-breaking attempt for dodgem car-riding was staged. A clever twist suggested by my programmers was that two presenters attempt the record, so their natural rivalry would keep each sufficiently interested during the cold dark hours. Sparky from the evening programme and Giuliano from the breakfast show admirably did their best and the latter stole the title by enduring almost twenty-seven hours in the hard-seated silly vehicle.

Another simple example came from Foxy and Giuliano, then hosting the Birmingham breakfast show, as they related an incidental, highly amusing anecdote about a visit to the sponsors of their daily Thousand Pound Minute contest. Amusing, relatable content followed, which served the client well. There are numerous other examples of genuinely creative responses to client briefs and I am proud of the work we did as an industry trendsetter.

The power of these devices was evident following an impressive series of commercial content at our East Midlands station, Gem, for a local timber merchants. A programme plot was developed in which overconfident breakfast presenter Sam was challenged to build a tree house. In general focus groups amongst casual listeners some months later, the activity was repeatedly cited, together with the client's name, as a piece of radio the listeners had genuinely enjoyed.

Other media are now also dreaming up innovative ideas for their clients on TV: from the *Coronation Street* meerkat activity devised by Zenith, CTM and VCCP, to ITV Creative's 'knitted ad break'. Podcasters who initially adopted the simple 'spot ad' now realise that a mention by the trusted presenter within the content can be much more powerful. As we compete against ever more imaginative offerings from other media, radio will need to continue to innovate beyond traditional ad spots.

Similarly, client brands will need to accept, just as they do with their social media presences, that some degree of freedom and trust must be given to their media channels, so that ideas can be tailored to audiences by the people who understand them best. Word of mouth is said to be the best recommendation for any product and no client can control every word of that incomparable communication.

53

NEWS JUST IN

Journalists are often a very particular sort of animal: serious, intelligent critical operators who just happen to pin their work on the radio platform. There are notable exceptions, but some journalists would agree that they could be just as happy on TV or online, and may not have listened back voluntarily to a bulletin they presented since their college days.

They are too sensible to catch the silly radio obsession; their hunger is for news; the thrill of chasing the story; the excitement of the exclusive. It would be a dangerous generalisation to suggest that they are a more cynical bunch than presenters, but one cannot expect the very people you hire to hold public figures to account and to see through glib press releases, simply to swallow jolly internal company announcements with a cheery smile.

During the balmy summer nights of 2011, widespread rioting and looting broke out in Birmingham, after a violent night in London following the death of Mark Duggan, who had been shot dead by police. Three men were killed in the West Midlands and shots were fired at police. For journalists, this was a big night.

Our stations were on alert as we prepared to cover what might happen and to keep our staff safe. Matters did not get off to a good start when a member of the commercial sales team sent round an all-staff afternoon email, repeating rumours that a huge swathe of troublemakers were descending and the city was effectively about to shut down. Staff scurried home. What can one do as a manager except allow those who are concerned about their safety to leave?

As night fell, the shops, restaurants and bars nearby pulled down their shutters. The usual evening laughter and chinking glasses were absent. One could just hear the ominous muffled growl of a mob of rebels in the distance. We prised open a window and tried to dangle a mic into the warm night air.

Sometimes, being in the media means you are left alone in any dispute and seen as an impartial observer. The mood on this occasion, however, suggested that media operations would themselves be a target. In Leeds, the BBC radio car was overturned and in Birmingham we knew the gangs were making for the BBC's premises in the Mailbox, which was just yards away from us.

Contingency arrangements were finely tuned, with plans A, B and C, dependent on both the extent to which we felt coverage should dominate our programming and how safe we felt in our building. Plan C would mean evacuation to our leafy Worcestershire premises whilst matters calmed down. Our chief executive was conveniently on holiday, so any judgements appeared to be mine.

I felt wary, despite being insulated from this insurrection by a couple of sets of double doors and the presence of a security guard. Several of our journalists, however, were anxious to get closer to the action. The sad truth about journalists is that they become excited about drama. Theirs is a compartmentalised existence. These characters are as sympathetic as anyone else when they need to be in real life, but, once on the job, you witness them grow in stature as adverse situations develop.

If you wanted to cast a throbbing journalist in a drama, you'd likely choose someone like our newsroom's Dan Dawson. As a kid, he probably won every argument with his teachers and, had he been in the business a generation ago, he'd likely have been the one throwing a typewriter intolerantly out of the window or screaming at his colleagues in the way no HR department would now tolerate. His nose for a story was superb and he was more than happy to take risks to get to the bottom of things.

This night was no exception. Dan and a few burly colleagues wanted to see the secrets this turbulent city held, as society's sediment was stirred to the surface.

I recall a midnight health and safety briefing with those about to leave the building. I duly read out the precautions which our hostile environment reporting team needed to observe, and agreed they could leave the building to report, but with certain limitations. Dan nodded and said all he knew I needed to hear. Frankly, I was glad we didn't argue. He's bigger than me.

'Hostile reporting' is a term particularly familiar to overseas correspondents as they wend their way into war zones. As the BBC's Robin Lustig explained to me recently, the BBC conduct lengthy courses where correspondents can even be brought to tears as potential risks are illustrated to a serious degree of reality.

Our team not only conducted themselves safely, they fed back some powerful audio. In one memorable clip, looters making off with electrical spoils from a smashed Currys window were questioned by a fearless Dan about their motives. The lack of a meaningful answer spoke volumes about the real justification for the disturbance. There wasn't any.

In radio, breakfast time is king. You know that whatever the timing of any incident, it is the early morning reports which will be most widely consumed. Although Dan had worked through the night, he was intent still on delivering the breakfast news bulletins. Whilst rival correspondents had retired to their beds, Dan delivered his eight o'clock morning bulletin with the conviction of a man who knew what he was talking about.

Dan's coverage and the efforts of all the news team that night was to earn a nomination for a Sony Radio Award, then the highest honour our industry could bestow. In the face of well-resourced BBC local competition, we rightly celebrated that achievement.

I know I should remember my West Midlands newsroom for its medals, its impeccable contemporary delivery, its quality journalism, its inventive programming and its truly brilliant leader in the majestic self-confessed 'biker chick', Vicky Breakwell, but I confess other moments stand out more in my memory.

There was the time when one bulletin comprised spells of silence, punctuated periodically by the voices on inserted reports, but no newsreader introducing them. Hurrying to check matters afterwards, it transpired that the journalist had omitted to push up the microphone fader to turn himself on as he spoke. What's more, he had not noticed he wasn't live as he had not troubled to wear headphones. He didn't like hearing his own voice, he later explained.

On another memorable occasion, one tired journalist had enjoyed a late night on the town and had chosen to sleep at the station, so that he might be on hand promptly next morning for his shift. Preparing to bed himself down comfortably in the corner of the studio, he decided to turn down the annoying music which was keeping him awake. Unfortunately, he turned the music down for everybody else too as he took us off air.

54

SET YOURSELF FREE

At an industry conference dinner, after a few glasses of wine, I started to reminisce embarrassingly with a time-served commercial radio figure. One by one, over the chewy leg of lamb, we recalled the full list of the first batch of the nineteen commercial stations. To the puzzled younger onlookers, our game appeared to resemble 'Mornington Crescent', the improvisational game featured on the BBC Radio 4 comedy panel show *I'm Sorry I Haven't a Clue*. The nonsense deteriorated as we then sought to recall the names of the first nineteen managing directors.

Those stations with their odd logos had a place in our hearts. Listening in had helped shape the rest of our lives. And, here I was, years later, playing a pivotal role in some of those stations whose very names spelt excitement and '70s sunshine summers. Those who knew our team at Orion knew our heritage and expected us to play our role in keeping the dream alive.

The last thing they expected was that we would engineer the end of the BRMB, Beacon, Mercia and Wyvern names.

The competitive backdrop was changing around us. Chris Moyles at Radio 1 had established a loyal breakfast following, and BBC Radio 2 had evolved with enviable skill from its cardigan days to a mainstream offering, with Evans, Wright and Mayo offering a warm welcome to those over thirty-five. In the commercial field, the Smooth brand, emerging from the old Saga stations, was now a well-programmed, soft adult contemporary and oldies mix, operated by Global Radio. That station's audience now butted neatly onto the greying end of Heart's demographic. At the other end of Heart territory, Galaxy had become Capital and was also performing well in Birmingham, spreading its format wings into mainstream young adult territory.

Our commercial competitors now covered the waterfront with well-defined brands, leaving no space for our 'one size fits all' station with a confused brand definition.

Our corner shop stations were also losing out on national revenue, by not being part of any recognised national network. London agencies, attending to the marketing needs of national clients, could buy radio exposure with ease across swathes of the UK from Global Radio or Bauer. Whilst we were well represented by the Global Radio sales team in London, our stations did not readily fit with their portfolio and, as they tidied up their stations' branding, our relative position deteriorated.

There was also a geographic challenge. London agencies knew the Birmingham market and found it attractive as England's second city. They did not attach the same importance to our neighbouring station, Beacon in Wolverhampton and the Black Country. BRMB, therefore, was in high demand and sold at a healthy price; Beacon fared less well. The situation was perverse given the huge overlap between the two stations. A BRMB listening hour commanded much more revenue than a Beacon listening hour, even though listeners tuning into the respective stations might live next door to each other in the overlapping town of Walsall.

The challenge was not new. When comparing national

revenue for Beacon and BRMB, *Music Week* magazine in 1976 reported: 'BRMB attracted the lion's share of national revenue.'

One of Beacon's early managing directors, Peter Tomlinson, suggested:

> When looking at the West Midlands conurbation on a national map, advertisers would see the name Birmingham prominently displayed, in larger letters than any of the other towns, including Wolverhampton. Seeing that BRMB was Birmingham's ILR station they therefore believed it provided for the whole conurbation, and therefore chose it in preference to Beacon.[43]

By the time of our ownership, in the twenty-first century, at last, the two formerly warring stations were in common ownership. We calculated that a greater Birmingham offering to London advertisers, under a single brand name, encompassing all listening to our services would equalise the benefits from the two stations in the populous hub of our region.

Marketing had also proved a challenge. Our rivals had ensured that their West Midlands stations had benefited from unprecedented levels of TV and poster advertising. The finely tuned Heart campaigns were now supplemented by a prolonged Capital campaign. The Kerrang! brand continued to benefit from its magazine profile and Smooth was now a Silk Cut-coloured, simple brand offering which was being well expressed.

Whilst we had come close to commissioning a TV campaign for BRMB, it would necessarily have been aired across the West Midlands ITV region, with huge wastage, as it would be seen by puzzled potential Mercia listeners in deepest Warwickshire. If we were to derive maximum value from our marketing investment, our four stations had to broadcast under a single name. The name we chose was Free Radio. Free to do whatever we wanted.

Whilst frequent advice to businesses is to zig when others zag, we felt that our position with separately branded stations had become untenable. Our thoroughly sensible strategy, which we had decided upon a couple of years before, was no longer so sensible.

The topic of brand change arose during an impromptu conversation in my office that I recall distinctly. Phil and I were chatting and we drifted from minor to major matters: 'Maybe we should just change our names too?' The unthinkable had been said. From that moment, it became a topic for real debate. Ultimately, we knew that for all the huge emotional attachment we had to the old station names, life would probably be easier if we adopted a more cohesive approach.

Whilst we all had experience of the mechanics of brand changes, not least the recent successful move to Gem 106 in the East Midlands, to change the names of what had become forty-year-old friends to our listeners was a different matter. Listeners were aghast, with the angriest response reserved for the change at our oldest station, BRMB.

'A piece of Birmingham heritage is set to vanish following the shock decision to change the name of BRMB after almost 40 years', reported the *Birmingham Mail*, citing also a Facebook campaign that had begun named 'Keep BRMB and Orion Stations as they are'.

'"This is a very strange decision indeed," observed Wolverhampton University's senior media lecturer.'[44] A BBC article bore the following headline: 'The decision taken by a West Midlands radio group to move away from its highly recognisable brand names after 40 years has struck some as bizarre.'[45]

The brand change project was a painstaking job, for which we were well equipped. However, long working days were not helped by returning home tired at night, only to savour the online forums that declared us all truly mad. I recall Phil Riley storming into my office one morning, hands raised, shouting that he was never, ever going to look at online comments again: 'They just don't understand,' he declared.

Admittedly, in our eagerness to disseminate our message, we'd released an early version of our new logo, in a shocking shade of pink, prompting one listener to comment online: 'Looks like a brand of Tampons FFS.'

Former long-serving BRMB presenter Les Ross was more stoic: 'Times change and you just have to get over it. Unfortunately for me, it is just another thing from my past that has gone into the past.'[46]

We'd like to have kissed those who expressed a more helpful view:

> Personally I don't see what all the fuss is about. There is [*sic*] clearly some sound commercial reasons for this decision. There have been reactions like this over other brand name changes over the years and they soon go away. The name? Is it so bad? Cheap and giveaway are not the first things that spring to mind for me. Isn't it more about free thinking? Feeling free?

As we moved through the change, our language showed deference to our past. We talked of retiring the old station names and I even volunteered for a podcast in which I allowed myself to be questioned by a sane sceptic. For some months, there was even a BRMB memorial room in our otherwise meticulously rebranded premises, decked out with fading memorabilia.

Unlike Capital, whose declared strategy in its opening moments was as a 'new radio station', we assured listeners on air: 'Nothing's changed – just the name.' The place in our hearts for our history was also clear on the fortieth anniversary of BRMB's launch in 2014, when we threw a fitting party for our childhood sweetheart.

On air and in our consumer-facing marketing, however, our focus was single-mindedly our proud new green Free Radio brand, as we seized the chance to create a clear contemporary identity.

We felt we had taken a difficult yet sensible decision at a time and place in British radio history. We knew it felt odd to listeners. On a personal level, it felt odd to us too.

55

THE HAMSTER

The meeting with our creative agency edged to a friendly close, and we patted ourselves on the back having created a decent launch TV campaign for the new Free Radio brand. As we shuffled our papers, one canny person from their side waved his finger and warned: 'You do know if you go with this campaign, you'll be associated with a hamster – for ever.' He was correct.

TV campaigns for radio stations in big markets had been tactical for many years, with stations buying spots to push towards exciting eight o'clock morning listening appointments, for attractions such as 'The Bong Game' or 'The Birthday Game'. Campaigns were relatively low budget in terms of both media spend and ad creative – and they served their purpose.

Polished brand advertising was a relatively recent arrival, as the major new stations sought to claim market share from their rivals and echo their brand awareness levels. Quality work from Galaxy, Magic and Heart and remarkable work from Capital set the benchmark, as did BBC radio's enviable TV promotional campaigns. In a world where our medium's promise to listeners sat alongside increasingly dextrous offerings from other entertainment media, we had to prove our worth. Similarly, in representing this centenarian medium to its clients, radio really needed to look sexy.

As we prepared to enter the fray, marketing Free to the 4 million potential listeners on our West Midlands patch, our brief was educated by yet more research. We knew music simply had to be the driver, yet the tone had to be less serious than that of Capital. We had to appear closer to our audience and suggest that we didn't take ourselves too seriously. The answer, provided by the Midlands-based agency Connect, was a hamster. One which sprang to life in its owner's absence – and danced to our music like no one was watching.

The concept was debated long and hard, with ideas refined and re-presented. As we, half a dozen grown-ups, met in the chief executive's office yet again, with light streaming through the Broad Street windows, having an earnest conversation about a hamster, the madness of our industry was apparent.

Just before we'd relaunched, a TV company had enquired whether we would be prepared to be observed as part of a fly-on-the-wall documentary. Whilst the exposure held some appeal, we chose to decline politely. Subsequently, each time a this-is-ridiculous moment occurred, which is relatively common in most radio stations, we'd wryly observe that it would have made a great scene for the documentary and imagined the Geordie narration that would have explained the episode.

The hamster TV ad was a simple concept, but one which demanded a deal of care in its production, not least because it necessitated using a real hamster. (I'm unsure whether directing Katy Perry on the Capital ad was more or less trouble than our furry friend.) There are more rules about working with animals than you would imagine and our hipster brand manager, Andy Price, supported the process diligently, calling on professional hamster handlers. The dancing was created by alarmingly expensive computer-generated imagery for which we turned to the same team who had worked on the film *War Horse*.

There's nothing quite like watching *Coronation Street* knowing that the ad for your radio station is going to appear during the break, although it's not a cheap hobby. As our debut spots aired, social media took the little hamster to its heart. Mention after mention of the cute little animal popped up, attributed to our correct new station name. Viewers grabbed their iPhones to seize screen shots and upload videos to YouTube. Aside from the painful TV spend, the viral value of the campaign was enormous. We should not have been surprised: the ad had been tested by the team at Millward Brown, who research many big brand TV ads in all sectors. Their conclusions suggested that this would be a particularly memorable campaign, scoring amongst the best of class. They were correct. The real proof came in later focus groups, where the ad was cited time and time again, with an affectionate smile, long after our ad budget had run out.

We had created something fresh and new, both on and off air. In the words of award-winning presenter Jo Russell it just 'felt better'; and Birmingham breakfast presenter, John 'Foxy' Fox, suggested he felt that inappropriate comparisons to the audiences, styles and presenters of a bygone era were no longer being drawn.

We had created an influential new radio brand for a key UK region and I struggled home with cardboard boxes of old branding and random grimy merchandise to add to my collection. They were now history.

56

RADIO TITANS

Few broadcasters enjoy such stature that their passing would be mentioned, from the heart, across all stations of all formats. Terry Wogan was the exception. Even the commercial radio industry, for which he had never worked, save for a few voice-overs, despatched an official message of condolence.

His home station of BBC Radio 2 broke the news in a bulletin in January 2016: 'Bob Shennan, the Controller of Radio 2, said "Terry established himself as one of the greatest and most popular radio hosts this country has ever heard".'

Mark Goodier followed the shock news in a fitting, instinctive programme, in which he simply reflected the mood of the listeners. In due course, we anticipated an immaculately produced tribute programme with reflections of celebrities mixed with clips of his performances and favourite Clifford T. Ward songs, but this was something far simpler. The official tribute programme would be the funeral. Mark's well-judged programme that day was the equivalent of a prompt phone call from a friend to say: 'I'm sorry – and I'm thinking of you.'

Mark told me: 'I kind of instinctively knew what we had to do. I knew I had to let the audience write the script.'[47]

Terry was remembered so fondly because he had simply done well what radio does best.

His whimsical storytelling was profound. Tales founded on fact would be embellished with a Wogan flight of fancy. A few words from a listener on Basildon Bond turned to gold in the hands of the master. A river of vocabulary flowed effortlessly from his wryly smiling face. He recognised that radio's intimate conversation continues in a listener's head: 'People think when they listen to radio. TV eschews thought, your thinking is done for you.'

Terry became an amusing, eccentric uncle muttering from behind his newspaper. He spoke to you and you alone. In the words of BBC Radio 4 *Today* presenter John Humphrys: 'Terry liked his audience – and they liked him. He wasn't broadcasting to them, he was talking to them.'

That connection serves to explain why listeners' grief was so intense on his passing. Each listener in each corner of Britain had lost a friend. To say that you'll miss someone is the greatest tribute of all.

A Facebook commenter posted: 'Such very sad news, the world will be a lesser place without you Terry. Will miss you X.' Terry's delivery always impressed: 'I can impose my own pausing, my own timing.' The Wogan pause meant that this high-earner took home almost as much for saying nothing as for saying something.

Broadcasters only reach their true potential when they can be themselves. Terry was himself on air. We acknowledge we witnessed a daily amplification of the most likeable and entertaining parts of his character, but we certainly know it was him. Radio exposes fakes like no other medium.

Despite his measured and common BBC grumbles, he reserved unconditional love and pride for his Auntie: 'It's the greatest broadcaster the world has ever seen.' Terry protested that his was an easy job, whilst quietly recognising the skill involved.

A crackly performance on the BBC Light Programme, 'down the line' from Ireland in 1966, was when the voice of Michael Terence Wogan was heard on the BBC for the first time. He had applied to the Corporation beforehand, only to be turned down by BBC 2 TV controller David Attenborough, who advised they already had one bloke from Dublin. Of course, Attenborough assured Terry limply that he'd pass the letter on to the head of presentation: 'If a suitable vacancy should occur, he will get in touch with you directly.'[48]

Terry's voice deepened and lilted a little less in the ensuing decades, but he was quickly to emerge as one of the radio industry's favourite performers.

After serving loyally on major BBC shows, Terry ascended the Radio 2 breakfast throne in 1972, entertaining the nation with his ramblings. Although television was to wag its beckoning finger for a brief brown-suited spell in the mid-'80s, he returned home to radio in 1993.

As the entertainment world changed beyond recognition, Terry continued to rule. By the end of his stint on the early show in 2009, he was attracting almost a fifth of all breakfast radio listening and almost 8 million weekly listeners.

The delivery of his famous farewell breakfast programme was a lesson to all broadcasters. I gather he was annoyed at the rabble of assorted bigwigs gathering in the adjacent control room to witness the end of an era. They were not even treated to a passing fond glance; his eyes were only for his listener.

Replaying the piece was to serve as a fitting farewell to life on his passing six years later. Just as it is said that sports stars die twice, so do broadcasters.

'They'll probably have to drag me away from the microphone when they decide to elbow me. I shall cling to it. There'll be a lot of tears and screaming.'[49]

Although many local markets also have characters who are worthy of recognition on their home patch, there are likely only a dozen true national radio greats whose legacy has been etched into radio's timeline forever.

The presenter who stepped into Wogan's shoes on the Radio 2 breakfast show, Chris Evans, would likely qualify. In his Lancashire youth, he hung around the Piccadilly Plaza until they let him in, soon speeding his way onto the national stage when he was appointed to the Radio 1 breakfast show. Matthew Bannister, who'd recognised his talent at the BBC local station in London, saw him in the '90s as the sort of character who would make a difference to the refocused Radio 1.

Whilst Chris's face had become popular on TV, radio was his natural home, and Matthew recalled to me how Chris had reacted when broached about assuming this coveted breakfast show: 'You don't have to sell this to me … because it makes me want to go to the toilet every time I think about it.'[50]

The programme was to last just two years, ending in a difficult fashion in 1997, with Chris's behaviour becoming increasingly unpredictable, and his infamous demand to work a four-day week. He was to return to national radio ten months later, assuming the breakfast mantle at the UK's original Virgin Radio. I recall sitting in the studio during one edition of the show, watching this ringmaster conduct his circus. Whoever held the title 'producer', Chris was clearly in charge.

Just months later, in an unusual move for a presenter, he bought the station, with support from an investment partner, snatching it away from Capital's grasp. Following its subsequent sale to SMG, which created much personal wealth for him, Chris was sacked from his breakfast programme in 2001.

Commercial radio stations unite as a network only when arms are twisted vigorously. They did so in early 2005 for UK Radio Aid, raising money for the victims of the Asian tsunami. All usual local output was dropped, in favour of a twelve-hour network show dedicated to the cause, live from Leicester Square with some regional opt-outs.

The programme, aired on 268 radio stations, including the national Classic and Virgin, amassed a potential audience of over 20 million, and raised around £3 million. At short notice, the programming initiative attracted a variety of names from within the radio industry and impressively beyond. Radio names included Zoe Ball and Simon Bates and we witnessed the return, after his radio wilderness years, of Chris Evans.

The fundraiser served to rehabilitate Evans and speed him to a suitable berth at BBC Radio 2 later in the year. A weekend stint led to a drivetime show and, in 2010, he assumed the breakfast show crown from Wogan. The transition was managed with skill. Dad handed over the family business to the son he loves but worries about. Chris Evans is one of the radio greats, and whatever his future holds, he will be remembered.

Wogan aside, a running theme of great broadcasters is their ability to be sacked. Liverpool's remarkable Kenny Everett perfected the art. His original pirate radio home, Radio London, had taken exception to him coughing during cigarette commercials and being rudely irreverent about their usefully funded proselytising American religious programmes. At Radio 1, Kenny was moved on following a gag about the Minister of Transport's wife passing her driving test after a fiver had been slipped to the examiner.

As former Radio 1 controller Johnny Beerling explained to me about the presenter he loved, the reasons for Kenny's BBC sacking were a little more complex: 'He was told he wasn't to speak to the press without a press officer present, but he couldn't button his lip.'[51]

Kenny had honed his skills at Radio London, before making his way to the BBC proper and even acquiring his own studio where he could indulge his creative instincts. Following his sudden Radio 1 exit, he managed to scratch his broadcasting itch at some BBC local stations, with a series of programmes which have become collector's items. He was to turn up later at the new Capital Radio, where he rose to the breakfast show, and was then rehabilitated at BBC Radio 2. Capital's new oldies station then beckoned, but he left in 1994 after the announcement that he had AIDS. This hugely talented broadcaster, born as a fitting gift to radio on Christmas Day 1944, died in 1995 at the tragically early age of fifty.

The stations Kenny appeared on are a little irrelevant. His talents transcended his platforms. His vocal abilities, gift with words, imagination and production skills have never been rivalled. It is refreshing to see that as the years go by, he remains celebrated by fans old and new.

Many in the radio industry muse as to whether today's more considered approach, in both the BBC and commercial sectors, would accommodate such creative talent. I believe it would. Technology and platform are now no longer barriers to entry. Great talent at this moment is sitting in back bedrooms creating sophisticated quality content which it can disseminate with ease. The broadcast industry has already shown its readiness to harness new talent from such sources.

Risks are also still taken in mainstream radio. Creativity is about more than being shocking. It is about interesting ideas, approaches and topic treatments. BBC radio's themed approaches to covering major anniversaries have made much use of schedule flexibility and digital spin-offs; and Radio 4 chose to broadcast live birdsong overnight as part of International Dawn Chorus Day. Over on commercial radio, the very best breakfast shows to this day are a ready home for creative content and powerful engaging communication; and, in general terms, Chris Moyles and Iain Lee are certainly not the safest of performers.

Gifted and experienced programme management is essential if we are to retain the creativity and engagement which has become the hallmark of our medium. UK programmers hold the keys to our medium's future and must be able to identify and hone real talent, recognising the distinction between creativity and self-indulgence. They must afford promising individuals the time to grow and flourish in the right home, then coach them to perfection, and support them when they err.

In October 2008, two creative souls making some entertaining radio went a step too far. They were not the first to do so, and I hope they will not be the last. As BBC Radio 2 sought to carve out a less comfortable reputation, the station paired Jonathan Ross with Russell Brand, and a prank call was recorded on the answerphone of actor Andrew Sachs. The content of the call, which related to Andrew's granddaughter, was ill judged. We are told that, after recording, this content was duly referred up for clearance. I lay no blame, however, given that any busy radio manager will know how many tough decisions there are to make on any day – and night. It is easy to go with the flow, and trust.

The issue grew out of all proportion. Its fallout probably says more about the press, BBC management and culture, and the challenging relationship the BBC is inevitably going to have with its various 'stakeholders', than it says about Jonathan Ross or Russell Brand.

A more confident BBC could have closed the issue down with speed. Leaders who choose a career in radio should appreciate that this unpredictable organic thing called radio can go wrong. You make good and apologise, take instant remedial action and tell the press and public with conviction what you have done. They have naughty children too.

The greatest damage was the displacement of top presentation, production and management talent, together with years of resultant paranoia and a disproportionate compliance process. Staff at BBC local radio stations are now still required to listen through to any recorded programme before it is broadcast, even a specialist weekly trombone show.

The day we don't have presenters who risk going too far is the day we should fear we are hiring the wrong talent.

57

SETTING MYSELF FREE

The most common question asked of anyone in radio by bright-eyed wannabees is: 'How do I get into the business?' I used to reply with a smile: 'Don't ask me, I'm trying to get out.' It wasn't true, but it helped to avoid answering the unanswerable.

From the excitement at the outset, a matter on the agenda of every board meeting of any well-run private equity-backed company is how they will manage their exit. Given they have indulged your dreams by funding the acquisition of your toy, they are rather keen to realise a return on their investment through disposal, by whatever route, when the time seems right. Accordingly, they ensure that every dribble in the game takes them closer to that goal.

Our backers for the Orion Media commercial radio venture in the Midlands, LDC, were excellent business partners, and our chairman, Geoff Percy, former CEO of skincare brand Simple, was a professional and supportive colleague. Having arrived from businesses driven by a range of interesting entrepreneurs, it was a welcome contrast for me to be working with calm yet enthusiastic evidence-driven investors. It fascinated me how LDC's canny representatives on our board always managed to ask exactly the right questions about the mad entertainment world they had just entered, not least because they had probably just left another meeting after discussing in equal depth the widgets produced by another of their investments. This is perhaps why they are wealthier than me.

I suspect our investors scratched their heads about our divining of the RAJAR audience figures. We would manage expectations, cautiously predicting a worrying result and then produce contradictory storming figures and vice versa. Had one of the more prosaic businesses in their portfolio predicted sales up or down 25 per cent, with the operators not knowing the likelihood of that change even the day before it was registered, I suspect they would have got short shrift. But this was radio.

The range of outcomes for the sale of any radio business is manifold. There are several potential buyers, such as existing radio operations; a diversifying media company; new blood, such as the acquisition by Global had been; a foreign buyer, as the Times of India had been; selling on equity to a secondary investor; management buy-outs and -ins – the list goes on. Then there's the matter of whether one sells the whole outfit or splits it. And there are outside influences which may affect the key matter of timing. I learned many years ago that no outcome is ever certain until ink has dried on the paper. And even if the outcome appears obvious once a deal has been concluded, it probably did not look that way at various stages of the journey. Courtships are complex and few people marry their first boyfriend or girlfriend.

The eventual purchase of our Midlands stations in 2016 by one of the two major UK radio groups, Bauer, was a good result for all. For Bauer it was a neat, strategic fit, filling in key geographic holes in their UK local station coverage. It also added useful bulk to their overall audiences, and afforded them solid coverage in England's second city. For us, it was a neat, clean arrangement and offered most of our staff some degree of welcome continuity.

Handover day is always an emotional one. You prepare to hand over control of something that has occupied almost every waking minute of your life for several years. The people with whom you'd shared more time each day than you had with your partner are set to become more than just casual acquaintances. But from this day on, you are no longer free to enter the buildings as you wish.

On the appointed final day of our company's existence, I was stationed in the premises at Gem 106, ready to give the East Midlands keys to Bauer. The new owners were represented in Nottingham that day by Dee Ford, the no-nonsense former local sales executive who had risen to rule her empire as group managing director for many years. Over in Birmingham one of her colleagues, Graham Bryce, prepared to assume control simultaneously of our West Midlands stations.

Dee first met with our Nottingham management team to break the news of their new head teacher, and we then proceeded to a full staff meeting. I doubt anyone was surprised by the agenda. The get-together was brilliantly and typically well handled by Dee and she delivered an engaging performance, with great generosity to us, which meant a lot.

A seven-year chapter had ended; one in which the business end of radio had featured more heavily than in any other episode of my radio life. I had worked with some hugely talented individuals, and it was reassuring to see many of them continue with the company we'd left, and indeed to be promoted, as larger companies are equipped to do.

At the end of the journey, I believe our legacy was strong

radio brands, operated by an efficient and focused business, equipped for life this century, and value was created for our shareholders. At the time of our farewell, it was good to boast that our stations were no. 1 by listening in every one of our markets amongst the key 25–44 age demographic. Against brilliant competition, much of it from people I count as friends, and an ever-changing backdrop, I think we did a reasonable job. The task was not as easy as we had imagined. Life rarely is. There are many things I wish we'd done differently.

Most importantly, I feel we created some truly memorable radio moments on air, which listeners enjoyed. We tried to provide for the people who worked for us an environment where they could do their best work and enjoy themselves. Had my first gig in radio been at our company, I hope I would have remembered my days there with the lifelong fondness that I still have for my days at Radio Trent in the '80s.

In the words of New York's Broadway Bill Lee from WCBS FM: 'Any radio station will necessarily take on the personality of its programme director.'[52]

58

COMMERCIAL RADIO'S FUTURE

Some people hold the wistful view that everything in UK commercial radio back in the 1970s and 1980s was perfect and that our current pasteurised programming is poor. It is a view frequently expressed with an angry red face – and one that suggests that if radio went back to just how it was in the days of Raleigh Chopper bikes, flared trousers and white dog poo, then life would be a whole lot better.

I am achingly fond of the past and I celebrate radio's rich history at every opportunity. I also relish the present day, and I'm extremely excited about the future. The present is not bad, it is just very different. I would suggest that the formal radio of the 1930s would have sounded odd to a listener in the 1970s, in the same way that radio of the 1970s would sound very odd now, were we to deliver it.

These critics, with their rose-tinted spectacles, love the music and radio of their youth. As they grow older, each chord reminds them of the excitement of those days: first song, first love, first drink, first home. You always remember the first time you did anything. The radio you grew up with is part of who you are. You chose one of very few stations, and it became the soundtrack to your life. Nothing will ever feel as good again.

If you heard the station you grew up with now, for the first time, what would you really make of it? More to the point, what would you make of it if you were now eighteen again?

Would you really seek out a station that plays a random selection of songs, of which you recognise but a few, when you could choose instead a station that plays all the songs you know and love, all the time?

Would you really prefer a station riddled with lengthy lists of lost and founds and swapshops, whilst at work and craving some background music, when another station can provide music with more flow?

When you're setting out on a long journey and need some company in the car, would you turn on a station that interrupts interesting conversation every few minutes with a song, if instead you can find a station which is all talk, all the time?

If you adore Johnny Cash, Carrie Underwood and Tammy Wynette, would you be loyal to a station that boasts only a Tuesday evening country slot, if you can choose another which plays country music all day, every day?

How would you feel about a station where the presenter allows you to write in only by post, and who may never respond – or may mention you when you're not listening in two weeks' time? Or would you prefer to text in or tweet them instantly?

When waiting to know if your school is open in the morning, would you really like to sit glued to the radio, listening to a lengthy list of everyone else's schools, hoping that yours will be mentioned before the school bus arrives? Or would you prefer to check the list of school closures online the night before?

Do you want five minutes of news on the station you have chosen for music or a ninety-second alert aimed at your generation?

Would you really like no other stations available in decent

quality? Or would you prefer a selection of hundreds, available by name on FM, DAB and online?

Radio simply could not continue as it was. For all the above reasons, no one would be listening.

Breakfast show recordings from long ago are a painful reminder of a hugely enjoyable, yet random, period. You went on air and you did it. Some natural communicators produced shows of the highest order. Many did not. Now, visit any sensible radio station just after ten o'clock and you'll find a gaggle of folk considering that day's show. What went well and what didn't? What are we planning for tomorrow? What angle or treatment should we adopt? How can we get listeners involved?

Nowadays, the informed specialists who select the music on many stations are better equipped to identify an audience and meet its needs than were the majority of presenters years ago, who attempted to serve everyone with no further insight into audience preferences than the weekly chart.

There are the business realities too. The cost of transmission has more than doubled, thanks to DAB and all the other platforms on which stations must appear. Key presenter fees have risen, thanks to market forces, with freelancers being tempted by rival stations – and rival media – at the ends of their contracts. Marketing budgets have rocketed as stations try to stay ahead of their competitors and clients have several stations to choose from when spending their advertising budgets. The BBC has become a direct audience competitor, its populist services now delivered on comparable platforms.

In the cyclical downturns, companies in the halcyon 1970s and 1980s often struggled to make ends meet. With today's extra pressures, the liquidators would have been at the door. In 2009, half of all commercial radio stations ran at a loss, with two thirds of all stations suffering a loss or only generating profits of less than £100,000 per year.[53]

There have been errors along the way as our business has carved out its future, and sometimes decisions have been made by both operators and regulators which do not serve listeners well. Radio remains strong, however, and is still consumed by almost everybody each week. Such a performance suggests mistakes must have been relatively few. It is important to separate our view, as radio fanatics, from the views of the average listener.

The huge change in the structure of commercial radio was necessary to engineer an industry which is sufficiently robust to face the future.

Radio as an advertising medium was slow to launch in the UK, having been delayed until the 1970s, by which time it was already well established in other countries and part of the fabric of advertising spend. Even then, its spread across the UK was pedestrian. After its penetration eventually grew and the network's structure started allowing a more cohesive sell to advertisers, it spent a little time in the promising spotlight – becoming the fastest-growing advertising medium through the '90s.

Tribute should be paid to the Radio Advertising Bureau for supporting this growth, under the early stewardship of the determined Douglas MacArthur, who fittingly shares his name with an icon of American military history. With typical bluntness, he described the challenge he faced in bringing together the disparate network: 'Getting 60 per cent [of radio owners on board] was easy – getting the rest was a pain in the ass.'

Douglas pointed out that audiences had doubled in the 1980s, yet revenues stayed static. When devising his strategy, he took counsel from distinguished leaders in the advertising world to establish the depth of their understanding of radio. Their average estimate of the size of the medium's 23 million audience was 12 million.[54]

Despite the welcome growth in the 1990s, however, radio still only accounted for but a very small percentage of all advertising monies. The sudden arrival of digital media then added a powerful extra competitor, now drawing £8.6 billion from the advertising economy.[55] Although record amounts of money are being spent by advertisers across all media, digital provides a new challenge for radio; a challenge that can only intensify in the years to come.

If it is to survive, commercial radio needs to ensure it continues to deliver significant audiences across the demographics and sells with conviction and creativity the impressively persuasive nature of radio's conversation with its audience.

59

THE FUTURE OF RADIO

On leaving school, the first thing I bought with my first month's wages was an Albatone clock radio with a fake teak front. My parents had much the same device by one side of their bed, with a teasmade machine by the other. Back then, radio and tea were necessary human requisites for the start of the day.

Now, we are more likely to be awakened by the annoying ringing of our mobile phone. Similarly, in the car, there are fears that radio will no longer enjoy hero status on the dashboard, as it is replaced by touchscreen media centres, of which radio forms just a part and several clicks away; as convenient as the multi-CD player in my old car, which puzzlingly lived in the boot.

Optimists would argue that radio is more accessible than ever, available on the mobile phones we carry around in our pockets and on the PC or tablet we have on our desks. Furthermore, the talented team at Radioplayer are squirrelling away to ensure that stations are readily accessible on smart speakers such as the Amazon Echo; thus, radio will be as available as ever in cars, once voice control is commonplace.

Never has it been so simple to track down a station, given we can now search by name rather than having to recall a string of digits. Radio frequencies certainly used to confuse my mother as she tuned from *Woman's Hour* to *Waggoners' Walk*. It is puzzling how we attracted any audience at all in the days when finding a station was akin to breaking into a security safe, as we twiddled the tuning knob and scanned the wave band, with no way of recognising any of the stations apart from by their content.

In marketing too, social media allows us to showcase what we do. Never before has it been possible to demonstrate radio's personalities so easily to non-listeners.

Radio is in rude health. In these fast-changing times, with an unprecedented volume of competition for the listening ear, almost nine out of ten adults[56] still choose to spend the equivalent of almost a complete day per week with radio – the same proportion of listeners as ten years before.

Live radio attracts around three quarters of 'ear-time'[57] amongst all adults, easily outshining audio on demand, podcasting, streaming or listening to one's own music – all by a considerable margin. I read with a smile that listening to music on cassettes and vinyl rose a little in recent surveys. I suspect it's not a renewed interest in some BASF C60s found in an old shoebox.

One speech I guiltily repurpose, whenever the need arises, adopts the theme 'If radio were invented today…' I consider what the news media would make of this universally popular medium which is portable, freely available and generates a relationship with its consumers which they call friendship. Radio bears all the traits of the sort of interactive medium which today's media pundits adore. Listeners even define themselves by it. They will readily boast 'I'm a Heart listener', in a way they would never say 'I'm an ITV viewer'.

In truth, this quiet, enduring, 100-year-old giant has never been given the credit it deserves. Against all expectations, it survived the onslaught of television's growth in the 1950s; and it coped easily with the arrival of portable music, as the Walkman and MP3 player gained popularity. In recent decades, radio has always been more popular and more powerful than its reputation would suggest.

It is only *in extremis*, and by accident, that radio attracts newspaper column inches. But when it does, it becomes front page news, with eager correspondents dashing off lengthy prose about the death of Wogan, the departure of Moyles or the 'Sachsgate' controversy. Many press stories arise too from those moments of honest radio conversation where news is made. From an LBC Ferrari clip which might change the course of a general election campaign, to BBC Radio 4's interview on the 'sexed-up' dossier on the Iraq war.

There is, therefore, compelling evidence that radio is currently far more influential than a media analyst might concede, particularly a young digital-native analyst with floppy hair and a straggly beard. It is important, however, to avoid complacency. I believe that radio is phenomenally strong, but that it is also under threat.

There is growing evidence that younger audiences are already less enthusiastic about radio than once they were. Any parent can vouch for the fact that their children do not enjoy the relationship with live radio that they themselves once had, and the same holds true for linear television. You wouldn't punish today's sixteen-year-old by taking away his radio.

No one yet knows whether this generation will grow into loving radio like teenagers once grew into an old 'hand-me-down' droopy sweater. The hope that touchscreen toddlers will graduate to our medium stems from the observation that radio audiences have traditionally grown more loyal as their faces get more wrinkled. But I fear that assumption is without foundation and that the penetration of radio will decline appreciably in the next twenty years, in both audience numbers reached and time spent listening. The pace of any decline will owe something to our own efforts to slow it. We need to continue to excite and not rest on radio's historic laurels.

Innovation now appears at unprecedented levels, and as it battles for ear-time, radio will be forced to combat threats that have yet to be invented. Nevertheless, radio will remain a mainstream medium for many decades to come. The irreplaceable content and friendship it provides, together with qualified music curation, plus the essentially live nature of radio, will keep it alive. I believe these elements, taken together with listen-again audio material and podcasting, will merge to form a new radio industry united principally by the spoken word. Existing mainstream music-intensive radio and streaming, taken together, may form a second rather different music entertainment medium.

The approach to radio presentation has already changed from the sombre deep voices or smiling energy which defined the various formats just decades ago, to a more conversational, natural tone. Today's broadcasters are authentic, the voices lighter, the content more personal. Many of those who aspire to a career in the medium now have already created a 'brand me' off the radio before they are appointed.

In 1922, Arthur Burrows delivered the first BBC news bulletin[58] from Marconi House in the Strand, telling of a 'rowdy meeting' involving Winston Churchill, a train robbery and detailing the latest billiard scores. This style of giving an hourly shopping list of stories remains essentially unchanged to this day, save for the absence of received pronunciation. This approach will surely change on entertainment stations. Listeners will not wait until 'on the hour' to be updated when they can get their news far more speedily elsewhere. And they will likely not tolerate their chosen entertainment medium pausing for this burst of sombre speech, a throwback to full service radio. But dynamic news coverage and analysis will remain a key part of radio's overall offering, with its purpose, tone and frequency redefined.

Whilst listeners currently still attach surprising value to travel news, I suspect radio will no longer be judged to be the best purveyor of this localised dull data, and that the bulletins will soon suffer the same fate as the chemists' rotas. When traffic delays are seriously bad, though, live radio will still prove to be the medium which empathises best with motorists.

And, at a time when just about every gadget apart from your kettle can tell you the time, maybe we will not need presenters to do the same in their curiously odd language: 'It's seventeen before eight'.

The production of radio content will change. Already, many high-quality 'stations' operate from PCs next to the linen basket in enthusiasts' back bedrooms, from where programmes can be voice-tracked. If any one of those 'stations' benefited from a broadcast platform and investment in staffing, they would attract a decent audience. Sovereign physical buildings may no longer define a radio 'station', giving way to remote operations where separate programmes originate from various locations.

In a future world, radio listening, I believe, will simply be driven by the very best communicators.

In terms of funding, BBC radio will survive although the

cost of providing digital content will eat into radio's budgets and impact on how it is produced. The legitimacy of the licence fee, similarly, will come under increasing pressure as the media diversifies. The Corporation will be obliged to run its radio services on less cash, and I dearly hope it chooses the right economies; I believe they are there to be made. The more 'broadcasting' is democratised, as it is through social media platforms and other online presence, the more the BBC's brand reputation as trusted curator will be valued. I see the merits, too, in Global Radio's strategy of labelling the output on all its stations with its parent brand for the same reasons.

In revenue generation for commercial radio, I anticipate that the commercial radio 'spot' advertising model will evolve into one ever more reliant on sponsorship and creative branded content. Attention spans will simply not tolerate interruptive advertising of the traditional kind, certainly not in current quantities. With ever growing ad breaks, and commercial sponsorships, promotions and calls to action, I worry we are at risk of killing the golden goose. Chief strategy officer at Saatchi and Saatchi Richard Huntington, when speaking at a radio conference, reminded us of the importance in any deal of 'leaving something on the table'. Our deal is with our listeners, and radio needs to retain their trust.

Whatever the future holds, people will always have two ears and will always want something to listen to. An appreciable number of people will always turn to engaging and interesting audio content.

60

TEASING AHEAD

To use a rather aged metaphor, I like to think I've not yet reached the red leader tape of my radio career, although I do dream of establishing a nursing home for ex-disc jockeys as we all reach retirement. We could all of us have a turn at the decks for the Friday night discos, and our doorbells could play JAM acapella namecheck jingles. Happy nurses would wear satin jackets with embroidered logos, and coffee would be served in red and blue 'Radio 1 247' mugs off a BBC tray. But that's some way off yet.

My new-found freedom enables me to wake up to Radio 4 without feeling guilty. It has also allowed me to travel and work with a host of stations at home and abroad. Given the number of us stalwarts plodding around labelled as 'consultants', I've determinedly avoided the phrase if I possibly can. I've lent a hand where I can in operations, both small and large, and it was wonderful recently waking up in southern Ireland and walking to work each day to help out at a small station where obituaries account for significant revenues.

It is not that I know all the answers; I simply remember the many things I've got wrong. I relish the opportunity to chat with programmers and presenters alike, tackling challenges and opportunities which are all too familiar.

I've provided quiet services for organisations seeking help

with a study or analysis, and it's good to have played a part as chairman of Notts TV, part of the new local TV network where challenges are familiar and radio lessons eerily relevant.

I've also had a chance to attend or speak at more conferences, not least the one in Aarhus in Denmark recently, where the efficient organisers introduced me gleefully on stage in smiling Danish. I only hope I was at the right conference talking about the right topic. European radio conferences are always fun, where keynote addresses are routinely delivered by jolly towering figures, speaking in near-perfect English, sporting an enviable head of hair and an old checked jacket from the wardrobe.

Whilst it might sound odd to suggest that being invited to record the announcements for the huge fleet of Nottingham City Transport buses was an unexpected recent career highlight, I concede it was.

Being on air was my dream as a callow youth, so I've thoroughly enjoyed being back in front of the mic too in recent months. Broadcasting in Nottingham for the first time for years, it was delightful to receive a text from a listener welcoming me home. 'Hearing your voice is like having a friend back,' she observed, in a comment which says all that needs to be said about this wonderful medium that has given me a life of happiness for which I shall be eternally grateful.

'Never forget that what you do is the most important thing in the world and, at the same time, joyously trivial.'[59]